YALE STUDIES IN ENGLISH

ALBERT S. COOK, Editor

VIII

THE CLASSICAL MYTHOLOGY

OF

MILTON'S ENGLISH POEMS

BY

CHARLES GROSVENOR OSGOOD, Ph.D.

HASKELL HOUSE

Publishers of Scholarly Books

NEW YORK

1964

published by

HASKELL HOUSE
Publishers of Scholarly Books
30 East 10th Street • New York, N. Y. 10003

Library of Congress Catalog Card Number: 65-15902

PRINTED IN UNITED STATES OF AMERICA

PREFACE

The student who diligently peruses the lines of a great poem may go far toward a realization of its character. He may appreciate, in a degree, its loveliness, strength, and direct hold upon the catholic truth of life. But he will be more sensitive to these appeals, and receive gifts that are richer and less perishable, according as he comprehends the forces by whose interaction the poem was produced. These are of two kinds— the innate forces of the poet's character, and certain more external forces, such as, in the case of Milton, are represented by Hellenism and Hebraism. Their activity is greatest where they meet and touch, and at this point their nature and measure are most easily discerned. From a contemplation of the poem in its genesis one returns to a deeper understanding and enjoyment of it as a completed whole. The present study, though it deals with but one of the important cultural influences affecting Milton, and with it but in part, endeavors by this method to deepen and clarify the appreciation of his art and teaching.

My interest in the present work has found support and encouragement in the opinions of Mr. Churton Collins, as expressed in his valuable book, *The Study of English Literature.* The particular subject was suggested by Miss Alice Sawtelle's study of the sources of Spenser's Mythology, which has served also as a helpful model. What is here printed as the second part was submitted as a doctoral thesis to the Philosophical Faculty of Yale University.

Any one who deals seriously with Milton's relation to his sources, especially to the classical ones, must become indebted in many ways to the scholarly editions of Newton and Todd, as well as to the increase of their wealth in the editions of Browne, Masson, Jerram, Verity, Hales, Cook, and Trent. In the tracing of the sources, however, I have, for the most part, worked independently of editorial annotations, and have found it both necessary and possible to carry the work beyond the limit of previous researches in this field. So thorough and extensive was Milton's reading that a study of his sources may be prolonged indefinitely before it fails of interest and profit. For this reason I have doubtless transgressed, in places, the strict boundary of my subject, as in my discussion of Milton's use of 'Chance,' or his allusion to the Chalybeans. The requisite apparatus included Roscher's *Lexikon der Griechischen und Römischen Mythologie*, Preller's *Griechische Mythologie*, and the Pauly-Wissowa *Realencyclopädie*, to which I may add Smith's *Dictionary of Greek and Roman Biography and Mythology*. The text used is generally that of Masson, but I have now and again taken liberties with respect to spelling and punctuation, usually with the aim of securing more perfect consistency. The principal translators cited are as follows: of the *Iliad,* Lang, Leaf, and Myers; of the *Odyssey,* Butcher and Lang; of Vergil, Lonsdale and Lee; of Plato, Jowett; of Ovid, Riley; of Theocritus, Lang; of Pindar, Myers; of Æschylus and Sophocles, Plumptre.

I speak with hesitation of my debt to my teachers, since I can hope to express but inadequately my gratitude to them. Of such indebtedness this work represents, indeed, but a small part. Had it not been for the advice and unfailing inspiration of Professor Albert S. Cook, it would never have been begun. To the enthusiasm and delicate appreciation of Professor Thomas D. Seymour I owe the beginning and deepening of an interest in Greek literature which has imparted zest to my labors. I am also grateful to Professor Seymour, to Miss Laura E. Lockwood, of Wellesley College, whose Milton Lexicon is shortly to appear, and especially to Professor Cook, for their care in reading the proof, and the freedom with which they have suggested corrections and improvements. To my brother, Mr. H. W. Osgood, I would record my acknowledgments for his assistance in compiling indexes and in preparing the manuscript for the press.

In the consciousness of one's mistakes and short-comings it is a comfort to find one's sentiments expressed, with his peculiar nobility of tone and phrase, by the great lexicographer and essayist of the last century, whose success in most things that he undertook must be the despair of lesser abilities: ' In things difficult there is danger from ignorance, and in things easy from confidence; the mind, afraid of greatness, and disdainful of littleness, hastily withdraws herself from painful searches, and passes with scornful rapidity over tasks not adequate to her powers, sometimes too secure for caution, and again too anxious for vigorous effort, sometimes idle in a plain path, and sometimes distracted in labyrinths, and dissipated by different intentions.'

C. G. O.

YALE UNIVERSITY, December 23, 1899.

INTRODUCTION

The importance of Greek and Roman mythology is proved by its unfailing vitality. After the visible forms of states and empires had passed away, the myths of the ancients survived with their politics and philosophy and poetry as a part of the heritage which the new peoples received from the old. This power of classical myths to survive is explained principally by two facts: first, they were the embodiment of the moral, religious, and artistic ideals of the Greeks and Romans; secondly, morality, religion, and art were serious and fundamental realities in ancient life.

These two facts explain also the kind of vitality by which the myths have survived. It consists not merely in the repetition of a tale through centuries, but also in the variation of its quality, and in its susceptibility to employment for various uses. The old mythology was a kind of plastic material which received through individuals a national impress. As the life of the Greeks became modified from century to century, so Greek mythology was similarly modified by the poets, teachers, philosophers, and artists who were the master-workmen of this people. The stories and conceptions of gods and heroes are strong, aspiring, or weak, as the people who invented and cherished them manifested the corresponding qualities. And when the Roman civilization adopted Greek culture, Greek mythology suffered modification, and became in some degree a reflex of the Roman life into which it had entered.

The poet who was religious, and hence peculiarly and continually sensitive to moral truth, found in existing mythology a partial expression of the truths dear to him, and in his poetic treatment added to the moral, religious, or imaginative value of the myth which he

employed. Reverence as well as imagination characterizes such treatment. We feel it in the mythology of poets
like Homer, Plato, and Vergil. Thus in the first book
of the *Iliad*, where Chryses prayed for revenge upon
Agamemnon, 'Phœbus Apollo heard him, and came down
from the peaks of Olympus wroth at heart, bearing on
his shoulders his bow and covered quiver. And the
arrows clanged upon his shoulders in his wrath, as the
god moved; and he descended like to night.'[1] This
passage not only shows Homer's imagination in its vividness and dramatic power, but contains moral enthusiasm for divine justice, and reverence for the superior
and majestic power of the god. But Homer's reverence had a lower object than that of either Plato or the
Christian. His ideal of conduct, as represented by his
heroes, and magnified in his divinities, was nourished by
a smaller life and a lower conception of the universe than
the Platonic or the Christian ideal. His greatest men
and women are brave, dignified, and generous, sometimes even tender. Yet they treat their enemies with
horrible cruelty, they violate our ideas of moral purity,
and they exhibit lack of self-control and fear of death.
Already in the palmy days of Greek civilization Plato
criticizes them for such shortcomings.[2]

The reverence of this poet-philosopher for mythology
was not based upon a literal belief in the old religion.
He appreciated the beauty of some of its myths, and
saw that they were sufficiently plastic to receive his
teaching. In his adaptation he has impressed them
with the imagination, and with the enthusiasm and reverence for truth which are exhibited in his philosophy.
Under the influence of his higher and larger ideals and
conceptions, mythology underwent a sort of expansion.
It was sublimated, rarefied, and projected into larger
space. It received a nobler form than that which it
possessed in Homer. At the same time, however, it

---

[1] 1.45.
[2] *Rep.* 3. 386.

assumed a new function; it became symbolic and almost allegorical. Thus in the *Phædrus*, where Plato is discussing the upward flight of the perfect soul, he says: 'Now the divine is beauty, wisdom, goodness, and the like; and by these the wing of the soul is nourished, and grows apace; . . . Zeus, the mighty lord holding the reins of a winged chariot, leads the way in heaven, ordering all and caring for all; and there follows him the heavenly array of gods and demi-gods, divided into eleven bands; for only Hestia is left at home in the house of heaven; but the rest of the twelve greater deities march in their appointed order. And they see in the interior of heaven many blessed sights; and there are ways to and fro, along which the happy gods are passing, each one fulfilling his own work; and any one may follow who pleases, for jealousy has no place in the heavenly choir. This is within the heaven. But when they go to feast and festival, then they move right up the steep ascent, and mount the top of the dome of heaven.'[1] To appreciate more fully the difference between Homer and Plato, this passage should be compared with the famous feast of the gods in the first book of the *Iliad*,[2] where jealous Hera stirs a quarrel with Zeus; but at his threats 'the ox-eyed queen was afraid, and sat in silence, curbing her heart; but throughout Zeus' palace the gods of heaven were troubled.' Then the drollery of Hephæstus made a truce, and 'laughter unquenchable arose amid the blessed gods to see Hephæstus bustling through the palace.'

An allegorical and naturalistic application of mythology was made by Plutarch. The attempt was afterwards made to identify many myths with early or sacred history through euhemeristic interpretation, or to discover in them an allegorical form of Christian and moral truth. Such uses of mythology find early prece-

---

[1] *Phædrus* 246, 247. Compare also the use of mythology in the story of the journey of Er, *Rep.* 10. 614–621.

[2] 1. 493–600.

dent in a euhemerist like Diodorus, or a moralist like
Plutarch. They were later practised by certain of the
fathers, such as Eusebius, and were resumed with great
enthusiasm by scientific writers of the Renaissance,
such as Bacon and Bochart.[1]

In the times of Greek and Roman decadence, when
faith in the old religion had died, leaving empty the
hearts of men, and when morality was by many
regarded as inconvenient and unnecessary, the treatment of a myth in art became correspondingly irreli-
gious and non-moral. As a diverting tale it admitted of
imaginative treatment only. A Horace or a Claudian
made it serve as a dainty and effective ornament. Ovid
clothed the old stories in new apparel and ornament,
and, thus renovated, they gave the world fresh amuse-
ment; his importance to us as a mythologist consists
much less in any moral or artistic excellence of his
treatment than in his great accumulation of mythological material from sources many of which have long
since disappeared.

Having thus considered the vitality of ancient myths
as illustrated by their varying quality and the various
ways in which they were applied, we may ask whether
this vitality has failed at last, or whether it is so
great that the myths may live with us a life in some
degree as intimate as that which they lived with the
ancients. When Christian civilization supplanted that
of Greece and Rome, it seemed likely that pagan mythology would perish with the old order of things.
It was too closely interwoven with earlier belief to
survive the antagonism of the new faith, which first
dreaded the ancient world, and then triumphed over it.
Within the last five hundred years classical mythology
has been partially revived, generally as a relic or a
plaything. But whether it can again receive the inspir-
ing power of revelation which it possessed for many of

---

[1] See pp. 7, 17, 26, 33, 34, 37, 43, 46, 49, 54, 68, 71, 84, 85.

the ancients remains a question. The answer to such a
question we may hope to find by a study of this element in the art of Milton.

Before passing to a detailed examination of Milton's
classical mythology, let us notice an architectural anal-
ogy which shows how a product of the classical civilization, by yielding to the transforming power of a new
faith, has been brought into a more beautiful life than
it had known before. In Greek temples of the purer
type, shafts and capitals play a conspicuous part, even
exceeding in size and number the requirement for the
support of the building, and existing in large measure
for the sake of their own splendor. Each column is
itself a complete and beautiful thing. It rises grandly
in heroic proportion, and is crowned with the glory of
its capital. It has the proud character of Athene or of
the far-darting Apollo, and in its definite and circumscribed perfection it reflects the finite nature of the old
religion.

It sometimes happens, as one wanders along the
ambulatory of an old cathedral, that he sees in the
apse, or in the triforium of the choir, a column which
reminds him of those in some of the Greek temples. It
has something of their individuality; it is distinguished
by volutes and a sort of acanthus foliage. It is indeed less conspicuous than they were. Its position is
a modest one; it may pass unnoticed in all the grandeur
of the building. The pagan pride is gone, but in its
new humility the column is more beautiful than of old.
Its beauty has fallen upon it from the infinite beauty of
the new faith in the service of which it has been established, and those who reared the column have given it
the tenderness, the strength, and the repose of their
religion.

Let us now consider some of the principal facts
revealed by an examination of the classical mythology
in Milton's poems. His methods of introducing such

allusions are principally three.   First, they may be
introduced in simile or comparison. Thus in the Second
Book of *Paradise Lost* he describes the turmoil of the
fiends who

> Rend up both rocks and hills, and ride the air
> In whirlwind; Hell scarce holds the wild uproar:—
> As when Alcides from Œchalia crowned
> With conquest, felt the envenomed robe, and tore
> Through pain up by the roots Thessalian pines,
> And Lichas from the top of Œta threw
> Into the Euboic sea.[1]

At times the comparison may be very brief, as when
the beasts are represented more obedient to the call of
Eve

> Than at Circean call the herd disguised.[2]

Or it may even not exceed the mere mention of
'Typhoean rage'[3] or 'Atlantean shoulders.'[4]

Milton often masses classical allusions of this kind,
piling them sometimes four or five deep, and obtaining
by means of this accumulation an effect of great richness.   Thus of the tempter disguised as a serpent he
says:

> Pleasing was his shape
> And lovely; never since of serpent kind
> Lovelier—not those that in Illyria changed
> Hermione and Cadmus, or the god
> In Epidaurus; nor to which transformed
> Ammonian Jove, or Capitoline, was seen,
> He with Olympias, this with her who bore
> Scipio the highth of Rome.[5]

Even supposing that the reader is not familiar with all
the allusions of this passage, the very succession of sono-
rous vowels and liquids, which Milton so often effected
by his choice and arrangement of proper names,

---

[1] *P. L.* 2. 540–546.
[2] *P. L.* 9. 522; cf. 4. 250; 5. 16, 378; 10. 559; *V. E.* 93.
[3] *P. L.* 2. 539.
[4] *P. L.* 2. 306; cf. 655; 3. 359; 10. 444; *Son.* 15. 7.
[5] *P. L.* 9. 503–510.

enhances the splendor of this massed comparison. In
some cases such comparisons are reinforced or extended
by allusions which are not mythological or even classical. Or mythological allusions introduced for another
purpose than comparison may occur in close connection
with these passages. It is by such treatment that the
description of Eden, in the Fourth Book of *Paradise
Lost*,[1] expresses through its own rich luxuriance the
luxuriance of the garden. We hear first the sound of
clear water running over beds of pearl and gold, now
sparkling in the sun, now lost in the green twilight of
deep woods. Against the dark foliage is the gleam of
fruits with golden rind, 'Hesperian fables true.' The
air is filled with the fragrance of gorgeous flowers,
and with the soft call of unseen birds. Where the
leafy branches part little vistas invite exploration.

> Airs, vernal airs,
> Breathing the smell of field and grove, attune
> The trembling leaves, while universal Pan,
> Knit with the Graces and the Hours in dance,
> Led on the eternal Spring. Not that fair field
> Of Enna, where Proserpin gathering flowers,
> Herself a fairer flower, by gloomy Dis
> Was gathered—which cost Ceres all that pain
> To seek her through the world—nor that sweet grove
> Of Daphne, by Orontes and the inspired
> Castalian spring, might with this Paradise
> Of Eden strive; nor that Nyseian isle,
> Girt with the river Triton, where old Cham,
> Whom Gentiles Ammon call and Libyan Jove,
> Hid Amalthea, and her florid son,
> Young Bacchus, from his stepdame Rhea's eye;
> Nor where Abassin kings their issue guard,
> Mount Amara, though this by some supposed
> True Paradise, under the Ethiop line
> By Nilus' head, enclosed with shining rock,
> A whole day's journey high, but wide remote
> From this Assyrian garden, where the Fiend
> Saw undelighted all delight, all kind
> Of living creatures, new to sight and strange.

---

[1] 205-287.

It will be noticed that Eden has been compared to three mythical gardens, and then to a garden of Abyssinia, and that besides these allusions, reference is also made to the Hesperides, to Pan, the Graces, and the Hours. This method of accumulation or massing of mythology is not confined to similes, but is also practised in other connections, as we shall see later.

Here we may pause to consider a characteristic of all great art which attempts to interpret the beauty of the natural world to men. Every work of art which maintains a strong and permanent influence over men contains some element which brings it in touch with humanity. However divine the truth which the artist feels, however radiant the beauty of nature is to him, his art is incomplete if his thoughts of these things are not brought home to men in terms of human life. It is for this reason that a painting or a description of a land-scape which reproduces simply the landscape itself is imperfect. The best art therefore personifies the forces cf nature, or perhaps is content with suggesting types or phases of human life which seem to correspond in spirit to the particular type or phase of nature. It is thus that in Corot's pictures of the glad morning, figures are seen dancing, or blithe and tuneful Orpheus appears, giving utterance to the joyful harmony around him. In Milton's description of Eden the same principle applies to the mention of Pan and the Hours. Furthermore, in the comparisons occurring here Milton has not stopped with mere allusions to myths, as in his description of the serpent-fiend, but has outlined in his concise and significant way the stories of Proserpina and Amalthea, and has suggested the voice heard in the Castalian spring sacred to the Apollo and Daphne of the Orient, thus furnishing appropriate personal types to reflect the natural beauty previously described.[1]

---

[1] Other examples of accumulated mythology in simile or comparison are *P. L.* 1. 196-208, 575-587; 2. 628; 4. 705-719; 5. 377-382; 9. 14-19, 386-396, 439-444; *P. R.* 2. 353-365; *Arc.* 18-23; *C.* 441-452; *Eleg.* 1. 63-73.

Of all the allusions to mythology in simile by far the greatest strength and finest balance are found in a certain double mythological simile in the Fourth Book of *Paradise Regained*, in which each member is firmly and concisely outlined. It is where Satan, in the last temptation, commands Christ to leap from a pinnacle of the temple :

> To whom thus Jesus : ' Also it is written
> " Tempt not the Lord thy God." ' He said, and stood.
> But Satan, smitten with amazement, fell.
> As when Earth's son, Antæus (to compare
> Small things with greatest), in Irassa strove
> With Jove's Alcides, and, oft foiled, still rose,
> Receiving from his mother Earth new strength,
> Fresh from his fall, and fiercer grapple joined,
> Throttled at length in the air expired and fell;
> So, after many a foil, the Tempter proud,
> Renewing fresh assaults, amidst his pride
> Fell whence he stood to see his victor fall.
> And, as that Theban monster that proposed
> Her riddle, and him who solved it not devoured,
> That once found out and solved, for grief and spite
> Cast herself headlong from the Ismenian steep,
> So, strook with dread and anguish, fell the Fiend.[1]

It may be observed that the similes and comparisons which have been cited are all from *Paradise Lost* and *Paradise Regained*. We may say that with few exceptions, principally in *Comus*, this manner of introducing mythological allusion is peculiar to these two longer and and later poems;[2] but it is not just to infer from this

---

[1] *P. R.* 4. 560–576. The strength of this passage is not due alone to the balance of these two similes, nor to the fact that not more than two are used. It lies partly in the grandeur of diction, but most of all in the deeper meaning common to the three solemn events here described. Each is the victory of a hero; each is the triumph of right over wrong, of light over darkness; and in each struggle is involved the fate of generations. The comparison of Christ to Heracles is implied in *Pass.* 13. The idea may have been suggested to Milton by some writer of the Renaissance, or more likely by one of the Fathers. Cf. *P. L.* 2. 1017–1020; 4. 713–719.

[2] In *Samson Agonistes*, the nature of the subject and the form in which it was cast naturally prevented almost entirely the use of Greek mythology. Neither Samson nor his friends and enemies could very appropriately be made to talk of things so far removed from them as classical myths, and in the drama the poet may not appear in person, as in

2

that Milton ultimately came to prefer such a form of allusion. It seems more likely that the subjects of the two epics offered so little opportunity for the incorporation of classical mythology within the story itself that, if the poems were to be enriched to any extent by means of pagan lore, it must be accomplished by the somewhat more remote method of simile and comparison.

A second method of introducing allusions to classical mythology is illustrated in nearly all the poems, though the earlier and so-called minor poems supply the best examples. It consists in the incorporation of a myth or the ancient conception of a divinity into a poetical setting of Milton's own creation.

This is accomplished in two distinct ways. First, the myth or conception, of which the several details may come from several different sources, may be removed, for example, from the peculiar setting of Homer, Apollonius, or Ovid, and placed in the different setting of *Comus*, *Il Penseroso*, or the First and Second Books of *Paradise Lost*. Thus the indefinite and shadowy classical idea of Chaos, as either a place or a divinity, or merely an unordered condition of things, has been elaborated under Milton's treatment, and separated into two distinct meanings in the cosmography of *Paradise Lost*. On the one hand, the word is applied to the deep and confused region between heaven and hell. On the other, it names the divinity who rules in this region. The principal source of the latter conception is in Hesiod, though his representation is much less definite than Milton's, and amounts to little more than

---

the epic, to make these allusions in his own name. Strictly, only one such allusion occurs in this dramatic poem, and that a very remote one. It is where Samson accuses himself of revealing God's secrets,

> a sin
> That Gentiles in their parables condemn
> To their abyss and horrid pains confined.
> (499–501.)

He evidently means Tantalus and Prometheus (see p. 80). But in addition to this one instance I have also discussed in their respective places the references to the Chalybeans (133), to 'dire Necessity' (1666), and to the phœnix (1699), as being mythological and having their probable sources among classical writers.

a personification of a condition in the order of nature's earliest development. In *Paradise Lost* the consort of Chaos, and his co-ruler, is Night. The Miltonic conception of Night is based upon that of the Orphic cosmogony, which makes her eldest and first of all things. Thus the two early Greek cosmogonies are combined, and introduced into the Second Book of Milton's great epic. By the same method, Saturn and Jove and the other Greek gods are made to appear among the devils, the most conspicuous of them all being Hephæstus, or Mulciber,[1] the skilful craftsman and architect of Pandemonium.[2] In *Paradise Regained*, Naiads, wood-nymphs, and the 'ladies of the Hesperides' figure in the temptation of Christ, and harpies snatch away the feast which has been spread by Satan.[3] Much of the mythology of the earlier poems is introduced in this manner. Thus in *Arcades* the Arcadian background is suggested by the presence of silver-buskined nymphs and gentle swains, these latter being the descendants

> Of that renownèd flood, so often sung,
> Divine Alpheus, who, by secret sluice,
> Stole under seas to meet his Arethuse.

And the last song of the poem is musical with the sweetness of such names as Ladon, Cyllene, Erymanth, and Lycæus, places dear to Pan and the nymphs. In *Comus* the element of enchantment and sensuality is largely composed of references to Bacchus and Circe It also includes the mention of dark-veiled Cotytto, who rides with Hecate through the night, concealing the wicked excesses of her worshippers. The magic song of Circe and the sirens quiets the rage of Scylla and Charybdis, and Comus is consigned to be girt with Harpies and Hydras, and

> With all the griesly legions that troop
> Under the sooty flag of Acheron.

---

[1] Cf. p. l.
[2] *P. L.* 1. 732-751.
[3] 2. 353-357, 403.

This element of sensuality in *Comus* is offset, on the
other hand, by an element of purity and benignity. The
latter is composed of references to the high air of
Jove's court, to the propitious aid of Neptune and all
sea-gods, to the glory of Iris, the sweetness of Echo, the
virgin majesty of Diana and Minerva. It is sustained
at the end by a description of the paradise of Virtue,
where the Hesperides sing, and whither the Graces and
Hours bring abundance. Here the air is cooled with
Elysian dew, and here sleeps the translated Adonis.
Here Love is reunited with Psyche, and to them are
born Youth and Joy.[1] *L'Allegro* and *Il Penseroso* should be
mentioned as important examples of this manner of
treatment. In these poems Milton has selected certain
conceptions of the ancient divinities, and expressed
them through the scenes and activities occurring in the
life of a refined man. It is the light spirit of Zephyr
and Aurora which predominates in the one poem, and the
sombre spirit of Vesta and Saturn which predominates
in the other. A more detailed analysis of these companion-pieces may be deferred until later in our discussion.[2]

Occasionally, instead of removing the whole myth

---

[1] It is worthy of notice in passing, that Milton, in making Youth and Joy the children
of Psyche and the celestial Cupid, has transcended the grosser treatment of Apuleius,
who makes Voluptas their daughter. Spenser is content with this version, and calls her
Pleasure. See p. 26; Spenser, *F. Q.* 3. 6. 50; *Hy. of Love* 288. A comparison of these
passages in Spenser with the closing speech of *Comus* reveals the principal difference
between Milton's method of treatment and Spenser's. The latter poet is nearly always
the more diffuse. Though the amount of mythology in his considerably larger body of
poetry appears to be much greater than in Milton, yet it represents less extensive reading
in the classics, and covers a range of allusion no wider, if as wide. Milton's wonderful con-
ciseness is of great artistic import, as one of the necessary elements of his classicism. Without the composure, reticence, and finish which this implies, no work of art is truly Hellenic.
We feel that Milton has gained these traits, or at least has developed them through direct
contact with pure Greek culture. We feel, on the other hand, that, however much Latin
and Greek Spenser read, he was in some degree perverted by the restless and unsettled
spirit of the early Renaissance from a deep and just sense of true classicism. He is therefore less faithful to originals. His mythology has more the nature of external ornament
rather profusely applied. There is evidence that, like the Italians, he was more charmed
with its sensuous and even sometimes fleshly aspect than with the deeper spiritual significance—which indeed he may not have perceived. It is in this way that his treatment
becomes more lavish of epithet, color, and circumstance than Milton's.

[2] See p. lii.

from its classical setting and inserting it in his own,
Milton adapts certain mythological events or features
by removing from them the persons and localities with
which they are connected in his sources, and substituting
his own persons and localities. This is the second way
in which mythology is incorporated or inwoven with his
story. One instance is Eve's story of discovering her
own beauty.[1] It is Ovid's story of Narcissus and his
love for the face that he saw reflected in the water of a
spring, except that Eve is put for Narcissus. Milton, as
usual, follows many of the details of his original, but
by a process of selection and exclusion renders them more
delicate.[2] The same sort of adaptation occurs when
Milton derives incidents from the visit of Odysseus
to Circe in the *Odyssey*,[3] and inserts them in his story
of Comus and the lady. As Circe by means of her
drug and wand changes all strangers to swine, so
Comus with his orient liquor and wand changes trav-
elers into brutish forms. As Odysseus was protected
against these charms by the moly, so the good spirit
checks the magic of Comus with a plant called hæmony.[4]
Again, in the battle between the rebel angels and the
army of God, many incidents are transferred from
Hesiod's battle of the Titans and the gods. Since the
occasion and general character of these two struggles,
as well as certain details, are similar, a comparison of
the two descriptions as a whole would be profitable.
We have space, however, only to point out a few details
in the *Theogony* which are adapted by Milton. Hesiod
tells us that the gods, taking great masses of rock in
their hands, hurled them upon the Titans. Zeus, without exerting his full strength, smote the Titans with his
thunderbolt, and drove them into the depths of Tartarus, whither an anvil could not fall in nine days. Here
they are confined for ever. Nearly the same incidents

---

[1] *P. L.* 4. 453-469.
[2] See p. 86.
[3] 10. 135-574.
[4] See p. 39.

are repeated in Hesiod's story of the fight between Zeus and Typhoeus. In Milton these details all appear with slight modification. As the Son of God advanced to battle, the steadfast empyrean shook beneath the wheels of his chariot, 'yet half his strength he put not forth.' His warriors

> plucked the seated hills, with all their load,
> Rocks, waters, woods, and, by the shaggy tops
> Uplifting, bore them in their hands.[1]

He himself hurled his thunders upon the host of Satan, who fell headlong from Heaven:

> Nine days they fell; confounded Chaos roared,
> And felt tenfold confusion in their fall
> Through his wild anarchy; so huge a rout
> Encumbered him with ruin. Hell at last,
> Yawning, received them whole, and on them closed.[2]

We may now consider the third method by which Milton introduces allusions to classical mythology. His

---

[1] *P. L.* 6. 644–646.

[2] *P. L.* 6. 871–875. Many instances of this treatment exist in Milton. The descent of Raphael in *P. L.* 5. 277–287 is derived in part from similar descriptions of Hermes in Vergil and Homer (*Æn.* 4. 222 ff.; *Il.* 24. 341). When in *P. L.* 8. 59, the poet says, speaking of Eve,

> With goddess-like demeanor forth she went,
> Not unattended; for on her as Queen
> A pomp of winning Graces waited still,

he is thinking of a conception of Venus, or Aphrodite, which is very common in the classics, and is illustrated in *Od.* 8. 364, where the Graces bathe and anoint the goddess. Cf. *Hom. Hy. to Aphrodite* 3. 61; Hor. *C.* 1. 4; 1. 30; 3. 21. In *P. L.* 8. 510, where Adam leads Eve to the nuptial bower, Earth and the powers of nature 'gave sign of gratulation.' The situation is similar to one in *Æn.* 4. 165, where Earth and the storm show approval of the union of Dido and Æneas in a cave. The amorous words addressed by guilty Adam to Eve (*P. L.* 9. 1029–1033) are much like those spoken by Paris to Helen in *Il.* 3. 442, or by Zeus to Hera in *Il.* 14. 315. In *P. L.* 11. 184–203 the eagle appears as a bird of omen in the manner of *Æn.* 1. 393–397; 12. 247–256. The description of the bounds of Hell in *P. L.* 2. 645 ff. bears traces of similar description in Homer, Hesiod, and Vergil. The sound of Hell's gates in *P. L.* 2. 879–882 suggests as an original *Æn.* 6. 573, 574. In *P. L.* 2. 252–258 Sin is represented as springing from the head of Satan, as Athene sprang from the head of Zeus. When Satan was wounded (*P. L.* 6. 320 ff.)

> A stream of nectarous humor issuing flowed
> Sanguine, such as celestial Spirits may bleed.

So Homer speaks of the wounded Aphrodite: 'Then flowed the goddess's immortal blood, such ichor as floweth in the blessed gods' (*Il.* 5. 339).

descriptions of nature are generally either mythological or touched with mythology. Especially is this true in descriptions of the dawn, of night, and of the progress of the sun and moon.[1]

We have already noticed how Milton can enliven and illuminate a description of natural beauty by throwing into it a touch of human life which reflects the spirit of that which he is describing. This is what Shakespeare does in peopling the forest of Arden with blithe spirits who make us forget that trees are not always green, and brooks merry; and in Milton the same result is produced by reflecting the spirit of nature from the personalities of the old gods, often slightly modified by the poet's art. It is thus that he tells of the beginning of another day:

> Now Morn, her rosy steps in the eastern clime
> Advancing, sowed the earth with orient pearl.[2]

And again he speaks of the Sun,

> who, scarce uprisen,
> With wheels yet hovering o'er the ocean-brim,
> Shot parallel to the earth his dewy ray,
> Discovering in wide landskip all the east.[3]

While it is true that Milton humanizes nature by means of mythology, we may go further, or perhaps reverse the statement, and say that in general, whatever the occasion of introducing the myth, if its persons or incidents connote even in the slightest degree the beauty or the power of nature, Milton makes us feel it. Thus broad meadows and shady places are made visible when he speaks in *Comus* of

> such court guise
> As Mercury did first devise
> With the mincing Dryades
> On the lawns, and on the leas.[4]

---

[1] Strictly speaking, the use of mythology in descriptions of nature is only another application of the second method by which myths are incorporated into Milton's poetry. Yet in a consideration of its artistic excellence it falls more conveniently under a separate head.

[2] *P. L.* 5. 1.; cf. p. xvi.

[3] *P. L.* 5. 139.

[4] *C.* 962.

The sound of the sea is suggested in the following lines:

>   Scylla wept,
> And chid her barking waves into attention,
> And fell Charybdis murmured soft applause.[1]

The luxuriance of spring is felt in a reference to the love of Zeus and Hera:

>   As Jupiter
> On Juno smiles when he impregns the clouds
> That shed May flowers.[2]

The name of Jove seems often to suggest the upper air and the broad sky.[3]

This consideration of the mythology in Milton's descriptions of nature is the most important of any thus far, since it opens the way to more thorough appreciation of his independence and originality, and of the true nature of his classicism and his artistic temperament.

As we approach these questions, the first thing for us to consider is that the part assigned to mythology in such descriptions varies widely in extent. One description may be entirely made up from mythology; another may reveal only a slight touch of it; in a third the mythical element may be wholly lacking, the personification employed being derived from another source. An analysis of several passages will clearly reveal the variation. In *Lycidas* the line,

> While the still morn went out with sandals gray,[4]

contains no mythological allusion. In the same poem occur the lines,

> Oft till the star that rose at evening bright
> Toward heaven's descent had sloped his westering wheel.[5]

---

[1] *C.* 257.

[2] *P. L.* 4. 499; see p. 49.

[3] This is evident in *Comus*, especially in the beginning, and in the lines *On the Death of a Fair Infant* 43-46.

[4] *Lyc.* 187. The ancients did not speak of the morning as 'gray.' Milton, however, seems to have delighted in this color as applied to the morning. See *P. L.* 7. 373; *P. R.* 4. 427; cf. the use in *P. L.* 5. 186; *L'Al.* 71.

[5] 30, 31.

This last passage contains only a slight mythical coloring. It consists in the allusion to the star's chariot, an idea which is more commonly associated with the sun, or moon, or night.[1] The mythological element is slightly increased in the following passage of *Paradise Regained:*

> Thus passed the night so foul, till Morning fair
> Came forth with pilgrim steps, in amice gray,
> Who with her radiant finger stilled the roar
> Of thunder, chased the clouds, and laid the winds.[2]

The mention of the Morning's 'radiant finger' appears to be an adaptation of the Homeric epithet 'rosy-fingered,' and her action in driving away the clouds may be partly suggested by the common idea that she puts the Night to rout, and partly by an expression which Vergil uses of Neptune.[3] The rest of the passage is peculiar to Milton. Again in the Fifth Book of *Paradise Lost* the Morning Star is addressed as

> Fairest of Stars, last in the train of Night,
> If better thou belong not to the Dawn,
> Sure pledge of day, that crown'st the smiling Morn
> With thy bright circlet.[4]

Of this passage the words 'last in the train of Night' are all that suggest the classical idea that the stars are attendant upon Night.[5]

Let us now examine a passage in which the mythological element is increased, even though it is not more conspicuous than the actual phenomenon of nature itself. Referring to sunset and sunrise, Milton says in *Lycidas:*

---

[1] Milton often used the chariot or moving throne as an accessory in myths. It occurs frequently in his reference to the sun, or moon, or night, and is often transferred to other connections. Examples are found in *P. L.* 1. 786; 2. 930; 3. 522; 5. 140, 166; 6. 100, 338, 358, 390, 711, 749-759, 770, 829, 881; 8. 162; 9. 65; *S. A.* 27; *D. F. I.* 15, 19, 56; *C. N.* 84, 145, 241; *Pens.* 53, 59, 121; *C.* 95, 134, 190, 892.

[2] *P. R.* 4. 426.

[3] *Æn.* 1. 143: 'Collectasque fugat nubes.'

[4] 5. 166.

[5] See p. 63.

> So sinks the day-star in the ocean bed,
> And yet anon repairs his drooping head,
> And tricks his beams, and with new-spangled ore
> Flames in the forehead of the morning sky.[1]

In the beginning of this passage we have the old figure of the god Helios sinking to rest in his bed at the end of a long day's journey. But as the passage proceeds this mythological idea fades, and in its place shines the brightness of the sun itself, like a flaming jewel in the forehead of the morning. Still more pronounced is the mythological character of the following lines :

> First in his east the glorious Lamp was seen,
> Regent of day, and all the horizon round
> Invested with bright rays, jocund to run
> His longitude through heaven's high road; the gray
> Dawn and the Pleiades before him danced
> Shedding sweet influence.[2]

Though this passage is founded principally upon the Bible, yet Milton, in combining the different parts, has given it a decided classical coloring, slightly modified by characterizing the Dawn as 'gray'; and so nicely are the parts fitted together that a seam is imperceptible, nor is it easy to tell where classical mythology ends and any other element begins.

The majority of natural descriptions in Milton resemble the last four examples in that they contain a more or less prominent suggestion of the mythical conception, together with a large element of Milton's elaboration.

We may now consider what is more rare, namely, a

---

[1] 168-171.

[2] *P. L.* 7. 370-375. At least two Biblical passages are represented by these lines. The more important one is Ps. 19. 4-6 : ' Their line is gone out through all the earth, and their words to the end of the world. In them hath he set a tabernacle for the sun, which is as a bridegroom coming out of his chamber, and rejoiceth as a strong man to run a race. His going forth is from the end of heaven, and his circuit unto the ends of it : and there is nothing hid from the heat thereof.' The second passage is Job 38. 31, where is mentioned ' the sweet influence of the Pleiades.' The resemblance of the dance of the Pleiades to the dance of seven figures, who may represent Pleiades, in Guido's picture of Aurora, has been remarked by Todd. Apparently this is the only classical antecedent of these lines.

description composed almost entirely of mythology. It occurs at the opening of the Sixth Book of *Paradise Lost.*

> All night the dreadless Angel, unpursued,
> Through Heaven's wide champaign held his way, till Morn,
> Waked by the circling Hours, with rosy hand
> Unbarred the gates of Light. There is a cave
> Within the Mount of God, fast by his throne,
> Where Light and Darkness in perpetual round
> Lodge and dislodge by turns, which makes through Heaven
> Grateful vicissitude, like day and night;
> Light issues forth, and at the other door
> Obsequious Darkness enters, till her hour
> To veil the Heaven, though darkness there might well
> Seem twilight here. And now went forth the Morn,
> Such as in highest Heaven, arrayed in gold
> Empyreal; from before her vanished Night,
> Shot through with orient beams.

In this passage there is an almost literal adaptation of at least four classical poets or poetic conceptions. The general idea of Dawn's opening the gates is from Ovid; the action of the Hours is from Homer; the cave of Light and Darkness is Hesiod's house of Day and Night; the final rout of Night before the beams of the sun is a common conception in Greek poetry, though perhaps in this case referable to Dante.[1]

We may notice that in this passage Milton intends to describe not the earthly dawn, but the grateful vicissitude of light and darkness in heaven. There is, however, in his description a beautiful reflection of the dayspring as it has appeared to many men, and this reveals to us a most important quality in Milton's treatment of mythology and nature. He appreciates the values of two things, nature and the myth, but to him the value of nature outweighs that of the myth. This accounts for the vividness and reality and enthusiasm, which, if the proportion of values were reversed, would tend to become pedantry and dry conventionality. With a view

---

[1] See pp. 15, 33.

to this statement, let us take the first lines of the preceding passage :

> Morn,
> Waked by the circling Hours, with rosy hand
> Unbarred the gates of Light.

Let us analyze this passage in comparison with its
originals. As already suggested, there are two passages in the classics which are here represented. The
first is in the Fifth Book of the *Iliad,* where Hera drives
forth her chariot from Olympus : ' Self-moving groaned
upon their hinges the gates of Heaven, whereof the
Hours are warders, to whom is committed great Heaven
and Olympus, whether to throw open the thick cloud or
set it to.' [1] The other passage is in the Second Book of
Ovid's *Metamorphoses:*

> Ecce vigil rutilo patefecit ab ortu
> Purpureas Aurora fores et plena rosarum
> Atria. [2]

We may first inquire what help Ovid has given Milton. He suggests the idea that the Dawn at her rising
throws open certain gates, but further than this his
influence can hardly be said to extend. As usual he has
made a tableau, overloading it with gay color. Milton,
however, in speaking of Aurora's rosy hand, lends color
enough, and stops before he smears. He is speaking of
dawn in Heaven, and the thought of gates naturally
leads him to think of the Hours, who are the warders
of Heaven's gates. They are therefore adapted from
Homer, with the addition of a beautiful epithet, 'circling,' from the common tradition of Greek poetry. But
the mere juxtaposition of these things is not enough.
Milton, like a true artist, realizes that though color is
lovely, something else is still lovelier, more important,
and more vital. He loves the morning for its freshness,
its action, its grace, its dignity, its progress toward glo-

---

[1] 5. 749-751.

[2] 2. 112. Lo, the watchful Aurora opened her purple doors in the ruddy east, and
her halls filled with roses.

rious climax, and all these qualities are present in his description. There is action in the words 'waked' and 'circling' and 'unbarred,' and in the intervening or accompanying movement which they suggest. There is freshness and grace in the swift Hours, in the modest but effective touch of color, and in the fact that we do not hear the harsh groan of the gates upon their hinges. There is dignity, because the movement, though rapid, is not hurried, and stays slightly at the words 'with rosy hand.' Lastly, there is progress toward a climax. Morn is waked by the Hours; she rises, throws back the bolt; the gates swing open without effort, and Light leaps forth and overspreads the sky. This action is suggested, if not expressed, and to feel the full effect of progress and climax the passage should be read aloud slowly with perfect enunciation. Much of its movement and progress is expressed in the effect of light consonants and liquids, and in the fine succession of vowels which seems to accompany the meaning and open out at the end.

It would be a mistake to assume that Milton deliberately and consciously went about arranging his description in this way. He rather felt deeply and keenly the glories of a new day at first hand, so deeply and keenly that his poetic sense of these things rushes in and informs his description, with a result such as this before us. Thus the myth does not remain or become, in his hands, a lifeless convention; nor is it a sort of mythological veil, through which we faintly see the loveliness of nature. Rather, on the one hand, he understands the spirit of nature, and is in harmony with it; on the other, he has sympathized with the Greek imagination until he imagines in part as a Greek. When, therefore, he hears from the Greek lyre, though echoed never so faintly, a note first stirred by the great harp of nature, he recognizes it, and sounds it again, loud and clear, inseparably mingling the qualities of the two instruments in one tone.

It follows from this as a sort of converse statement that Milton was also independent in his use of the myth. It never threatens to get the best of him, for his use of it is governed by an unfailing sense of things more serious and important to the human heart and mind. However extensive the mythological element in a given passage, the result is no less vivid and imaginative. The myth never encumbers the poet and gets in his way. It does not have the appearance of something in the wrong place, which makes itself the excuse for being there. Rather it is properly related to the more important thing, and falls into the place where it belongs.

After this somewhat detailed analysis and consideration of the more apparent facts in connection with Milton's treatment of nature, let us endeavor to weigh the value of the mythological element in Milton's art, and discover, if possible, the true benefit of its influence upon him.

As we have already seen, mythology is not the product of one man, possessing the marks of his peculiarities, but is the reflection of national character and ideas. It is only in part subject to the personal variation of the individual who treats it. Its nature is therefore chiefly universal, containing qualities and truths which appeal not to men of a certain narrow class, but to nearly all men. For this reason classical myths, when presented in an artistic and appreciative manner, exert a strong and refining influence, and many have therefore insisted upon a study of them as an element in the best culture. For culture is not an exaggeration and development of the oddities and idiosyncrasies of the individual, but is rather the result of assimilating in one soul, so far as may be, the best part of the past and contemporary life of men, that is, the part which is most permanent and universal. It is according to such a principle that mythology possesses artistic value. The best and most permanent qualities of the Greek people are to be found there; and the artist who selects his material from it, and who treats it lovingly and with understanding, may be sure of a certain steadiness and universality in his art, while at the same time the material is of such a pliant nature that he may express with it much of the best that he has within himself. Take, for example, the passage which we have already discussed:

> Morn,
> Waked by the circling Hours, with rosy hand
> Unbarred the gates of Light.

We have seen already the extent and importance of the classical element in this passage. The pure and beautiful imagery is wholly classical. It possesses Greek dignity and repose. It contains the elements of expectancy, action, progress, and climax, and these qualities are the essential and universal ones by which the beauty of the dawn appeals to men. But thoroughly mingled with the universal elements of these lines are some of the best personal qualities of Milton himself. They are not introduced in the form of a curious and outlandish conceit; by his selection of certain qualities from the Greek, and his emphasis of them, he reflects the same qualities in his own nature. Such are his delicacy, dignity, and repose. Then we feel also his purity of thought and emotion, and his high reserve, which is felt elsewhere, in nearly every line, as a distinguishing trait of the poet.

Milton lived in a time when the importance and development of individuality had become the importance and development of personal peculiarity. Much of the poetry of his time suffered from this fact, and as a result is full of conceits and curious figures, while generally it no longer appeals strongly to men, and is now read only at the promptings of an idle interest in its quaintness. Milton himself did not always escape this tendency to conceit and oddity. Whether he was aware of it or not, the fact remains that mythology often

served in his case as a sort of safeguard against such mistakes, for while it suffered some modification under the
influence of his individuality, it kept his poetry within
the bounds of universal appeal.

For the sake of illustration let us compare with the
passage last quoted two or three others, which, as it
happens, all describe the dawn or the sun. The first is
in *L'Allegro*, where the poet is walking upon high ground
at sunrise,

> Right against the eastern gate
> Where the great Sun begins his state,
> Robed in flames and amber light,
> The clouds in thousand liveries dight.[1]

Here also is the figure of the opening gates as in the
other description, but notice the difference between its
two applications. There the figure was simply suggested. Here it has been developed into a conceit
whose artificiality is not in keeping with the freedom of
nature. The sunrise is a grand ceremony. The Sun is
ushered forth in all the pride of state and of gorgeous,
shining robes, attended by numberless clouds in gay
and pompous livery. The figure has lost some of its
former appropriateness. There is now a sort of dis-
crepancy between its formality and the unrestrained
grandeur of the sunrise. The image has been slightly
overworked, so that it begins to resemble an odd fancy.
It is impressionistic in character, and seems to be the
effluence of a single, changeful mood of the poet. It
follows that, in so far as this is true, no man is subject
to the full appeal of this passage, unless, at the moment
when he considers it, his mood coincides with the mood
in which the poet first conceived it. As moods are
superficial as well as occasional in character, the art
which is dependent upon them for its value must be
narrowly confined both in the range and depth of its
appeal, and must be in a corresponding degree weak.

---

[1] *L'Al.* 59-62

Another example of the same tendency to conceit on the part of Milton is found in a speech of Comus, who prays that Hecate may befriend his nocturnal orgies

> till utmost end
> Of all thy dues be done, and none left out,
> Ere the blabbing eastern scout,
> The nice Morn on the Indian steep,
> From her cabined loophole peep,
> And to the telltale Sun descry
> Our concealed solemnity.[1]

There is possibly a mythological allusion in the epithet 'telltale,'[2] but the description of the Dawn is peculiar and odd—so much so that we think only of this curious figure and not of the natural phenomenon which it would typify.[3]

One more instance remains which is even more fantastic and unusual than those already cited, and mars the serious close of the beautiful *Ode on the Nativity:*

> So, when the sun in bed,
> Curtained with cloudy red,
> Pillows his chin upon an orient wave,
> The flocking shadows pale
> Troop to the infernal jail.[4]

Here is a figure so overwrought that it becomes almost a burlesque. It may be that to a few men, who are in a sufficiently light mood, the sunrise might suggest a figure of this kind, but to the multitude it can only remain far-fetched and meaningless.

Before going on, let us notice one passage in which mythology and the personality of Milton are balanced in almost equal proportion. It is in *Il Penseroso*, where the poet wishes to be hidden in a shady nook near a running stream,

---

[1] *C.* 136-142.

[2] See p. 11.

[3] The odd imagery of this passage may be partly intentional, since the words are spoken by Comus, whose life is irregular, and who therefore hates the light of day as unfavorable to his wickedness.

[4] 229-233.

3

> While the bee with honeyed thigh,
> That at her flowery work doth sing,
> And the waters murmuring,
> With such consort as they keep,
> Entice the dewy-feathered Sleep.
> And let some strange mysterious dream
> Wave at his wings in airy stream
> Of lively portraiture displayed,
> Softly on my eyelids laid.[1]

The substance of this passage is mythological. It is practically contained in the epithet 'dewy-feathered.' The conception of sleep as a dew falling upon wearied limbs is expressive at once of its gentleness and its power to refresh, and holds good also in the fact that the night brings both. The figure is a classical tradition, and appears in Homer, Vergil, and Statius. No less common is the conception of Sleep as winged, which also appears in Homer, Vergil, Ovid, and other Latin poets. These two conceptions are united by Statius in the expression 'humentes alæ,' and again with lighter and softer effect by Milton in his 'dewy-feathered.' Silius Italicus has elaborated this conception in describing the dreams of Hannibal, as the great general lies before the walls of Rome.[2] As the god descends to the soldier,

> quatit inde soporas
> Devexo capiti pennas, oculisque quietem
> Inrorat, tangens Lethæa tempora virga.[3]

This is followed by a long train of dreams in solemn succession. The passage in Silius is enough like Milton's to be its original, but, whether it is or not, Milton gains by the comparison. The meaning of his lines has never been definitely explained, and we almost shrink at the thought of defining it closely. This very indefiniteness is in harmony with the evasive and shadowy

---

[1] 142–150.
[2] *Punici* 10. 337–371.
[3] 'Then waves he his sleepy wings over the bowed head, and sheds the dew of rest upon his eyes, touching his temples with his Lethean wand.'

character of dreams. In view of Silius, however, the thought seems to be that in an airy and graceful line move faint, mysterious figures of a dream, following the motion of the wings of Sleep, as he gently waves them above the slumbering mortal. With these facts in mind, we may perceive more clearly how the dignity and grace and gentleness of Milton's soul, together with his deep love and knowledge of nature, have here met the beauty and truth of classical imagery, and how all are inseparably blended in the single loveliness of the whole passage.

To return now to the beginning of the Sixth Book of *Paradise Lost*, the description of celestial dawn quoted at length above, brings to mind another important characteristic of Milton's treatment of classical mythology. Taken as a whole, it is a beautiful synthesis, or fitting together, of three or four very distinct classical ideas. As we have seen, Homer and Ovid are united, these are joined to Hesiod, and the group is finished with a tradition common to classical poets. We have already noticed in the treatment of similes the tendency to accumulation or synthesis, and it occurs frequently in the use of mythology throughout Milton's poetry. In the description of Eden, Pan, the Graces and the Hours, Proserpina, Daphne, and Amalthea were all gathered to illustrate the beauty of the garden, like petals about the honeyed center of a flower. So also in the Second Book of *Paradise Lost*, the description of the terrors of Hell is reinforced by a reference to 'Typhoean rage,' and by describing the death agony of Hercules, when, mad with pain, he slew his own companion. The infernal rivers are mentioned—hated Styx, Lethe, Acheron, Cocytus, 'named of lamentation loud,' and Phlegethon, the torrent of flames. There also is the wretched Tantalus, together with Medusa and the other Gorgons, and Hydras and Chimeras dire. At the bounds of Hell are two monsters, the one, like Scylla, girt with wide Cerberean mouths, the other black as

Night, and fierce as ten Furies. Here again the allusions are all arranged about one idea and focused upon
it, thus emphasizing it and throwing it into relief.

But by far the best example of this grouped arrangement occurs in *Comus*, or, more accurately, contains
Comus. It consists in bringing together the earth and
sea and sky to serve as a kind of setting or background
for the poem.   At the beginning of the masque is this
stage direction: 'The first scene discovers a wild wood.'
We soon hear of the nodding horror of its shady brows,
and of fountain-brims where wood-nymphs play.   Here
wanders the Lady, singing her song of Echo, who lives
in an airy shell

> By slow Meander's margent green,
> And in the violet-embroidered vale.

Here prevails the good influence of Pan or Sylvan,
while through green alley and bushy dell steals the son
of Circe.   There is mention, too, of quivered nymphs and
flowery-kirtled Naiads, of Diana, queen of the woods,
and of a shepherd who, sitting on the tender grass,
discourses of hæmony and moly, while others in the
green meadows offer wreaths of pansies and gaudy
daffodils to the nymph of the river.   Thus it is that
Milton has not merely set a circumscribed background
of woods for the action of *Comus*, but has filled it with
the larger atmosphere of forest and field, and has suggested beyond the bounds of his scene the wide extent
of the green earth.   Such a result is hardly accomplished by the representation of a single limited landscape.   The landscape is likely to exhibit nature in one
of her moods, and, since she is changeful and fickle, it
may not contain, or at least may not effectively show
forth, her permanent and underlying qualities.   Milton
has therefore endeavored to suggest these permanent
qualities of Nature, such as her mystery, her sweet playfulness, her terror, her dignity, and he has done it largely
by his use of mythology.   Thus Echo embodies her

sweetness, the nymphs her playfulness, Circe and
Comus her terror, Diana her dignity, and all of them
her mystery.   And the myths thus arranged blend in a
certain harmony through their parts in the plot, while
they give to nature a human and personal character,
and thus bring her nearer to men.

But the earth is not the only manifestation of nature
in *Comus*. Now and then, not far away, we hear the
sound of a quiet ocean, and may sometimes look off
over its expanse, or feel the mystery of its blue depths.
Its influence is first felt in these lines:

> Neptune, besides the sway
> Of every salt flood and each ebbing stream,
> Took in by lot, 'twixt high and nether Jove,
> Imperial rule of all the sea-girt isles
> That, like to rich and various gems, inlay
> The unadornèd bosom of the deep;
> Which he, to grace his tributary gods,
> By course commits to several government,
> And gives them leave to wear their sapphire crowns
> And wield their little tridents.[1]

And again:

> The sounds and seas, with all their finny drove,
> Now to the moon in wavering morrice move;
> And on the tawny sands and shelves,
> Trip the pert fairies and the dapper elves.[2]

Comus speaks of a swelling sea and unsought diamonds
which

> Would so emblaze the forehead of the deep,
> And so bestud with stars, that they below
> Would grow inured to light, and come at last
> To gaze upon the sun with shameless brows.[3]

In the end comes Sabrina, the nymph of Severn, from
under the glassy, cool, translucent wave.   She is invoked

---

[1] 18–27.
[2] 115–118.
[3] 732–735.

> In name of great Oceanus,
> By the earth-shaking Neptune's mace,
> And Tethys' grave majestic pace;
> By hoary Nereus' wrinkled look,
> And the Carpathian wizard's hook;
> By scaly Triton's winding shell,
> And old sooth-saying Glaucus' spell;
> By Leucothea's lovely hands,
> And her son that rules the strands;
> By Thetis' tinsel-slippered feet,
> And the songs of Sirens sweet;
> By dead Parthenope's dear tomb,
> And fair Ligea's golden comb,
> Wherewith she sits on diamond rocks,
> Sleeking her soft alluring locks;
> By all the nymphs that nightly dance
> Upon thy streams with wily glance.[1]

Sabrina appears in a chariot

> Thick set with agate, and the azurn sheen
> Of turkis blue, and emerald green,
> That in the channel strays.[2]

By means of such lines as these the spirit of the sea is present in *Comus*.

But around and above the earth and the sea of *Comus* is the sky. It is now seen inwrought with bright stars, and now flooded with the light of day. It is, throughout, the home and symbol of purity and virtue, the palace of eternal happiness. It is the heaven where aspiration to good things receives its reward, and in pity for the weak it stoops to help them. As the earth is included by the sea, both earth and sea are surrounded by the air of heaven, for with it the poem begins and ends. It opens with these lines of the Attendant Spirit:

> Before the starry threshold of Jove's court
> My mansion is, where those immortal shapes
> Of bright aerial spirits live insphered
> In regions mild of calm and serene air.

---

[1] 868–884.
[2] 893.

Here and there throughout the poem one may look out into the infinite depth of the sky as through an open window in the pictures of old Dutch and Flemish masters. At the command of Jove, the good spirit doffs his sky-robes, spun out of Iris' woof, and descends 'swift as the sparkle of a glancing star' to convey wanderers through the precincts of Comus. The magician and his rout enter with these words:

> The star that bids the shepherd fold
> Now the top of heaven doth hold;
> And the gilded car of day
> His glowing axle doth allay
> In the steep Atlantic stream;
> And the slope sun his upward beam
> Shoots against the dusky pole,
> Pacing toward the other goal
> Of his chamber in the east.[1]

Comus speaks of the starry quire

> Who, in their nightly watchful spheres,
> Lead in swift round the months and years.[2]

Again he compares the two brothers to gay creatures of the element

> That in the colors of the rainbow live,
> And play i' the plighted clouds.[3]

While at the end of the poem the good spirit flies away to

> those happy climes that lie
> Where day never shuts his eye,
> Up in the broad fields of the sky.
> There I suck the liquid air,
> All amidst the gardens fair
> Of Hesperus, and his daughters three
> That sing about the golden tree.
> Along the crispèd shades and bowers
> Revels the spruce and jocund spring;
> The Graces and the rosy-bosomed Hours
> Thither all their bounties bring.

---

[1] 93-101.
[2] 113.
[3] 300.

There eternal Summer dwells,
And west winds with musky wing
About the cedarn alleys fling
Nard and cassia's balmy smells.
Iris there with humid bow
Waters the odorous banks, that blow
Flowers of more mingled hue
Than her purfled scarf can shew,
And drenches with Elysian dew
(List, mortals, if your ears be true)
Beds of hyacinth and roses,
Where young Adonis oft reposes,
Waxing well of his deep wound,
In slumber soft, and on the ground
Sadly sits the Assyrian queen.
But far above, in spangled sheen,
Celestial Cupid, her famed son, advanced
Holds his dear Psyche, sweet entranced
After her wandering labors long,
Till free consent the gods among
Make her his eternal bride,
And from her fair unspotted side
Two blissful twins are to be born,
Youth and Joy; so Jove hath sworn.[1]

We have now seen how Milton's imagination transcends the particular locality of *Comus*, and in so doing surrounds it with the large exterior world of earth and sky and sea. Nor is the action unrelated to this outer atmosphere, but rather draws sky and sea and earth together on one horizon, as the Attendant Spirit and Sabrina come from their distant homes to mingle with the lives of men on earth. In accomplishing this result, classical mythology plays the important part of poetic suggestion which we have already seen assigned to it in other descriptions of nature.

But these examples taken from *Comus* illustrate also another quality of Milton's art—a quality which it is difficult to define. I refer to a certain width of range and sweep, which often, as in this case, accompanies a synthesis of mythological legends; the myths seem to

---

[1] 977-1011.

be transformed from their original state into something large and exalted. Milton seems to carry them into a larger universe, where through his poetic imagination and his sense of truth he expands and purges them, somewhat as Plato has done in the passage from the *Phædrus* quoted near the beginning of our discussion. It is this quality of range which distinguishes a passage in the lines for a *Vacation Exercise*, where the poet apostrophizes his native language:

> Yet I had rather, if I were to choose,
> Thy service in some graver subject use,
> Such as may make thee search thy coffers round,
> Before thou clothe my fancy in fit sound:
> Such where the deep transported mind may soar
> Above the wheeling poles, and at Heaven's door
> Look in, and see each blissful deity
> How he before the thunderous throne doth lie,
> Listening to what unshorn Apollo sings
> To the touch of golden wires, while Hebe brings
> Immortal nectar to her kingly sire;
> Then, passing through the spheres of watchful fire,
> And misty regions of wide air next under,
> And hills of snow and lofts of pilèd thunder,
> May tell at length how green-eyed Neptune raves,
> In Heaven's defiance mustering all his waves;
> Then sing of secret things that came to pass
> When beldam Nature in her cradle was;
> And last, of kings and queens and heroes old,
> Such as the wise Demodocus once told
> In solemn songs at king Alcinous' feast,
> While sad Ulysses' soul, and all the rest
> Are held, with his melodious harmony,
> In willing chains and sweet captivity.[1]

Behind these two qualities of synthesis and range there lie two conditions. The first is the enormous extent of Milton's learning. The second may be called his inclusion of material, that is, his power of mastering it and making it subservient to the truths embodied in his poetry. The first qualification is extensive, the second intensive.

---

[1] 30–52.

A study of Milton's mythology, being limited to a particular kind of subject-matter, cannot furnish complete evidence, but only an indication, of his attainments and preferences in reading. Yet with but this partial knowledge, we may justly wonder at the greatness of these attainments. There are four poets from whom he certainly derived more help than from any others. These are Homer, Hesiod, Vergil, and Ovid. Hesiod, in proportion to the body of his poetry, probably furnished Milton with the greatest amount of material, and nearly all of this comes from the *Theogony*. That Milton should have known Hesiod so well is not unnatural, since the character of both poets is dignified and austere. Of the *Iliad* we find most frequent allusions to the First Book, especially to its closing episode, and to the Second, Fifth, and Eighteenth Books. Of the *Odyssey* the Eighth, Tenth, and Eleventh Books are the favorites. The First and the Sixth Books of the *Æneid* are apparently much preferred to any others, though not infrequent use is made of the Third, Fourth, and Fifth. Ovid's *Metamorphoses* and *Fasti* would naturally appeal to Milton more strongly than the same poet's rather sordid love-poetry. Of the *Metamorphoses* the First Book is most often used, and the Twelfth is the only one which I have not had occasion to cite. Such preferences are what we should expect of Milton. He listened most gladly to the songs that tell the solemn origin of the world, that celebrate the noble character of a hero, declare the sanctity of poet and prophet, or reveal the mysteries of the after-life.

Next in importance to these four sources are Euripides, Pindar, Theocritus, and the *Homeric Hymns*. With these we may mention also the prose writers, Pausanias and Apollodorus. Milton has also drawn some of his mythology from Æschylus, Sophocles, Plato, the *Orphic Hymns*, and Apollonius of Rhodes; from Herodotus, Plutarch, Pliny, Diodorus, and Strabo; from Horace, Statius, Claudian, and the tragedies of Seneca. To these we may add, though the list will be by no means exhaustive, Cicero, Athenæus, Hyginus, Aratus, Macrobius, Lucretius, and most of the minor poets of the empire.[1]

Having thus considered the extent of Milton's reading, we may see how it becomes a condition of the two qualities of range and synthesis already mentioned as qualities of his poetry. These qualities are simply the reflex of corresponding ones in the poet himself. To Milton an extension of his reading was an extension of his own life, with all its experience, sympathies, and understanding, into the life and times of which he read. It is not in the enormous store of information revealed in his poems that this quality of range is principally felt; it lies rather in the dignity and impressiveness with which each myth has been treated, in an underlying consciousness of the high and universal truth of these myths, which frees them from the limitations of time and space. It is a commonplace that travel enlarges a man's nature. For the high and sensitive mind books do the same, and in the case of Milton the quality of wide range in his poetic utterance was a direct consequence of the range of his own mind, which his reading had done much to extend.

The broader and more universal knowledge and sympathy which he thus acquired reinforced his tendency to synthesis. When he came to deal with a given idea or truth, he dealt with it more authoritatively and universally, since he was able to summon from widely divergent sources such instances as, converging upon this truth, would uphold and illustrate it.

We may pause at this point to consider two or three inferences, less significant in themselves, which follow from a detailed study of Milton's classical sources. The sources of his mythology served him in one or both of two ways. They either furnished him with mythological information, or contained poetic sugges-

---

[1] For a more complete idea of the topics discussed here the reader may consult the index of sources on pp. 89 ff.

tion of which he made use in his own treatment. It may
even be said that nearly every writer of whom he made
any considerable use assisted him to some extent in
both of these ways, though some of them did so principally in the former way, some principally in the latter,
and several about equally in both. The writings of the
prose mythographers, Apollodorus and Hyginus, are
little more than storehouses of legend, and serve Milton
as such. He makes a similar use of the historians,
and some of the poets, such as Apollonius. Yet hard
lines of division are impossible, for even so prosy a
writer as Apollodorus may contain a word which Milton
transforms by the magic of poetry.[1] On the other hand,
Vergil, Pindar, Theocritus, and Horace generally contain
poetic beginnings for Milton—the seeds which he brings
to flower in a single finished epithet or expression, or
which, increasing, give color to an entire poem.[2] Lastly,
the poets who served Milton most equally in both ways
are Homer, Hesiod, and Ovid.

The question of Milton's conformity with his originals is also an interesting one. It may be said, in spite
of well-known apparent exceptions to the contrary,[3]
that he follows the details of his originals with strict
accuracy. The present discussion has already furnished striking instances of this fact, and almost every
mythological allusion illustrates it in some way.[4] Yet

---

[1] Cf. the use of 'throttled' at the head of a fine climax in *P. R.* 4. 568. This detail of the fight with Antæus is drawn from the account by Apollodorus. See p. 8. Other instances may be found in a comparison of Apollodorus 1. 6 with the poetical condensation in *C. N.* 226, and of Aristotle with the catalogue of winds in *P. L.* 10. 695–706. See pp. 83, 86.

[2] Cf. 'rosy-bosomed Hours,' p. 44; 'Plutonian hall,' p. 70; 'flowery-kirtled Naiads,' pp. 58, 59; cf. also the relation of *L'Allegro* to Pindar's Fourteenth Olympian ode, pp. liv, 39.

[3] For example the genealogies in *L'Allegro* and *Il Penseroso;* but see pp. lii ff., lviii ff.

[4] I can hardly refrain from calling attention to a typical example in *Arcades*, where the poet speaks of

> Divine Alpheus, who, by secret sluice,
> Stole under seas to meet his Arethuse.

'Secret sluice' is apparently a pretty combination of Vergil's 'occultas vias' and Statius' 'demerso canali.' See p. 5. Of course Milton's accuracy here, as always, is not observed merely for its own sake, but rather for the purpose of keeping, and, if possible, of refining the poetic quality of the originals.

with all his careful adherence to his sources, it seems impossible that he ever adapted them directly from the printed text, or that his relation to them was sustained in any degree by the open book. Though his treatment of a given myth may reveal the use of Homer, Hesiod, and Ovid, even in minutest details, yet the elements are united and mingled only as they could be after not merely a process of memory, but of absorption and appropriation by the poet.

It is in the spirit of his treatment, however, that Milton departs from his originals, for while the mythology of his poetry contains a great deal which is classical in the best sense, and while it may contain something which resembles the directness of Homer, the austerity of Hesiod, the exaltation of Plato, the dignity of Vergil, or even the facility of Ovid, it possesses the grandeur and purity that characterize Milton, and it has been removed from its old surroundings that it might be subservient to a new faith.[1]

More essential than the extent of Milton's learning is what we have called his inclusion of it. His treatment of mythology is throughout characterized by firmness and control. It is felt in his compression of myths, and in the freedom with which he moves among them and groups them. It is felt more distinctly in the subjection to which he reduces every myth. Frequently as they occur, it is impossible to find one of them which is not in some way subordinate to a ruling idea or truth. Whether in simile, or in description of nature, or in the development of a great theme, the function of the myth

---

[1] Strongly imbued with the classics as Milton was, it would of course be wrong to suppose that his mythology was not frequently modified by intermediate influences, such as the patristic writings, but more often the poets, painters, and scientists of the Renaissance. The names of Lactantius, Eusebius, Dante, Boccaccio, Chaucer, Spenser, Boiardo, Guido, Tasso, Ariosto, are only a few of a list which careful investigation could make much longer. Yet it can hardly be doubted that when Milton turned to account in his own poems a mediæval or modern treatment of mythology, he would at the same time be conscious of its original in classical literature. This being the case, the influence of the original upon him was likely to mingle with that of the later treatment, so that his relation to the classics could hardly ever become wholly second-hand.

in Milton's poetry is always subservient. He never treats it for its own sake, that is, merely for the sake of the story or invention which it contains. Such an employment of the myth would have been to him a mere dissipation or idle indulgence. Even the story of Bacchus and Circe, which plays an important part in Comus, stands for the basest forces in humanity, and these are met and overcome by others which are high and purifying. In order to gain a clearer idea of the sense in which Milton included his material it is necessary to inquire into his theory concerning mythology.

Both the early and the late poems contain direct evidence of his view in this respect. The patristic and mediæval idea that, being pagan, mythology was at war with Christianity, appears in the *Nativity Hymn*, where heathen gods flee before ' the dreaded Infant's hand.' In *Paradise Lost* all the Ionian gods—Oceanus, Saturn, Jove, and the rest—belong to the host of Satan. In three places Milton speaks of their oracles as abominable, or as the diguised voice of Satan. While these opinions were common in the Middle Ages, they were foreshadowed in the writings of Plutarch, especially in his treatise on the *Cessation of Oracles*, nor is it unlikely that in each expression of this opinion Milton may have had Plutarch in mind. Thus he says in the *Nativity Hymn*, ' The oracles are dumb,' actually quoting Plutarch; and again in *Paradise Regained* he says, 'Henceforth the oracles are ceased.' [1]

Milton sometimes represents the myths themselves as of Satanic origin, invented to deceive men, or he speaks of the gods as disguises assumed by the devils in order to practise more successfully their wickedness among men. The fallen angels are said to have fabled

---

[1] See Plutarch, *Cess. of Oracles* 38; *P. R.* 1. 456; compare also Plutarch 15 with *P. R.* 2. 173–191. Other traces of this work are to be found in Milton. Thus Night's ' shadowy cone' of *P. L.* 4. 776 may be compared with *Cess. Or.* 4, where the earth's shadow is called conical. In *Cess. Or.* 7 Apollo is called ' lord and father of the sun,' and in 13 the moon is called the ' province of Hecate.' Both expressions resemble a line in Milton's twelfth sonnet referring to

Latona's twin-born progeny,
Which after held the sun and moon in fee.

how the Serpent, whom they called
Ophion, with Eurynome (the wide-
Encroaching Eve perhaps), had first the rule
Of high Olympus, thence by Saturn driven
And Ops, ere yet Dictæan Jove was born.[1]

Satan accuses Belial of hiding to waylay

Some beauty rare, Calisto, Clymene,
Daphne, or Semele, Antiopa,
Or Amymone, Syrinx, many more
Too long, then lay'st thy scapes on names adored,
Apollo, Neptune, Jupiter, or Pan,
Satyr, or Faun, or Silvan.[2]

---

[1] *P. L.* 10. 580–584. This passage illustrates a theory which began with the euhemeristic method of interpreting mythology, and which seems to have been very popular in Milton's time. It first consisted in explaining mythology by identifying the gods with mortals mentioned in the earliest traditions. Thus Saturn was said to have been an early king of men, and Æolus a weatherwise friend of sailors. Cf. pp. lviii, 43. Christian writers seized upon this method of condemning mythology for its false origin, and went further in identifying the classical divinities with characters of Biblical history. Thus Eurynome, whose name means 'wide-encroaching,' or rather 'wide-ruling,' is identified with Eve, to whom these epithets are quite as appropriate. Ophion is said to be the same as the serpent of Eden, by virtue of the etymological idea of 'serpent' which the name contains. Such identification often rested upon etymology, as that of Hammon with Ham, p. 7. The theory is stated in *P. R.* 4. 334 ff. Instances are noted on pp. 17, 46, 57. The most beautiful use which Milton made of this idea is found in *C. N.* 85 ff.:

> The shepherds on the lawn,
> Or ere the point of dawn,
> Sat simply chatting in a rustic row;
> Full little thought they than
> That the mighty Pan
> Was kindly come to live with them below.

The identification of Pan with Christ is implied in Spenser, *Shepheards Calender, May* 53. E. K., in a gloss on the passage, says : '"Great Pan" is Christ, the very god of all shepheards, which calleth himselfe the greate, and good shepherd. The name is most rightly (methinkes) applyed to him; for Pan signifieth all, or omnipotent, which is onely the Lord Jesus.' E. K. cites as an authority the *Præparatio Evangelica* of Eusebius, but the latter (5. 17. 13), on the basis of the wonderful story of Thamus at Paxi, first related by Plutarch (*Cess. of Oracles* 17) and recounted by E. K., seems to make Pan merely a type of paganism overcome by Christianity. Plutarch relates that Thamus, an Egyptian mariner, when once becalmed near the islands of Paxi, heard a loud voice admonishing him to carry to Palodes the message that Great Pan was dead. At Palodes Thamus in a loud voice uttered the words, 'Great Pan is dead,' and forthwith the air was filled with the noise of groans and dreadful lamentations. Tiberius was at that time emperor in Rome, and when he heard of the matter from Thamus inquired earnestly of the wise men who this Pan was. E. K. also cites Lavater, a writer of the Renaissance, who in his book, *De Spectris, etc.* (pp. 114-116), after mentioning Eusebius says : 'Alii religionis nostræ sanctissimi viri asserunt, ut Paulus Marsus in suis annotationibus in librum I. Fastorum Ovidii annotavit, eam vocem auditam e Paxis ea nocte, quæ secuta est passionis Dominicæ diem, decimo nono anno Tiberii, quo quidem Christus passus est: qua voce miraculo quodam ex solitudine desertorum scopulorum edita, nuntiatum illud sit Dominum et Deum nostrum passum. Pan enim totum significat. Totius autem et universæ naturæ dominus passus erat.'

[2] *P. R.* 2. 185-191.

Milton often speaks of the myths as fables, or affects to entertain a doubt of their literal truth. He mentions 'Elysian fields (if such there were).'[1] He refers to 'Hesperian fables,'[2] to Titans and Giants, 'whom fables name of monstrous size,' and to the 'fable' of Deucalion and Pyrrha.[3] He contrasts the Greek Muse Calliope with his own Heavenly Muse, as an 'empty dream.'[4] He avers that the Greeks derived their songs from the Hebrews,

> Ill imitated while they loudest sing
> The vices of their deities, and their own,
> In fable, hymn, or song, so personating
> Their gods ridiculous, and themselves past shame.
> Remove their swelling epithets, thick-laid
> As varnish on a harlot's cheek, the rest,
> Thin-sown with aught of profit or delight,
> Will far be found unworthy to compare
> With Sion's songs, to all true tastes excelling,
> Where God is praised aright, and godlike men.[5]

The above passages seem to prove that Milton assumed an attitude of antagonism and contempt toward classical mythology, regarding it as empty, false, and unprofitable. Taking this last quotation from *Paradise Regained* as the most elaborate and explicit statement of his view, it cannot be denied that he is right in charging classical myths with much that is ridiculous, shameful, and even vicious. On the other hand, how are we to reconcile this view with his frequent and loving and reverent treatment of the myths in his poetry?

There are two passages which, presenting as strongly as they do the opposite position, are most important in helping us to effect such a reconciliation. The first of these passages occurs in the Ninth Book of *Paradise*

---

[1] *D. F. I.* 40.
[2] *P. L.* 4. 250.
[3] *P. L.* 1. 197; *P. R.* 2. 215; cf. *P. L.* 2. 628; 4. 706; 5. 381; 9. 431; 11. 11; *P. R.* 2. 358.
[4] *P. L.* 7. 39.
[5] *P. R.* 4. 339-348.

Lost, where Milton calls the place in which the serpent appeared to Eve

> Spot more delicious than those gardens feigned
> Or of revived Adonis, or renowned
> Alcinous, host of old Laertes' son;
> Or that, not mystic, where the sapient king
> Held dalliance with his fair Egyptian spouse.[1]

And again in *Comus* the good spirit says:

> 'Tis not vain or fabulous
> (Though so esteemed by shallow ignorance)
> What the sage poets, taught by the Heavenly Muse,
> Storied of old in high immortal verse
> Of dire Chimeras and enchanted isles
> And rifted rocks whose entrance leads to Hell;
> For such there be, but unbelief is blind.[2]

In the first of these quotations Milton plainly asserts that the classical legends are mystic, intending thereby not merely an antithesis to historical or true narrative, but also the additional idea that they contain hidden or deep truth of which they are the symbolic expression.[3] In the second quotation he says that they are in the best sense true, implying that they contain the deep truths of life. More than that, he calls the poets who treat them sage, and their poetry high and immortal, and above all says that the myths are the gift of divine inspiration. What more could he say of them? We are likely to lose some of the emphasis of his statement unless we remember well what divine inspiration meant

---

[1] *P. L.* 9. 439–443.

[2] *C.* 513–519.

[3] A similar idea of poetic legend occurs in *Pens.* 120:

> And if aught else great bards beside
> In sage and solemn tunes have sung,
> Of turneys, and of trophies hung,
> Of forests, and enchantments drear,
> Where more is meant than meets the ear.

The last line is almost a paraphrase of Seneca, *Ep.* 114. 1: 'in quibus plus intellegendum esset quam audiendum.' Cf. *Ep.* 59. 5: 'Plus significas quam loqueris.'

4

to Milton, with his pure and steadfast faith in Christianity, and his regard for sacred history, both Christian and Hebraic, as shown in the passage already quoted from *Paradise Regained*.[1]

With these two apparently contradictory opinions over against each other, it is only fair to make allowance for a certain amount of inconsistency in Milton's position. It is possible that at the moment of broader conception he may have felt the community of truth existing between Christianity and Hebraism on the one hand, and Hellenism on the other,[2] while at a moment when for some reason his view was narrowed, the weakness and uncertain utterance of Greek teaching may have condemned it in his mind. Along with this goes the fact already suggested that classical mythology contains at once that which is both good and bad, both profound and superficial, both pure and defiling. As treated by one poet it becomes the outgrowth of high living and aspiration; as treated by another it reflects an idle and vicious imagination. These facts impose upon Milton the necessity of choice. He therefore distinguishes clearly between the good and the bad, exalting the one and condemning the other, or passing it over in silence. Thus in one place the conception of Zeus as just and powerful and beneficent is magnified;[3] in another this divinity and his associates are thrust down for their vices and depravity.[4] The same may be said concerning Milton's use of other divinities, such as the nymphs and Apollo and the Graces, and in every case for his opposed conceptions there is abundant support in classical lore.[5] He prefers, too, those myths which are sublime and noble, or pure and sweet. Thus he deals often, as we have seen, with the mythology of

---

[1] The entire passage, *P. R.* 4. 286-364, should be read.

[2] Cf. *S. A.* 497-501 and p. 80.

[3] Cf. *P. R.* 4. 565; *D. F. I.* 45; *V. E.* 39; *Pens.* 48; *Arc.* 44; *C.* 1, 20, 41, 78, etc.; *Lyc.* 82.

[4] Cf. *P. L.* 1. 512; 10. 580; *P. R.* 2. 190, 214.

[5] See pp. 38, 39, and lviii with N. 1.

the after-life, with heroes like Heracles and Odysseus, and dwells upon their manliness, while he is silent concerning their ungoverned passions. He loves the purity of Artemis and Athene, and the gentleness of the gods of the sea.

In all this Milton is not the victim of idle or change-ful preference, since nothing inspired his imagination without relation to his one purpose, namely, by his utterance to make the soul of man purer and wiser and stronger. It is the ruling force of this conscious pur-pose which gives not only his treatment of mythology, but all his art, its strength, completeness, and positive appeal. In a time when men travel in the circle of 'art for art's sake,' and turn from Milton because he is 'moral,' and therefore certainly not an artist, as they say, the necessary relation of a definite philosophic pur-pose to art, as illustrated in his poetry, should not be unheeded.

It will now be better understood what is meant by Milton's inclusion of his material, in which he renders it subservient to a definite idea or expression. Every occurrence of mythology in his poems illustrates the quality of this inclusion in some way, but none of them better than the companion-pieces *L'Allegro* and *Il Penseroso*.

Perhaps the most noticeable thing, in a first reading of these poems, is the existence throughout each of cor-respondence and contrast with the other. Editors com-monly say that they represent the world as seen under the influence of two distinct moods, and therefore the melancholy so hateful at one time becomes attractive at another, while of the spirit of mirth the reverse is true. This merely raises the problem instead of solving it, for it implies either that Milton was insincere in at least one of these poems, or that he was so largely a man of moods, and therefore so superficial and unphilosophical, that the world which he endeavored to interpret might assume, at various times, appearances diametrically opposed. Either implication is hardly reconcilable with the order and positive consistency which generally characterize his art.

As Milton achieved the expression of his thought in these poems by means of mythology, so we may most profitably approach them through the same medium. The keynote of them both, that is, the deeper truth which lies beneath them, is discoverable in a thorough analysis of their mythology—an analysis which indeed, in a few cases, has been carried on in the right direction, but has never been made sufficiently exhaustive in any. Let us begin with *L'Allegro*.[1]

We are to notice first of all that the poem is largely concerned with the external aspect of things, and especially with their sound and color. This fact is illustrated by the opening lines:

> Hence, loathed Melancholy,
>   Of Cerberus and blackest Midnight born
> In Stygian cave forlorn
>   'Mongst horrid shapes, and shrieks, and sights unholy!
> Find out some uncouth cell,
>   Where brooding Darkness spreads his jealous wings,
> And the night-raven sings;
>   There, under ebon shades and low-browed rocks,
> As ragged as thy locks,
>   In dark Cimmerian desert ever dwell.

The genealogy of Melancholy was invented by Milton. It is based upon the etymology of the word, which is derived from the Greek μελαγχολία, composed of μέλας, *black*, and χολή, *bile*. The first element is represented by blackest Midnight, as one of the parents, and is borne out by the mention of brooding Darkness, the night-raven, ebon shades, and the dark Cimmerian desert. The second element, meaning *bile*, and often used by poets in the sense of anger, is typified by the fierce and implacable Cerberus more successfully per-

---

[1] As the poems are too long to quote at length, the analysis will be more intelligible to the reader if he follows it with the text before him.

haps than by any other mythical figure.[1] This is further carried out by the mention of the Stygian cave forlorn, of horrid shapes and unholy sights, of the jealous wings of brooding darkness, and the ragged, low-browed rocks of his abode. Sounds also, in harmony with the general conception, are suggested by the shrieks heard in infernal caves, and by the dissonant song of the night-raven.

After this introduction the poem proper begins with the invocation of Euphrosyne or Mirth. The poet first mentions a late classical genealogy of the Graces, by which they are made the daughters of Bacchus and Venus.[2] He rejects this, however, for obvious reasons. The Bacchus of the ancients always denotes, in his interpretation, a force antagonistic to high poetic and

---

[1] This idea of Cerebus is prominent in Vergil and Dante, both of whom Milton doubtless had in mind. Thus Vergil says (*Æn.* 6. 417-422):

> Cerberus hæc ingens latratu regna trifauci
> Personat, adverso recubans immanis in antro.
> Cui vates, horrere videns jam colla colubris,
> Melle soporatam et medicatis frugibus offam
> Objicit

Dante's description is even more elaborate (*Inf.* 6. 13-33):

> Cerbero, fiera crudele e diversa,
>   Con tre gole caninamente latra
>   Sovra la gente, che quivi è sommersa.
> Gli occhi ha vermigli, e la barba unta ed atra,
>   E 'l ventre largo, ed unghiate le mani;
>   Graffia gli spirti, gli scuoia ed isquatra.

> .   .   .   .   .

> Quando ci scorse Cerbero, il gran vermo,
>   Le bocche aperse, e mostrocci le sanne:
>   Non avea membro che tenesse fermo.
> E 'l Duca mio distese le sue spanne,
>   Prese la terra, e con piene le pugna
>   La gittò dentro alle bramose canne.
> Quale quel cane, ch' abbaiando agugna,
>   E si racqueta poi che 'l pasto morde,
>   Chè solo a divorarlo intende e pugna;
> Cotai si fecer quelle facce lorde
>   Dello demonio Cerbero, che introna
>   L' anime sì, ch' esser vorrebber sorde.

[2] This genealogy is found only in a scholium of Servius on the *Æneid*. See pp. 38, 39.

spiritual attainment,[1] and therefore not in harmony with the present theme. Moreover, there is something in common between the elevation and purity of Milton and the elevation and purity of a poet like Pindar, of whose conception of the Graces, as exemplified in the Fourteenth Olympian ode, certain traces are visible in this poem. Milton seems to have perceived the discord between such a conception and the later and grosser Græco-Latin ideas of Bacchus and Venus. In preference to this he cites from the song of 'sager poets' another origin of Mirth, namely, Zephyr and Aurora.[2] This genealogy is usually explained as meaning that the merry man's day begins at dawn, when the soft west wind is blowing, but in addition to this it seems to contain another idea. We have spoken already of the sensuousness of these poems, especially with reference to color and sound. The spirit of Melancholy is reflected in blackness and gruesome sounds. In contrast with this is Aurora, who in Milton, as at all times, suggests bright color,[3] Mirth being thus not unnaturally associated with the enjoyment of bright hues. Milton causes Euphrosyne to inherit her mother's power of suggestion by filling this poem with color, both through direct description and through allusion. Thus the conception of Mirth took place on beds of violets blue and fresh-blown roses. The poet speaks of the dappled dawn, of the sweet-briar and eglantine which grow near his window, of the hoar hill at a distance. Beneath elms and over green hills he goes to meet the sun, which comes forth

> Robed in flames and amber light,
> The clouds in thousand liveries dight.

---

[1] Not only here is the god in effect condemned, but also by his position in *Comus* as the father of an evil spirit. Especially clear is the idea in *P. L.* 7. 30 ff. where Milton prays for the heavenly inspiration which repels the barbarous dissonance of Bacchus and his revelers. See also *Eleg.* 6. 55-78, quoted on p. lx; *Pens.* 45-48.

[2] Who the sager poets are I have not discovered. It is not unlikely that Milton had some original in mind, whether classical or not, and after working some time in search of his sources, one is inclined to think that he had. Until it is proved, however, the possibility remains that his words, 'as some sager sing,' are only a modest way of saying that in this case he prefers his own invention to a classical tradition.

[3] Cf. *P. L.* 5. 1, 2; 6. 3, 12; 7. 30; 11. 175; *P. R.* 4, 428; *Pens.* 123.

The landscape reveals warm brown furrows and russet lawns. On the barren breasts of the mountains repose the clouds. The meadows are bright with daisies. Old towers are seen, 'bosomed high in tufted trees,' the home, perhaps, of a fair lady. Not far away arises the blue smoke from a humbler hearth. We hear too of 'tanned haycocks in the mead,' of dances 'in the chequered shade' on sunshine holidays. At night comes the nut-brown ale, with stories of the hairy goblin and his shadowy flail, and after that dreams of bright-eyed ladies:

> There let Hymen oft appear
> In saffron robe, with taper clear,
> And pomp, and feast, and revelry,
> With mask and antique pageantry;
> Such sights as youthful poets dream
> On summer eves by haunted stream.

And last comes the music which would wake Orpheus from his golden slumber on heaped Elysian flowers.

But fully as important as the color-element is the element of sound in this poem. The origin of Mirth is in the combination of bright color with cheerful sound As Aurora represents the former, so Zephyr stands for the latter. Milton elsewhere twice speaks of the sound of the west wind,[1] and this general conception is extended throughout the poem. After the song of the lark

> From his watch-tower in the skies,

comes the shrill clarion of the cock, and after that the voices of hounds and horn multiplied in echoes. Then is heard the ploughman's cheerful whistle and the song of the milkmaid, with the merry rhythm of the whetstone on the scythe. On a holiday the bells ring gaily all

---

[1] These are two out of the four references which he makes to Zephyr. In *P. L.* 5. 15 Adam speaks

> with voice
> Mild as when Zephyrus on Flora breathes.

Cf. *L'Al.* 20 and *Son.* 20. 6. In *P. L.* 10. 705 Milton speaks of the lateral noise of Zephyrus.

about, and young people come to dance to the tune of
jocund rebecks. At night whispering winds bring sleep,
and with it dreams of towered cities and the busy hum
of men.   Then also the poet would hear

> sweetest Shakespeare, Fancy's child,
> Warble his native wood-notes wild.
> And ever, against eating cares.
> Lap me in soft Lydian airs,
> Married to immortal verse,
> Such as the meeting soul may pierce,
> In notes with many a winding bout
> Of linkèd sweetness long drawn out
> With wanton heed and giddy cunning.
> The melting voice through mazes running,
> Untwisting all the chains that tie
> The hidden soul of harmony;
> That Orpheus' self may heave his head
> From golden slumber on a bed
> Of heaped Elysian flowers, and hear
> Such strains as would have won the ear
> Of Pluto to have quite set free
> His half-regained Eurydice.

This perhaps will be sufficient to show how the poet
has adapted certain conceptions from mythology, and
has informed the poem throughout with their spirit.

The same thing is true of *Il Penseroso*, although in
that poem it is not the color and sound which are suggested by the mythologies at its opening. The color-
element is rather a reflection of the etymological idea
of darkness contained in the word melancholy, and the
element of sound supplements it in order to complete
the correspondence and contrast to *L'Allegro*. First the
joys of Mirth are bidden to depart and possess fond
fancies with gaudy shapes

> As thick and numberless
> As the gay motes that people the sunbeams.

Then Melancholy comes veiled in black, staid Wisdom's
hue, such as becomes the sister of Memnon or the ill-

fated Cassiopeia,[1] and wears a robe of darkest grain,
'and sable stole of cypress lawn.' With her may she
bring Abstinence, who best hears the song of the Muses
about the altar of Jove; may she come at night with
silence or the song of the nightingale, when the moon
sheds her pale light and fills the trees with dark
shadows, or when on the stillness is borne

> the far-off curfew sound,
> Over some wide-watered shore,
> Swinging slow with sullen roar.

Within, the fire on the hearth with flickering glow
teaches the 'light to counterfeit a gloom,' while the
cricket sings, and from without is heard faintly the
sound of the bellman's drowsy charm. In some lonely
tower the poet would consort with gorgeous Tragedy,
moving by in sceptred pall, or listen to the sage and
solemn tunes of old bards and such music as that with
which Eurydice was won.

> Thus, Night, oft see me in thy pale career,
> Till civil-suited Morn appear,
> Not tricked and frounced, as she was wont
> With the Attic boy to hunt,
> But kerchieft in a comely cloud,
> While rocking winds are piping loud,
> Or ushered with a shower still,
> When the gust hath blown his fill,
> Ending on the rustling leaves,
> With minute-drops from off the eaves.
> And, when the sun begins to fling
> His flaring beams, me, Goddess, bring
> To archèd walks of twilight groves,
> And shadows brown, that Sylvan loves,
> Of pine, or monumental oak.

There the hum of the bee mingles drowsily with the
sound of murmuring waters, and there is heard the

---

[1] Cassiopeia and the sister of Memnon, being Ethiopians, are types of dark beauty.
Classical accounts agree that Cassiopeia was punished for boasting not her own beauty,
but that of Andromeda, her daughter. Verity says, 'It is said that Apollonius the Grammarian told the story in this [Milton's] way.'

sweet music of spirits of the wood.   Thence the poet
seeks the dim, colored light of a great church where
voices mingle with the solemn organ, and bring heaven
to earth.

It is thus that sound and color play throughout this
poem.   But these rather external elements are less conspicuous than in *L'Allegro* by reason of others, which lie
deeper, and are represented by Saturn and Vesta as the
father and mother of Melancholy.   Two characteristics
of the ancient Saturn or Cronus are here suggested by
Milton: first, his fondness for solitude and retirement;
second, his generally gloomy or melancholy disposition.[1]
The classical conceptions of Saturn in this respect were
harsh, and Milton has softened and purified them in his
use of them here.   More distinct, however, than these
ideas of Saturn are the ideas of Vesta, which are principally three of classical origin, and a fourth, which is in
reality a sort of modern corollary.[2]   First, Vesta is the
goddess of the hearth, that is, of domestic retirement,
and in respect to her fondness for seclusion she possesses
something in common with Saturn.[3]   Thus they met in
glimmering bowers and glades, and in the secret places
of woody Ida's inmost grove, and there was Melancholy
conceived.   She is invoked to bring with her Peace and
Quiet, and to

> add to these retirèd Leisure,
> That in trim gardens takes his pleasure.

---

[1] The former trait seems nowhere in the classics to be explicitly attributed to him.   It
is true that he lived in banishment in the western isles after being dethroned, but Milton
refers to his life in Crete.   Possibly his solitude, as has been suggested, is to be inferred
from his hatred and suspicious fear of his wife and sons, and the plots of each against the
other, as well as from the fact that, though the youngest of six brothers, he usurped their
rights by plotting against his father and seizing the throne.   See pp. 82, 74.   He is also
generally represented by later euhemeristic writers as a king who, unlike the other gods,
ruled upon earth rather than in heaven.   Diodorus Siculus says that he was remarkable
for his greed and impiety, and that Zeus, his son, by pursuing a mode of life the opposite
of his father's, and by rendering himself agreeable and kindly disposed to everybody,
drove out his father. (3. 61.) See also 5. 66, 70 and the excellent article *Kronos* in
Roscher's *Lexikon der Griech. und Röm. Mythologie*, especially the section on euhemeristic interpretation.

[2] See Preller, *Griechische Mythologie*, pp. 422, 423.

[3] The original distinctness of this trait in Vesta may have suggested to Milton the
possibility of attributing it to Saturn, on the basis of stories already cited, though it is
nowhere emphasized in the classics.

The poet meets her near a secluded oak or in the woods, where all is silence beneath the wandering moon, except for the song of Philomel,

> Sweet bird, that shunn'st the noise of folly,
> Most musical, most melancholy!

In stormy weather the poet seeks Melancholy in the still, removed nook beside the fireplace, 'far from all resort of mirth,' or with solitary lamp at midnight he would be found in a high lonely tower deep in philosophy or poetry. When morning comes he retires into the woods, beyond the reach of woodman:

> There, in close covert, by some brook,
> Where no profaner eye may look,
> Hide me from day's garish eye.

Often he would walk in the secluded cloister or steal into the retirement of a great church. At last in old age his refuge becomes the mossy cell of the hermit, where he may attain a ripeness of knowledge like very prophecy.

A second characteristic of Vesta is that of fixity or constancy, as opposed to instability, or by Milton to fickleness or instability of mind.[1] The idea appears at the very beginning of the poem, where the poet, addressing the joys of Mirth, exclaims:

> How little you bested,
> Or fill the fixèd mind with all your toys!

He compares them also to 'hovering dreams, The fickle pensioners of Morpheus' train.' But Melancholy, steadfast and demure, is to come in different manner, keeping her wonted dignity, 'with even step and musing gait.' Forgetting herself to marble, she fixes her eyes constantly upon the earth with sad, leaden, downward cast. Throughout the poem the thought of permanence

---

[1] This is illustrated by the passage from the *Phædrus* of Plato, quoted in part on p. xi, where Hestia, or Vesta, remains seated in heaven while the other gods move to and fro.

and stately dignity is present in the references to
tragedy, philosophy, and great poetry, and in all the
suggestions of movement and music and architecture.[1]

A third characteristic of the classical Vesta was her
virgin purity.[2] This, however, has been extended by
Milton to apply not only to moral purity, but also to
the general idea of abstinence as an indispensable condition of highest meditation and poetic utterance.[3] In

---

[1] This is especially true in 31–44, 85–102, 135 (where the poet mentions the shadows of
pine or monumental oak), 157–174.

[2] This trait is emphasized in the *Homeric Hymns*, especially in the hymn to Aphrodite,
21 ff.

[3] This thought, so important to Milton, must constantly be kept in mind in an intel-
ligent reading of his poetry. Besides its beautiful elaboration in the present poem (cf.
esp. 45–48) it is set forth in a wonderful passage of the Sixth Latin Elegy, which for its
noble loveliness I cannot refrain from quoting at length. To his friend Diodati, who is
enjoying the festivities of Christmas with friends near Chester, he admits that convivial
pleasures find a certain place in poetry, though not a noble one :

> Namque Elegia levis multorum cura deorum est,
>   Et vocat ad numeros quemlibet illa suos;
> Liber adest elegis, Eratoque, Ceresque, Venusque,
>   Et cum purpurea matre tenellus Amor.
> Talibus inde licent convivia larga poetis,
>   Saepius et veteri commaduisse mero.
> At qui bella refert, et adulto sub Jove caelum,
>   Heroasque pios, semideosque duces,
> Et nunc sancta canit superûm consulta deorum,
>   Nunc latrata fero regna profunda cane,
> Ille quidem parce, Samii pro more magistri,
>   Vivat, et innocuos praebeat herba cibos;
> Stet prope fagineo pellucida lympha catillo,
>   Sobriaque e puro pocula fonte bibat.
> Additur huic scelerisque vacans et casta juventus,
>   Et rigidi mores, et sine labe manus;
> Qualis veste nitens sacra, et lustralibus undis,
>   Surgis ad infensos augur iture Deos.
> Hoc ritu vixisse ferunt post rapta sagacem
>   Lumina Tiresian, Ogygiumque Linon,
> Et lare devoto profugum Calchanta, senemque
>   Orpheon edomitis sola per antra feris;
> Sic dapis exiguus, sic rivi potor Homerus
>   Dulichium vexit per freta longa virum,
> Et per monstrificam Perseiæ Phœbados aulam,
>   Et vada fœmineis insidiosa sonis,
> Perque tuas, rex ime, domos, ubi sanguine nigro
>   Dicitur umbrarum detinuisse greges :
> Diis etenim sacer est vates, divûmque sacerdos,
>   Spirat et occultum pectus et ora Jovem.
> At tu si quid agam scitabere (si modo) saltem
>   Esse putas tanti noscere siquid agam).

so doing he includes with the ancient and more limited conception a modern adaptation or corollary of it,
by which the word 'vestal,' originally the vowed purity
of the pagan priestess, becomes nearly synonymous

> Paciferum canimus cælesti semine regem,
>   Faustaque sacratis sæcula pacta libris;
> Vagitumque Dei, et stabulantem paupere tecto
>   Qui suprema suo cum patre regna colit;
> Stelliparumque polum, modulantesque æthere turmas,
>   Et subito elisos ad sua fana Deos,
> Dona quidem dedimus Christi natalibus illa;
>   Illa sub auroram lux mihi prima tulit.

The following translation of these lines is taken from the Cambridge edition of Milton's poems: 'For light elegy is the care of many gods, and calls to its numbers whom it will; Erato, Ceres, Venus, all gladly come, and tender stripling Love with his rosy mother. But the poet who will tell of wars, and of Heaven under adult Jove, and of pious heroes, and leaders half-divine, singing now the holy counsels of the gods above, and now the realms profound where Cerberus howls,—such a poet must live sparely, after the manner of Pythagoras, the Samian teacher. Herbs must furnish him his innocent food; clear water in a beechen cup, sober draughts from the pure spring, must be his drink. His youth must be chaste and void of offence; his manners strict, his hands without stain. He shall be like a priest shining in sacred vestment, washed with lustral waters, who goes up to make augury before the jealous gods. Thus righteously, they say, wise Tiresias lived, after his eyes were darkened; and Linus, and Calchas, who fled from his doomed hearth, and Orpheus, roaming in old age through lonely caverns, quelling the wild beasts with his music. So, a spare eater and a drinker of water, Homer carried Odysseus through the long straits, through the monster-haunted hall of Circe, and the shoals where the sirens made insidious music; and through thy realms, nether-most king, where they say he held with a spell of black blood the troops of the shades. Yea, for the bard is sacred to the god; he is their priest; mysteriously from his lips and his breast he breathes Jove. But if you will know what I am doing, I will tell you, if indeed you think my doings worth your concern. I am singing the King of Heaven, bringer of peace, and the fortunate days promised by the holy book; the wanderings of God, and the stabling under a poor roof of Him who rules with his father the realms above; the star that led the wizards, the hymning of angels in the air, and the gods flying to their endangered fanes. This poem I made as a birthday gift for Christ; the first light of Christmas dawn brought me the theme.'

The reference to the *Nativity Hymn*, in view of the sublimity of that poem, seems like an unconscious proof of the poet's statement. The same thought occurs in Comus 453–463:

> So dear to Heaven is saintly chastity
> That, when a soul is found sincerely so,
> A thousand liveried angels lackey her,
> Driving far off each thing of sin and guilt,
> And in clear dream and solemn vision
> Tell her of things that no gross ear can hear;
> Till oft converse with heavenly habitants
> Begin to cast a beam on the outward shape,
> The unpolluted temple of the mind,
> And turns it by degrees to the soul's essence,
> Till all be made immortal.

See also *P. L.* 7. 30–39; cf. *C.* 702–705, 784–787.

with the word 'nun' and its connotation of a temperate
or abstemious life, devoted to truth and goodness. A
somewhat similar idea appears in Shakespeare's *Venus
and Adonis:*

> Love-lacking vestals and self-loving nuns,[1]

and in *Pericles:*

> A vestal livery will I take me to,
> And never more have joy.[2]

In Milton, the invocation of Melancholy reflects the
same association of ideas:

> Come, pensive Nun, devout and pure,
> Sober, steadfast, and demure.

It is continued in the lines,

> Come; but keep thy wonted state,
> With even step, and musing gait.

Melancholy is again addressed as 'sad Virgin, sage and
holy,' and is represented as hidden from profane eyes.
The idea of holy retirement is continued in the reference to the cloister and the cathedral, and receives its
highest and broadest expression in the closing lines,

> And may at last my weary age
> Find out the peaceful hermitage,
> The hairy gown and mossy cell,
> Where I may sit and rightly spell
> Of every star that heaven doth shew,
> And every herb that sips the dew,
> Till old experience do attain
> To something like prophetic strain.

In addition to these leading mythological ideas of
Il Penseroso there may also be another. Vesta was primarily the goddess of fire, with which element her
name is thought to be etymologically connected. Under-

---

[1] 752.
[2] 3. 4. 10; cf. 4. 5. 7; *R. and J.* 2. 2. 8; 3. 3. 38.

neath Milton's poem a sort of dazzling brightness or
fire appears to smolder, which here and there breaks
through into sight, and is again covered. Thus Melancholy is a celestial being at first:

> But, hail! thou Goddess sage and holy!
> Hail, divinest Melancholy!
> Whose saintly visage is too bright
> To hit the sense of human sight,
> And therefore to our weaker view
> O'erlaid with black, staid Wisdom's hue.

So Melancholy is brought from the glory of her heavenly abode into the lower life of men. There is a touch
of light in the mention of ' bright-haired Vesta,' and
again in those

> looks commercing with the skies,
> Thy rapt soul sitting in thine eyes;
> There, held in holy passion still,
> Forget thyself to marble.

Dying out with Melancholy's 'sad, leaden, downward
cast,' it reappears in the lines,

> But, first and chiefest, with thee bring
> Him that yon soars on golden wing,
> Guiding the fiery-wheelèd throne,
> The Cherub Contemplation.

There is another suggestion of it in the glowing embers
on the retired hearth, and in the far-reaching gleam of
the lamp at midnight from the high, lonely tower, and
possibly in the suggestion of rich, burning colors of
cathedral windows. It is difficult to explain the meaning of this fiery element. It would seem, however, to
signify the burning enthusiasm of true and lofty genius,
or perhaps the flame of pure truth—the flame that fires
genius in a contact effected only by temperance and
retirement.

The course pursued by our analysis has of necessity
been intersected by its own line more than once. This,
however, is simply a proof of Milton's great artistic

power in blending the different ideas so that they are
inextricably mingled in one word or expression. Thus
the epithet 'pensive' suggests a steady as well as a
retiring nature, and the downcast eyes are significant of
both reticence and purity.

With the aid of this detailed inquiry we may come,
perhaps, to a better understanding of these two poems,
and realize that after all they are not directly anti-
podal, but rather complemental. Thus, as we have
already noticed, the general aspect of things in *L'Allegro* is more external than in *Il Penseroso*. It charms
most of all with its gaiety of color and sound.
These elements are present also in the more serious
poem, but being in this case unessential, are not suggested by the mythology. The most important difference between the two is marked by the fact that
mythology is here reserved for the expression of
deeper and more permanent thoughts, to which sound
and color bear an incidental relation. We may look
upon the two poems as harmonized expressions of a
great personality, the one presenting the world as it
appears to the poet in his less thoughtful contemplation of it, the other a more penetrating view, using the
world as the interpreter of a permanent and devout
philosophy by which all life proves to be serious and
full of meaning, though still deeply and constantly joyous, because its meaning is understood.

Somewhat the same thought may be approached
from another direction. It will be noticed that the
monstrous Melancholy at the beginning of *L'Allegro* is
not in any sense the same as the 'Goddess sage and
holy' of *Il Penseroso*, nor is the meretricious Folly in the
prelude of the latter the same as the Euphrosyne of the
former. Each prelude seems rather to represent an
extreme of which the poems proper are the corrective.
The gaudy and uncertain brood of Folly designates the
joys of the man who has no philosophy or religion,
whose entire life is lived only in view of the present

moment, with the one hope that the next moment will in some way vary the sensual enjoyment of this. On the other hand, the daughter of Cerberus and blackest Midnight typifies a morbid brooding over self and the world, in disregard of the joyous aspect of life, ending in monstrous pessimism, which looks upon all things asquint. But true joy of heart, however spontaneous and buoyant, is never gross and fleshly. It is good and lovely by reason of an underlying temperance which gives it gentleness, and makes it positively moral and artistic. Likewise true melancholy in its retirement and meditation does not forget innocent playfulness and the sound of sweet laughter, but is kept pure by a consciousness of these things. Taken in this sense, each of these poems represents a sort of prerequisite for the enjoyments and appreciations set forth in the other. Only the man who is pure in heart and able to withdraw into himself can with safety and genuine delight enjoy the pleasures described in *L'Allegro*. Only the man who knows these joys can safely and truly be his own philosopher or the teacher of other men.

That Milton deliberately set about the exposition of this abstract truth by means of these two poems is improbable. He is himself a beautiful example of the nature which insists upon knowing both the joyous and the serious side of life, and upon harmonizing the two in his own manner of living. It is such a character that pervades both of these poems through and through, and it is the artistic and moral quality of this character which we feel more distinctly the more we reflect upon them.

We shall now better understand in what sense Milton included his poetic material, or, in this case, his mythology. Without detracting from its ancient richness and significance, he has refined and exalted it to become the medium through which he gives himself to the world.

5

But in order to fit his mythology for this purpose, the process of inclusion had first to affect it in a different way. I refer to Milton's quick and accurate perception of the highest poetic quality and possibilities in the mythology of which he made use. This has already been illustrated in our analysis of the descriptions of nature.[1] Once having felt the poetic value of any mythical representation or oft-repeated tradition, he has the great artist's power of purging away the grosser elements, and of reducing it to the pure and final form. Take, for example, a refence in *Comus* to 'the flowery-kirtled Naiades.'[2] This little epithet includes in a beautifully chaste manner a tradition which recurs a number of times in the classics, and is occasionally adapted in modern times.[3] It consists in the natural association of flowers with the apparel, particularly the robes, of wood-nymphs or water-nymphs, or with the Hours who come leading the Spring. The idea is found as early as a fragment of the *Cypria*, quoted by Athenæus,[4] where it is somewhat elaborate. It is seen again in the *Orphic Hymns*,[5] in a fragment of Hermippus,[6] in Ovid,[7] and possibly in Plato.[8] Two instances of its modern adaptation may also be mentioned. The one is the figure of Primavera in Botticelli's Spring. Her robe, loose and flowing, is richly embroidered all over with a pattern consisting of little bunches of flowers. The other instance is in Watson's translation of Italian madrigals:

> Zephyrus, breathing, now calls nymphs from out there bowres,
> To play and wanton, in roobes of sundry flow'rs.[9]

---

[1] See pp. xxviii, xxix; cf. xxxiv.
[2] *C.* 254.
[3] See pp. 58, 59.
[4] 15. 682.
[5] 42. 6.
[6] Kock, *Com. Att. Frag.* 3. 226.
[7] *Fast.* 5. 217; cf. *Ars Am.* 3. 173 ff.
[8] *Rep.* 8. 557 C.
[9] See *The Journal of Germanic Philology* 2. 337, in an article, *Watson's ' Italian Madrigals Englished*,' by F. I. Carpenter. To Professor Albert S. Cook I owe acknowledgment for calling my attention to this instance.

The idea is here introduced by the translator, and does not occur in the original.

Between these several instances the conception varies. In some it evidently is that of an embroidered flower-pattern, as in Botticelli and possibly Ovid, in others of garments dyed in the variegated colors of flowers, as in the *Cypria* and in a comparison of the two citations from Ovid; in others still of robes of fresh flowers actually woven together, as in the close of the fragment of the *Cypria*, and in the Orphic hymn, and the fragment of Hermippus. The question of the comparative artistic value of these conceptions seems hardly significant, for each, if defined too closely, loses suggestiveness and illusion by that very fact. Ovid seems to have realized this, and in speaking of the Hours as 'pictis incinctæ vestibus' he apparently depends upon his context and the general nature of these divinities for any suggestion of flowers.[1] It anything, he has gone too far in the opposite direction, and lacks sufficient definiteness. The epithet 'flowery-kirtled,' however, contains a more vivid suggestion of flowers and of dainty and graceful dress. Yet it does not go far enough to define the particular mode of applying the one to the other. It is thus that Milton establishes the just balance between the definite and the indefinite, and includes the full content of the classical tradition within an expression at once brief, restrained, and finished. The sweetness of many an ancient verse has been gathered and distilled, like the honey of Hymettus, into this single pellucid and quintessential epithet.[2]

These examples are enough to show that, in the relation of Milton to the myths which he used, his mere

---

[1] The passage is *Fast.* 5. 217, 218:

> Conveniunt pictis incinctæ vestibus Horæ
> Inque leves calathos munera nostra legunt.

[2] Milton's power of touching a thing lightly, and leaving it richly charged with suggestion by the avoidance of hard definition, is found in his characterization of Sleep in *Il Penseroso*. See p. xxxiv.

acquaintance with the facts or story—that which often
seems like the most wonderful thing, by reason of its
extent—is after all the least significant and profitable to
us.   What we are rather to consider is the power of the
artist, the teacher, the great character, which perceives
and adds to the value of the fables, and makes them a
new and living revelation.

In attempting to explain Milton's power over his
material one word suggests itself, but it names a characteristic of the poet which differentiates him from his
period, and, in fact, from all the movement known as
the Renaissance.   It is his clearness of vision.   With
the detailed scrutiny of the Renaissance added to the
exalted faith of the Middle Ages, and the clearness
and intellectuality of true classicism, he looked upon
the world with a more perfect comprehension of its
meaning and of the right purpose in life.   Throughout
his poems there is passionate but steady contemplation
of things which men of his time either failed to see, or
saw but faintly and apart from life itself.   They are the
eternal truths which lie around and above this life, and
through which all things act in cooperation, and not in
contradiction, as it appears to the worldly man.   Of
such a vision the poet is conscious in the beautiful
lament for his blindness at the opening of the Third
Book of *Paradise Lost:*[1]

> So much the rather thou, Celestial Light,
> Shine inward, and the mind through all her powers
> Irradiate; there plant eyes; all mist from thence
> Purge and disperse, that I may see and tell
> Of things invisible to mortal sight.

This light shines through the passage already quoted
from the *Vacation Exercise,*[2] in which the poet apostrophizes his native language.   Milton's starting-point
in this passage is evidently Homer.   One remembers Homer's famous picture of the gods gathered on

---

[1] 3. 51–55.
[2] p. xli.

Olympus, enjoying feast and song, upon which the opening of Milton's lines is based.[1]   So the song of Demodocus, further on, is drawn from the *Odyssey*, and the raging of Neptune may be a reminiscence of the god's oppo-
sition to Zeus in the *Iliad*.[2] Hesiod and the *Orphic
Hymns* and Ovid, who sang of the early beginnings of
things, are suggested.   But Milton's use of the old
authors in this case implies an extension of their original meaning.   For example he could not have believed
that it requires a deep transported mind to enjoy
Homer's Olympus.   Nor were circumstances all that he
would call blissful on the occasion described in the
Iliad. He would not wholly approve the song which
Homer was likely to put into the mouth of Apollo,
and he certainly would not suffer sweet captivity
at the songs of Demodocus about the sordid intrigue
of Ares with Aphrodite, and the desperate fight at
Troy. He did not, as a poet, attempt to subject men to
the bondage imposed by such tales.

This whole passage seems to be informed with the
high philosophy of Milton, and though this philosophy
is at first hardly perceived for the sensuous richness of
the lines, yet, when once discovered, it is beautifully
illuminated by the very cause of the former obscurity.
The deep transported mind, rising above the temporal
and incomplete things of life, looks in at Heaven's door,
and there beholds in unclouded vision the infinite and
eternal ideals of bravery, purity, wisdom, love, power,
constancy, justice.   Each is in harmony with the rest,
and all are in harmony with final and perfect truth.   In
loving consciousness of such ideals life is to be measured, determined, and directed, that it may not be in
vain.   Only with the sense of the true values revealed
in such a vision is the poet to interpret the world to
men, to sing of origins and causes, to contemplate hills
of snow and lofts of piled thunder, or the raging sea,

---

[1] *Il*. 1. 584 ff.; see p. 40.
[2] *Od*. 8; *Il*. 1. 399; 15. 162 ff.; see p. 62.

and to recount histories of kings and queens and heroes old. Such songs transcend those of Demodocus and Hesiod and Ovid, for they reveal a profounder vision to men, and captivate them to a bondage which alone liberates the pent-up energies of the spirit.

This perception of the organic and concordant nature of the universe—a perception which should control and beautify even the lowliest acts—often suggested to Milton the harmonious sound of perfect music. The conception of truth and noble conduct as sweet music is Platonic, but it is exalted by Milton into the solemnity of Christian worship and service, just as the Greek chant may have become by religious transformation the pure and uplifting Gregorian. The Platonic thought appears in these lines of *Arcades*, spoken by the Genius of the Wood:

> But else, in deep of night, when drowsiness
> Hath locked up mortal sense, then listen I
> To the celestial Sirens' harmony,
> That sit upon the nine infolded spheres,
> And sing to those that hold the vital shears,
> And turn the adamantine spindle round
> On which the fate of gods and men is wound.
> Such sweet compulsion doth in music lie,
> To lull the daughters of Necessity,
> And keep unsteady Nature to her law,
> And the low world in measured motion draw
> After the heavenly tune, which none can hear
> Of human mold with gross unpurgèd ear.[1]

But Milton's most perfect expression of this truth is the poem known as the *Solemn Music:*

> Blest pair of Sirens, pledges of Heaven's joy,
> Sphere-born harmonious sisters, Voice and Verse,
> Wed your divine sounds, and mixed power employ,
> Dead things with inbreathed sense able to pierce;
> And to our high-raised phantasy present
> That undisturbèd song of pure concent,
> Aye sung before the sapphire-colored throne

---

[1] *Arc.* 61–73.

To Him that sits thereon,
With saintly shout and solemn jubilee;
Where the bright Seraphim in burning row
Their loud uplifted angel-trumpets blow,
And the Cherubic host in thousand quires
Touch their immortal harps of golden wires,
With those just Spirits that wear victorious palms,
Hymns devout and holy psalms
Singing everlastingly:
That we on earth, with undiscording voice
May rightly answer that melodious noise;
As once we did, till disproportioned sin
Jarred against nature's chime, and with harsh din
Broke the fair music that all creatures made
To their great Lord, whose love their motion swayed
In perfect diapason, whilst they stood
In first obedience, and their state of good.
O, may we soon again renew that song,
And keep in tune with Heaven, till God ere long
To his celestial consort us unite,
To live with Him, and sing in endless morn of light!

It has already been remarked that Milton's inclusive vision distinguishes him from his age and from the spirit of the Renaissance. The nature of this difference is essentially described by certain words of Ruskin in *The Stones of Venice.* He says at the beginning of his chapter on the Roman Renaissance: 'The moral, or immoral, elements which unite to form the spirit of Central Renaissance architecture are, I believe, in the main two—pride and infidelity.' Of these we may set aside infidelity as the natural consequence of pride, and extend Ruskin's statement by saying that in greater or less degree pride formed an element in the life and art of the Renaissance wherever the influence of this movement was felt.

The pride of the Renaissance consisted in its humanism, that is, its extreme yet often narrow interest, not in humanity as a whole composed of interdependent parts, but in the human individual. So absorbing did this interest tend to become that men forgot to think of things which are higher and more important than even the single human life. Their attention was devoted to the facts and phenomena of this world. Their ideal of beauty was the human body. They were absorbed in contemplation of the individual heart and mind, not as a revelation of divine truth, but simply as interesting and curious in themselves. They devoted themselves body and soul to the studies which most supported and satisfied this interest, namely the classics. They dwelt long upon the humanistic element in classical literature, and generally missed the finer and more elevating influence of Hellenism.

One of the commonplaces of the art of drawing is the necessity of perfect proportion. If in a picture every line and mass is not justly related to every other in size, shape, direction, and quality, the representation is not a true one, and loses value according to these shortcomings. Any one who has tried to draw will remember his encounter with this principle. He may have attempted to draw a house with a tree beside it. He sets out to draw the house first, and becomes so interested in it that he entirely forgets the tree; then in turn the operation of reproducing the tree drives any thought of the house out of his mind. The result is two pictures, one of a house, the other of a tree, not one picture in which the tree and house serve each to reveal the character of the other.

The pride of the Renaissance is at bottom just such a fault, and consists in an imperfect sense of values and proportions. It exaggerates out of all proportion the human individual and his earthly interests, and disregards the divine and transcendent things which give human life its real and highest value.

In two ways this pride of the Renaissance makes itself manifest. In its first phase it appears as the wonder and enthusiasm which accompany the discovery and revelation of strange new things in the world and in human life. It must be admitted that this spirit of enthusiasm is most charming and attractive, especially as it is felt in the paintings of Holbein or Rembrandt, or in the plays of Shakespeare. Men who were possessed with it seem thrilled with the strangeness of human nature and human beauty. They were determined to become familiar with these wonderful things. They examined, experimented, measured, and reflected, in order to gain the power of holding the mirror up to nature. Each man, according to his peculiar nature and power, might be fascinated with a particular phase of human life, and would devote his entire energy to an expression of it, but in whatever direction he worked the general result was the same, and all labored, in effect, to exalt and glorify the individual man.

The pictures of Holbein, for example, demonstrate first of all the glory of the human intellect. He was the artist who could most fully express the intellectual vigor of Erasmus, More, and Amerbach. His other portraits reveal the same mental energy, and it appears in many of his compositions. It is marked by the full brow, the firm lips, the spare face, and the keen eye. Especially in the portraits are felt the repose and confidence which go with power of intellect. The glance of the eye is direct and searching, and so intense that the artist makes it a rule to turn the face aside. When he does not do so, the penetrating gaze of the eyes is almost violent. Holbein's manner of working is itself intellectual. His expression is distinct and clear-cut. He draws only the most significant lines, but each one is as fine and incisive and telling as expert argument. He makes most effective use of contrast. Though he does not become cold and hard, yet at his best he lacks the geniality of the great Dutch artists, a lack which often goes with great intellectual power.

If Holbein glorifies the human intellect, Rembrandt glorifies human state and bearing. Not by gorgeous colors or the display of dazzling physical beauty and gigan-

tic muscular strength does he produce his result, but by
dignity of proportion and movement and attitude and
countenance. Whether the expression is grave, as it
more often is, or jovial, one can always see in it the same
assured repose, the same sense of great attainment, of
mastery and superiority. Rembrandt prefers large and
noble features. He often throws a warm shadow over
the eyes, thus increasing the impressive mystery of
their power. The glory of his subject is enhanced by a
certain Oriental richness, due perhaps to the large
Hebraic element in his art, and consisting partly in the
peculiar use of chiaroscuro. While the most important
part of his picture is flooded with a soft light, the rest
is enveloped in a deep golden gloom, through which
objects only half appear. The effect of richness is
increased by Rembrandt's choice of these objects. Perhaps he suggests the heavy texture of velvets and furs
and brocades, or we catch the subtile gleam from a
jewel or a gold chain. Sometimes it is the splendid
line of a long plume in a portrait, or in composition
a grand architectural background of tall pillars and
high vaulting and broad steps. Whatever the detail it
contributes in some way to the glory of the central
figure or group.

In these two examples of northern Renaissance art,
the humanistic interest concerns itself with the physical aspects principally as a means of expressing that
which lies beneath. The interest in physical beauty
itself is more characteristic of the south, and one of
many examples is the so-called portrait of Mona Lisa by
Leonardo da Vinci. In spite of what the picture has
suffered from restoration, Mona Lisa is still generally
regarded as one of the most beautiful women in art. In
the sense of purely superficial appearance this may be
true, but when it comes to the question of Mona Lisa's
character the world is divided. The picture is one of a
woman sitting, slightly turned to the left, with her
crossed hands resting upon some low support in front

of her. Her head is erect, and she looks straight out of
the picture. Her dress is simple—not even rich. The
hair, partly covered by a veil, falls in fine, loose curls to
either shoulder. All the outlines are unobtrusive, and
the head and features are extremely regular and well-
proportioned. A faint smile emphasizes the fulness of
the face, especially above and under the eyes and about
the mouth. No less beautiful are the hands. They are
neither so full that they are flabby, nor so thin that
they are angular, but a perfect combination of softness
and firmness. They seem to be not painted, but molded,
so that their fine form and texture can almost be felt.
The whole figure is gentle, graceful, and dignified. So
great is its external charm that we are likely to forget
for a time that there is aught beside to be considered.
Yet something is evidently meant by those eyes, partly
covered as they are with the lids, by the arched brow,
by the rising oblique shadows at the corner of the
mouth, by the half visible curl of the under lip. What
are we to think? Is this lady gentle, and pure, and
sweet? Or is she, as one feels convinced at times, a
woman versed and practised in all the vice and iniquity
of the Italian Renaissance, quietly regarding the world
with shameless defiance? The case of Mona Lisa
remains just this. The picture is valuable merely as an
expression of the exterior beauty of a woman. The
problem to which it gives rise may furnish gossip, but
it does not make the picture a great work of art, any
more than the problem of Hamlet's madness proves the
essential excellence of Shakespeare's drama.

The sincere interest and enthusiasm with which
these artists worked is charming enough to make us
often forget that their vision was limited to this world,
and that the celestial light in the pictures of Memling
and VanEyck does not find its way into theirs. The real
danger of a vision thus limited is better understood
when we consider the second way in which the pride of
the Renaissance is manifest. The early enthusiastic

ardor of humanism remained fresh in the hearts of many men. Especially was this true in the north, where their study of the individual always offered them something new and fascinating. But where the lively interest did pass away, it left in its place the ambition to exalt self, to perform some astonishing feat which should dazzle the world and cover the performer with vainglory. It was the spirit of self-conscious achievement which characterized the works of art and scholarship. The painter was proud of his technique, the scholar became a pedant, the artist exulted in fulsome extravagance and oppressive bigness, and painter and scholar and architect alike forgot the glory of God, which they of all men should uphold. It was such a spirit which produced quantities of hollow and artificial neo-Latin poetry. It built a cathedral like St. Paul's in London, with its heavy piers, and low-browed, ponderous cornices, and tawdry grossness, and filled it with tombs hideous as a nightmare. It painted the religious pictures of Rubens, tricky and meretricious and insincere as they are. Perhaps the most wonderful thing about Rubens is his technique, that is, his ready power to perform brilliant feats of drawing and coloring, and to throw into his pictures a certain superficial unity of arrangement. Since the only value of these pictures is spectacular, any deeper unity of meaning is absent. He aims, furthermore, by violent and sensational means to impress and stagger men, with a view only to the first effect. He forgot, or perhaps never knew, that the influence of the best art is not violent or sudden, but gradual and incessant.

Let us take, for example, the Christ on the Cross in the Antwerp Museum. Rubens has produced his unity by dividing his figures into five groups, and putting one in each corner and one in the middle. The two upper corners are occupied each by a thief. In the lower left-hand corner are the soldiers, in the lower right are the women, and the figure of Christ, as the centre of inter-

est, is raised somewhat above the middle of the canvas.
This grouping is further emphasized by a system of
strongly contrasted lights and shadows. These are so
skilfully thrown into relief that they mark lines of direction which lead the eyes from outside the picture to the
central figure of Christ, placed full in the highest and
most conspicuous light of all. Thus from the lower
left-hand corner the glance is easily carried along by
lights on the tail and neck of a horse, and on the soldiers'
long spears. Above, the body and arms of a prisoner
serve the same purpose. On the right side the line of
direction is first assumed in the lower corner by the
weak and voluptuous lines of the Virgin's hands and
drapery, and the light on her averted face. The line is
then picked up by the trunk of the cross on which the
right hand prisoner hangs, and thus transferred to his
distorted legs. One of these is stretched down, tho
other drawn up under his body until his knee nearly
touches the body of Christ, thus extending the line of
direction and carrying it to the centre. Another line
descends from above along the arm of the prisoner and
tho high light on his body. So much for the tricks by
which Rubens gains his effect of apotheosis.

As much might be said of his violence. It pervades
the picture, from the agonized writhing of the man
whose legs are being broken to the restless hoof of a
horse, and the hard gleam of light on the armor of a
Roman soldier. The prisoner's enormous muscles are
swollen and twisted with his struggle. The soldier
below rests a moment to enjoy the suffering of his
victim and so holds the bar of iron that it stands in cruel
relief against the legs of Christ. The other prisoner is
worn out and relaxed with pain. His eyes are rolled
up, his jaw dropped. Beneath, with horribly deliberate
precision, another soldier thrusts his spear into the side
of Christ. But not merely in this violence does the sensational excitement of the picture consist. It is due
quite as much to the theatrical arrangement, bearing,

and facial expression of the figures, especially of the women. At the foot of the cross kneels the Magdalene as in a tableau, with plump arms outstretched to the soldiers in deprecation. The languid behavior and fleshly beauty of the other women amount to the same thing. All facial expression is treated by Rubens according to rote. One red stroke in one corner of the eye stands for pity, another in another corner for grief, and so on. The result is as meaningless as the expression assumed by an unskilful and shallow actress, and lacks any refinement of distinction or conception.

These characteristics are the most important which Rubens exhibits. The result is that, returning to his pictures for the twelfth or twentieth time, one finds nothing new, nothing but the same trick, now no longer astonishing, the same violence and pride and self-satisfaction.

It is in contrast with this narrow and more disturbed life and art of the Renaissance that we are to consider the art of Milton. He was himself in part a product of the Renaissance, and embodied the best qualities of that movement. As we have seen in his treatment of mythology, he possessed the expert technique which the Renaissance made vastly important. As a man of his times, he greatly appreciated the beauty and wonderful significance of the human individual and the world about him. He realized the necessity in art of studying man and nature until the artist can reproduce them as they are, whether he idealizes them or not. Lastly, Milton stands as a most eminent type of the Renaissance by reason of his enormous store of learning, especially of classical learning. All this gave him much in common with the men of his times. He resembles them in his brilliant accomplishments. He differs from them in the most important consideration, namely, the use to which he put these accomplishments. His knowledge of classical mythology represents only a part of his attainments, but his relation to it, and his use of it, reveal a nature which not only included the best that his times had to give, but established the true value of these gifts and their true relation to the infinite and everlasting Power whom men had forgotten. Milton was not in the narrower sense either classicist or romanticist; he was not exclusively Platonic, Hellenic, Hebraic, mediæval, or modern. He rather includes in the compass of his great nature the best of each manner of culture, and, by using them all in the expression of his personality, shows their common truth and vitality as related to the highest conduct of life. His clear, high vision did not belittle the value of even an obscure, quaint myth, but exalted it above the height of its own intrinsic worth, just as at Chartres or Lincoln the cathedral exalts above meanness or narrow ostentation the least detail of its ornament.

Thus it was with the column, mentioned in an earlier illustration. In the Greek temple it was conspicuous and proud. Its power to delight and benefit men was almost entirely confined to itself, and to appreciate it there was no need of considering facts or truth which lay far beyond its own strength and beauty. But the centuries have brought to men a new faith and a larger vision; they have humbled the pride of this column and devoted it to a higher service. Its glory does not now depend upon itself; to understand it we must feel the infinite peace and strength and duration of the building to which it belongs. As we remain within its walls the sense of these things reaches us continually in many ways. It comes through the beatific faces of saints and prophets crowded within the niches of the doorways. It comes through the stillness and sanctity within. It comes through the multitude of varied forms converging in one plan and one thought. We feel it in the quiet seclusion of a side aisle with the soft light and shadow alternating along its length, and in the form of the great, solemn cross which, marked on the ground by the

foundations, is transformed as it rises in the superstruc-
ture, and lost in the glory above.   We feel it in

> the high embowèd roof,
> With antique pillars massy-proof,
> And storied windows richly dight,
> Casting a dim, religious light.
> There let the pealing organ blow
> To the full-voiced quire below,
> In service high and anthems clear,
> As may with sweetness, through mine ear,
> Dissolve me into ecstasies,
> And bring all Heaven before mine eyes.

The influence of the place drives away the turmoil and
perplexity of life. It causes one to feel the security
of some new and mighty support, and the most serious
question of life is resolved naturally and easily.   There
is no longer any difficulty in deciding what things are
really desirable in life and what are worthless, for their
real and permanent value is no longer obscure.   Clarity
of vision, consciousness of infinite support, sense of true
value, belonged to the man who shaped our column, and
carved the volutes and acanthus of its capital.   Not in
pride, but in love, not in the hope of having his work
praised and admired, but of showing forth the glory
of God he wrought, and the meaning of the whole
cathedral has passed through his heart and mind into
his handiwork.   How beautiful is the shaft! Springing
easily near the altar, it rises without effort.   It bears a
burden, but does not seem to feel the weight.   Its stone
and mortar have been transformed to spirit, and, passing the glory of its capital, it loses itself in soft celestial
light above.   It is the transfiguring power of a pure
faith and a clear vision, such as form the essential
greatness of Milton's poetry.   Not the extent of his
acquaintance with the generations of men, not his brilliant execution, but his perception of universal truth,
and his infusion of truth into the smallest detail of his
work, are the cause of its immortal influence.

There remains yet one aspect of Milton's treatment of mythology for us to consider. The work of an artist, viewed as a whole, reveals changes of spirit and method which occur along the way from youth to old age. In the case of Milton these changes are superficial modifications of permanent and underlying character. He was always temperate, and upright, and devoted to high ideals. These qualities are felt in both the early and the late poems, but their aspect is modified by certain differences between the two, as though the poet's quality were at first more sensuous, and afterward became more severe. The principal differences are clearly perceptible in his treatment of myths, and no instance shows them more distinctly than four occurrences of the story of Orpheus.

In *L'Allegro* the poet calls for soft Lydian airs,

> Untwisting all the chains that tie
> The hidden soul of harmony;
> That Orpheus' self may heave his head
> From golden slumber on a bed
> Of heaped Elysian flowers, and hear
> Such strains as would have won the ear
> Of Pluto to have quite set free
> His half-regained Eurydice.[1]

The second occurrence, which may be regarded as contemporary with the first, is from *Il Penseroso:*

> But, O sad Virgin! that thy power
> Might raise Musæus from his bower;
> Or bid the soul of Orpheus sing
> Such notes as, warbled to the string,
> Drew iron tears down Pluto's cheek,
> And made Hell grant what Love did seek.[2]

The third is from *Lycidas,* where the poet reproaches the nymphs for neglecting his friend:

[1] 143–150.
[2] 103–108.

6

> Ay me! I fondly dream
> ' Had ye been there,' . . . for what could that have done?
> What could the Muse herself that Orpheus bore,
> The Muse herself, for her enchanting son,
> Whom universal nature did lament,
> When, by the rout that made the hideous roar,
> His gory visage down the stream was sent,
> Down the swift Hebrus to the Lesbian shore?[1]

The fourth is from the Seventh Book of *Paradise Lost*, where the poet, modulating his theme from Heaven to sing in lower key of earthly things, invokes the Muse:

> Still govern thou my song,
> Urania, and fit audience find, though few.
> But drive far off the barbarous dissonance
> Of Bacchus and his revelers, the race
> Of that wild rout that tore the Thracian bard
> In Rhodope, where woods and rocks had ears
> To rapture, till the savage clamor drowned
> Both harp and voice; nor could the Muse defend
> Her son.[2]

Of all these passages the last is the most concise, that is, it contains the greatest amount of meaning and specific reference in proportion to its length. It includes a suggestion of the ecstatic sweetness of Orpheus' song, found in the first two passages, together with the harsh violence of the lines in *Lycidas*. It is generally more specific than the others in the mention of Bacchus and his revelers, of their discordant clamor and confusion, of Rhodope, and woods and rocks. This compression of many significant details into small space is a characteristic of mythological allusions in the late poems.

We may observe, in the second place, that in the earlier poems the meaning or application of a myth is more deeply buried beneath its sensuous element, and therefore less conspicuous than in the later poems. In the first two citations the application of the myth consists in its

---

[1] 56–63.
[2] *P. L.* 7. 30–38.

appropriateness of content and presentation to the
mood which controls either poem. Though we feel the
effect of this application, we are partly or wholly unconscious of it, while our conscious thought dwells upon
the story of Orpheus and Eurydice itself. In the passage from *Lycidas* the reader is more aware of the underlying thought that divine poetry could not save Orpheus
from death in an evil hour, nor could it save Lycidas.
In the passage from *Paradise Lost* the meaning is so prominent that Milton's treatment almost makes allegory of
the myth. His thought is that only the true inspiration
which comes from heaven can protect the poet against
the babble and revelry of the world and the appeal of
earthly and temporal pleasures, and for such inspiration
Milton seeks. Thus as he grew old the sensuous veil
which hung between him and pure spiritual truth grew
thinner and more pervious to the white light beyond.

Not only does the proportion of the spiritual and
sensuous elements change with increasing years, but
with it there is a change in the poet's choice and application of myths. We have already seen that Milton at
any time selects a story for its inherent sweetness or
delicacy or sublimity, or for the element of moral and
æsthetic truth which it contains. But the later poems
show a modification of his preference and treatment
such as may also be traced through his use of the
Orpheus myth. In his first citations of it he has
selected the gentlest and tenderest and most pathetic
episode from the life of Orpheus, namely the recovery
of Eurydice, which he unites with a suggestion of the
blissful reward of Orpheus in Elysium. In *Lycidas* he
uses the tragic story of the Mænads, but its violence is
tempered with some of the earlier pathos, and the dom-
inant note is not harsh, but plaintive. The same story
is employed in the latest allusion to Orpheus. It is no
longer tender or pathetic or plaintive, but informed
with the sublime austerity which characterized the
later life and art of Milton. So it may be said, in gen-

eral, that his epics contain less frequent reference to
Apollo and the nymphs and the milder legends than the
earlier poems. Their mythology is grave and impressive, and is often drawn from the primitive poets, such
as Hesiod and Homer. It concerns itself with the deeds
of heroes, the certain and terrible punishment of wrong-
doing, the awful majesty of the gods, and their victories
over grim monsters and the powers of darkness. We
hear of Hercules and Bellerophon, of Epimetheus and
Tantalus, of Jove and the Titans, of Chaos and Night
and Rhea and Saturn.[1] Milton's treatment of these
stories reveals a deep and unfailing sensitiveness to the
grand and awful truths of life.

To explain the growing austerity of Milton by any
one of the many influences which entered into his life is
impossible. It must rather have been the combined
effect of several large elements in his culture, each of
which is essentially austere. Such are certain aspects
of Hellenism, to which he was strongly attracted,
especially those represented by Homer, Hesiod, and
Æschylus. More important is the Hebraic element,
and the sublime influence of the Psalms and the Prophets. Something similar he must also have felt in his
devoted study of patristic learning and early Christianity, whose simple severity was largely that of the
Hebrews. Closely akin to both are the Puritanism of
Milton's England and his own Presbyterianism, both of
which would tend to nourish such influences of culture
and intercept any others. Nor must we forget the
afflictions of his private life. We may say, then, that it
was the conspiracy of these different elements within
his deep and serious nature which rendered him more
susceptible to the solemn aspects of the human life of
all times.

After all, the true and complete nature of the poet is
of most importance, and upon that the details of

See p. li.

our study should converge. We shall not, then, be far astray if, recalling the words with which Christ, when tempted with all the learning of the world, repelled Satan, we find in them a summation of the power by which Milton triumphed over the world, and as victor claimed the riches of its poetry and learning for the kingdom of God:

> Many books,
> Wise men have said, are wearisome; who reads
> Incessantly, and to his reading brings not
> A spirit and judgment equal or superior,
> (And what he brings what needs he elsewhere seek?)
> Uncertain and unsettled still remains,
> Deep-versed in books and shallow in himself,
> Crude or intoxicate, collecting toys
> And trifles for choice matters, worth a sponge,
> As children gathering pebbles on the shore.

THE SOURCES

OF

MILTON'S CLASSICAL MYTHOLOGY

THE SOURCES

ACHERON.—P. L. 2, 578; C. 604. See **Rivers of Hell.**

ACHILLES.—P. L. 9. 15.

The subject of the Iliad is 'the wrath of Achilles, Peleus' son, the ruinous wrath that brought on the Achæans woes innumerable' (*Il.* 1. 1 f.). *Il.* 22 tells of Achilles' fight with Hector. Cf. 22. 165 f.:

> ὡς τὼ τρὶς Πριάμοιο πόλιν περιδινηθήτην
> καρπαλίμοισι πόδεσσι.

'Stern' is not a Homeric epithet of the hero. Vergil calls him 'immitis' (*Æn.* 1. 34; 3. 87).

ADES.—P. L. 2. 964.

Hades or Ades, after the Homeric spelling Aides, was a son of Cronus (*Il.* 15. 188), 'who drew as his domain the murky darkness,' and was 'ruler of the folk in the under-world.' In *Il.* 9. 158 f. he is 'not to be softened, neither overcome, and therefore is he hate-fullest of all gods to mortals.' Cf. *Orcus* and *Pluto.*

ADONIS.—P. L. 1. 446; 9. 440; C. 999; (C. N. 204).

The story of Adonis or Adon is of Oriental origin. He is identi-fied with the Syrian Thammuz (cf. Ezek. 8. 14), and one center of his worship was the region of Lebanon (Strabo 16. 755, and Lucian, *De Dea Syria* 6 ff.). Ovid (*Met.* 10. 503 ff.) tells the love of Venus and Adonis in Cyprus. In disregard of her warning he entered the chase, and was killed by a wild boar. Venus laments him saying (727):

> repetitaque mortis imago
> Annua plangoris peraget simulamina nostri.

Lucian (*De Dea Syria* 6 ff.) says that the people of Byblus, near Lebanon, relate the story of Adonis' death as occurring in Mount Lebanon. The river Adonis, which flows from that mountain, became tinted annually with his blood at the festival of mourn-ing for the youth, and thence derived its name. Lucian also speaks of the festival of Adonis' revival (cf. Theoc. 15. 102, 136, 144). The scholium on 102 speaks of his returning from Hades for intervals of six months, and the Orphic hymn to Adonis (55. 12) says that he brings with him the fruits. His return is thought to signify the annual revival of Nature.

The epithet 'Assyrian queen' (*C.* 1003) is not only appropriate to the legend, but consistent with the statement of Pausanias (1. 14. 6), that the Assyrians were 'the first of men to pay reverence to Celestial Aphrodite.'

In *P. L.* 9. 439 Eden is described as fairer than the gardens of Adonis or Alcinous, and according to Pliny (*N. H.* 19. 4 .19),'antiquitas nihil prius mirata est, quam Hesperidum hortos, ac regum Adonis et Alcinoi.' Ancient writers have little else to say about the gardens of Adonis. Hesychius defines the Ἀδώνιδος κῆποι as the plants used at the festival Adonia, as in Theocritus 15. 112 ff. In connection with *P. L.* 9. 439 should be read *C.* 976-1011, which Todd refers to Spenser's elaborate description of the gardens of Adonis, *F. Q.* 3. 6. 29-51, and *Hymn of Love* 41, 42. As Milton refers to actual gardens of 'revived Adonis,' he may be thinking of Spenser, who describes his revival and his union with Venus.

Milton refers to the legend of Adonis in *Nat. non pati Sen.* 63; *Eleg.* 1. 62; *Eikonoklastes, P. W.* 1. 330. Baudissin discusses the identification of Thammuz with Adonis in *Stud. z. Semit. Religions-gesch.* 1.295.

AFER.—P. L. 10. 702. See Winds.

ALCESTIS.—Son. 23. 2.

Milton's version of Alcestis' surrender to Death in place of her husband, Admetus, is the one given by Euripides in his drama of *Alcestis.* Other accounts make Hades the scene of the capture, instead of the tomb. Heracles speaks of himself (1119) as 'Jove's son.' Browne suggests τι φάσμα νερτέρων (1127), as an original of 'pale and faint.'

ALCINOUS.—P. L. 5. 341; 9. 441; V. E. 49.

Alcinous was king of the Phæacians in the island of Scheria. He received and entertained Odysseus (*Od.* 6-13. 92), who was cast upon this island after his long wanderings. About the palace were the gardens, described in *Od.* 7. 112 ff. There are many kinds of trees whose fruit 'never perisheth, neither faileth, winter or summer, enduring through all the year. . . . There too, skirting the farthest line, are all manner of garden beds, planted trimly, that are perpetually fresh, and therein are two fountains of water, whereof one scatters his streams all about the garden, and the other runs over against it beneath the threshold of the courtyard, and issues by the lofty house, and thence did the townsfolk draw water.' These gardens are mentioned by Eustathius Macrembolites (12th cent.) in his *Hysmin. and Hysm.* 1. 4, as though they were a familiar example of luxuriance, and Pliny (*N. H.* 19. 4. 19) says that these gardens and those of Adonis were greatly admired by antiquity. *V. E.* 49 refers to the two feasts given by Alcinous (*Od.* 8. 40 ff., 470 ff.). At the first banquet Demodocus sang of the quarrel of Odysseus and Achilles (73 ff.), and at the second of the capture of Troy (499 ff.). His theme after the games which intervened was the love of Ares and Aphrodite (266 ff.). All the Phæacians were delighted, but when Odysseus heard his own deeds sung, he wept bitterly (83–93, 368, 521–531). Demodocus was 'the beloved minstrel whom the muse loved dearly, and she gave him both good and evil; of his sight she reft him, but granted him sweet song ' (62–64). He was both ' divine ' and ' famous ' (43,83).

ALPHEUS.—Arc. 30 ; Lyc. 132.

Alpheus, the river-god of Elis, was much honored as early as Homer (cf. *Il.* 11. 725 ff.), and ' often sung' by later poets (cf. Pind. *Ol.* 13. 48; Moschus, *Id.* 7; Statius, *Theb.* 1. 271; 4. 239). Seneca (*Nat. Quæst.* 6. 8) calls Alpheus 'celebratum poetis.' In Ovid, *Met.* 5. 572–641, Arethusa tells the story of Alpheus' love for her as she bathed in his upper waters in Arcadia, and of the pursuit into Sicily, where she became the spring which bears her name in Ortygia near Syracuse. Vergil, *Æn.* 3. 694, refers to the legend:

> Alpheum fama est huc Elidis amnem
> Occultas egisse vias subter mare· qui nunc
> Ore, Arethusa, tuo Siculis confunditur undis.

Statius (*Silv.* 1. 2. 205) says Alpheus passed under the sea ' demerso canali.' Arethusa and Alpheus are used by Milton as suggestive of Sicily and Arcadia, the lands of pastorals (*Lyc.* 85, 132); cf. Verg. *Ecl.* 10. 1:

> Extremum hunc, Arethusa, mihi concede laborem.

In the *Epitaph of Bion* (Mosch. 3), Bion is said to have drunk of Arethusa (77; cf. 10).

AMALTHEA.—P. L. 4. 278 ; P. R. 2. 356.

According to Apollodorus (2. 7. 5), the river-god Achelous contended in the form of a bull with Heracles for the hand of Deianeira. Heracles tore off one of his horns, which Achelous ransomed with the horn of Amalthea. Amalthea, he says, was a daughter of Haimonios, who had in her possession a bull's horn which yields either food or drink whichever anyone desires. In 1. 1. 6 he mentions the belief that she was the goat which nourished the boy Zeus in Crete. Strabo (10. p. 458) says that the two horns were identified by many, as appears in Ovid (*Met.* 9. 87 ff.), where Achelous himself tells the story of his lost horn, which, ' heaped with fruit and odoriferous flowers, the Naiads have consecrated, and the bounteous goddess, Plenty, is enriched by my horn.' Milton's mention of the Hesperides may have been suggested by the account of Hyginus (*Fab.* 31), where Hercules gave the horn to the Hesperides or the nymphs.

For Amalthea, as mother of Bacchus, see *Rhea.*

AMARYLLIS.—Lyc. 68.

With Milton's line:

> To sport with Amaryllis in the shade,

compare Verg. *Ecl.* 1. 4:

> Tu, Tityre, lentus in umbra
> Formosam resonare doces Amaryllida sylvas.

In Theoc. 3 a goatherd serenades his Amaryllis. These examples explain the general association of the name with pastoral poetry.

AMAZONS.—P. L. 9. 1111.

The Amazons are mentioned by Homer (*Il.* 3. 189; 6. 186), who calls them ἀντιάνειραι, 'women peers of men.' Vergil (*Æn.* 1. 490 ff.) describes Penthesilea leading them to the aid of the Trojans. They are armed 'lunatis peltis' (cf. *Æn.* 11. 660 ff.). Pollux in the *Greek Onomasticon* 1. 134 speaks of the πέλτη 'Αμαζονική as resembling, according to Xenophon, an ivy leaf. The πέλτη was a small rhomboid shield (Paus. 1. 41. 7; Plut. *Thes.* 27).

AMBROSIA AND NECTAR.—P. L. 2. 245; 4. 240; 5. 57, 633, 642; 6. 332; 9. 838; 11. 279; P. R. 4. 590; D. F. I. 49; V. E. 39; C 16, 838, 840; Lyc. 175.

Ambrosia and nectar are primarily the meat and drink of the gods (Hom. *Od.* 5. 92 ff.; *Il.* 1. 598), but the corresponding adjectives are used in the sense of 'immortal' (cf. ἀμβρόσιος). In *Il.* 5. 331 ff. Diomed has wounded Aphrodite; 'straight through the ambrosial raiment (cf. *C.* 16) that the Graces themselves had woven her, pierced the dart into the flesh. . . . Then flowed the goddess's immortal blood, such ichor as floweth in the blessed gods; for they eat no bread neither drink they gleaming wine, wherefore they are bloodless and are named immortals.' Cf. *P. L.* 6. 331. Milton is faithful to the classical usage of these words. Homer speaks of 'ambrosial night' (*Il.* 2. 57); cf. *P. L.* 5. 642. Zeus has ambrosial locks (*Il.* 1. 529); cf. *P. L.* 5. 57. Euripides (*Hippol.* 748) mentions the ambrosial fountains in the gardens of the Hesperides; cf. *P. L.* 11. 279. With the 'ambrosial oils' of *C.* 840 compare the anointing of Sarpedon's wounds with ambrosia, *Il.* 16. 680. In *Il.* 14. 169 ff., where Hera prepared to meet Zeus, she anointed herself with ambrosia, and 'plaited her shining tresses, fair and ambrosial'; cf. *P. L.* 5. 57. The fragrance of ambrosia is referred to by Milton in *P. L.* 2. 245. It is suggested in such passages as *Il.* 23. 187; *Od.* 4. 445. Cf. ὀδμῆς ἀμβροσίης of Theognis 9.

Nectar also is an ointment in *D. F. I.* 49 and *Lyc.* 175. The suggestion of fragrance may be added to that of immortality. Cf. *Il.* 3. 385; Ov. *Met.* 4. 250. As Homer speaks of νέκταρ ἐρυθρόν (*Il.* 19. 38; *Od.* 5. 93), Milton speaks of 'rubied nectar' (*P. L.* 5. 633).

AMMON.—P. L. 4. 277; 9. 508; C. N. 203.

Ammon or Hammon was one of the chief divinities of the Africans, whom the Greek colonists called Zeus Ammon, and the Romans Jupiter Ammon.

In *P. L.* 4. 277 Ammon is identified with Cham or Ham, the son of Noah, as in 4. 717 Iapetus is called Japhet. Samuel Bochart, who in 1646 published his *Geographia Sacra*, discusses this correspondence, and says (1. 1) that the learned had for some time maintained that Noah and Saturn were the same. Among other reasons for believing that Cham was Ammon, he says that Ham is the same word as Hammon, and that Ham and Zeus both mean 'hot,' and he adds that each was his father's youngest son. He mentions also the fact that Egypt, 'the land of Ham,' was the home of Ham's descendants. The identification rests upon the 'poetarum judicium' (2. 1). Ralegh says that Cham was no other than Saturnus Egyptius, and gives his reasons in his *History of the World* 2. 2. 4.

A passage which throws some light upon *C. N.* 203 may be found in Macrobius, *Sat.* 1. 21: 'Ideo et Ammonem, quem deum solem occidentem Libyes existimant, arietibus cornibus fingunt, quibus maxime id animal valet, sicut sol radiis.'

The love of 'Ammoulan Jove' and Olympias, mother of Alexander (*P. L.* 9.508; *P. R.* 3.84), may be referred to Plutarch's *Alexander* 2. Among other accounts of Alexander's birth, Plutarch says, 'A serpent was also seen lying by Olympias as she slept;' and in 3, 'Apollo commanded him (Philip) to sacrifice to Jupiter Ammon and to pay his homage principally to that god.' The story is told afterwards by Justin 11. 11; 12.16. Milton refers to it again in *Eleg.* 4.26. See *Rhea*.

AMPHITRITE.—C. 921.

Amphitrite was a daughter of Nereus (cf. *C.* 835), who with her sisters 'calmed the blasts of the divine winds' (Hesiod, *Theog.* 243, 254.) She became the wife of Poseidon (Pindar, *Ol.* 6. 104 f.). The name Amphitrite is sometimes used of the sea, as in Ovid, *Met.* 1. 14; Hom. *Od.* 12. 60.

AMYMONE.—P. R. 2. 188.

Apollodorus (2. 1. 4, 5) tells the story of Amymone, one of the fifty daughters of Danaus, who, having fled from Egypt, were seeking water in Argos. Amymone threw her weapon at a deer, but struck a sleeping satyr, who offered her violence. Poseidon, who came to the rescue, won her love. Lucian (*Dial. Mar.* 6) speaks of her beauty, and relates that Poseidon stole her away into the sea. Cf. Hyginus, *Fab.* 169.

ANCHISES.—C. 923.

Locrine was the son of Brutus, first king of Britain, who was the 'son of Silvius: he of Ascanius; whose father was Æneas,' son of Anchises of Troy. Cf. Milton's *History of Britain*, *P. W.* 5. 168. The legend is related by Geoffrey of Monmouth in his history, Chap. 3.

ANTÆUS.—P. R. 4. 563.

Antæus was the giant son of Poseidon and Ge, the Earth (Apollod. 2. 5.11), and king of Libya. The name Irassa, of the city of Antæus, seems to have been taken by Milton from Pind. *P.* 9. 106:

ἔβαν
Ἴρασα πρὸς πόλιν, ᾿Ανταίου μετὰ καλλίκομον
μναστῆρες ἀγακλέα κούραν.

The scholiast on Pindar says, however, that the Antæus living in the city Irassa was not the one who strove with Heracles, but he adds that, among others, Pherecydes says that the latter Antæus came from Irassa (neut. plur.) on Lake Tritonis in Cyrene. Herodotus mentions Irassa (neut. plur.) as a locality of Libya (4. 159). That Milton says '*in* Irassa' indicates reference rather to a region as the home of Antæus, for which he has the scholiast's authority.

The story told by Milton is a later version, related by Apollodorus (2. 5. 11) and Lucan (4. 597 ff.). The incidents of the fight with Hercules coincide with Lucan's longer description, except that ἀράμενος ἄμμασι of Apollodorus gives the cue to 'throttled' (*P. R.* 4.568). See also *Hercules*.

ANTIOPA.—P. R. 2. 187.

Pausanias (2. 6. 1) says that Antiopa, daughter of Nykteus of Thebes, was famous among the Greeks for her beauty. Apollonius (4.1090) calls her εὐώψ. Ovid (*Met.* 6. 110), in a list of the loves of the disguised Jove, mentions Antiopa, whom the god embraced in the form of a satyr.

AONIAN MOUNT.—P. L. 1. 15. See **Muses.**

APOLLO.—P. L. 1, 517; 4. 273; 10. 296; P. R. 2. 190; D. F. I. 23; C. 662; Lyc. 106; Son. 12. 6; See also **Apollo as God of Prophecy,** and as **Sun god.**

> The aggregated soil
> Death with his mace petrific, cold and dry,
> As with a trident smote, and fixed as firm
> As Delos, floating once.

In these lines (*P. L.* 10. 293 ff.) Milton refers to the myth of Delos as the birthplace of Apollo. The earliest source of the myth in this form is a quotation from Pindar by Strabo (10. 485). He says, in speaking of Delos: 'For here, as the story goes, Leto suffered in the birth of Apollo and Artemis; "For of old time," says Pindar, "it drifted before the waves and stress of winds from every side; but when she of Koios set foot thereon, as the swift pains of her travailing drew nigh, then verily from roots deep down in earth there sprang upright four pillars with adamantine base, and on their capitals they held up the rock: there was the goddess delivered, and looked upon her blessed brood." ' But another story, told by Aristides (7. 77), says that Apollo himself, according to the poets, caused Delos to become stationary, 'planting it firmly in the sea, because he had been born there.' Cf. Verg. *Æn.* 3. 75.

The story of the hinds 'that were transformed to frogs' (*Son.* 12. 6) is told by Ovid, *Met.* 6. 337 ff. This was their punishment for refusing the waters of a Lycian spring to the thirsty Leto and her new-born babes (358 ff.). Cf. *Apollo as Sun-god.*

The story of Apollo's love and pursuit of Daphne (*P. L.* 4. 273; *P. R.* 2. 187; *C.* 661) is related by Ovid, *Met.* 1. 453 ff. As she fled,

> Pes, modo tam velox, pigris radicibus hæret.

She was changed to the laurel, which thenceforth was sacred to the god.

In *P. L.* 4. 272 ff. Eden is lovelier than

> that sweet grove
> Of Daphne, by Orontes and the inspired
> Castalian spring.

The legend of Daphne was transferred to the banks of the Orontes (Paus. 8. 20), and its centre was the famous gardens of Daphne at Antioch. As described by Strabo (16. 750), they were about forty stadia above the city, 'a great and thickly shaded grove traversed by streams of spring water.' Libanius in his *Antiocheus* (*Orations*) gives a detailed description of these gardens, and praises the springs ecstatically. He says (p. 352, ed. Reiske) that they were the abode of the nymphs, in which these delighted as much as Apollo in Delphi. According to Philostratus (*Life of Apollonius of Tyana* 1. 16) several names of places associated with Apollo and Daphne were transferred to Antioch, and thus the spring mentioned above was called 'Castalian' (Johannes Phocas, *Compend. Descriptio* p. 2). We learn from Sozomen, in his *Historia Ecclesiastica* 5. 19, that this Castalian spring ('aqua divinatrix') had the same prophetic power as the one at Delphi, and that on one occasion a prophecy was obtained by dipping in the spring a laurel-leaf, which came forth bearing a prophetic inscription. Accounts seem generally to point to an utterance of some sort from the spring itself, rather than from a priest of the spring. Ammian (22. 12. 8) mentions the 'venæ fatidicæ Castalii fontis' and the 'præcinentes aquæ.' The same belief seems to have been held with regard to the Castalian spring at Delphi. Gregory Nazianzen (*Or.* 5. 31) says that Castalia 'is now silent, no longer giving forth prophecies.' The same idea appears in Claudian (81. 1): 'Castalio de gurgite Phœbus anhelat'; cf. 4. 7.

Clymene, who is mentioned in *P. R.* 2. 186, was the wife of Merops of Æthiopia, and the mother of Phaethon by Apollo. Phaethon's high origin was disputed by Epaphus, but confirmed by Clymene's appeal to Apollo (Ov. *Met.* 1. 748 ff.; cf. *Trist.* 3. 4. 30).

The arraignment of the gods in *P. R.* 2. 186 ff. is not unlike that in the *Protrepticus* of Clement of Alexandria, 27 P ff., where among others, Poseidon, Apollo, and Zeus are named with Amymone, Daphne, Semele, and others. In Ovid, *Met.* 6. 70 ff., is a recital of the loves of Jupiter, Neptune, Apollo, and Bacchus, but excepting Antiopa the names of the women aré other than those mentioned by Milton.

The story of Apollo's love for *Hyacinth* is touched upon in *D. F. I.* 25; *Lyc.* 106. Ovid (*Met.* 10. 162 ff.) tells how by accident the discus from the hand of Apollo struck and killed Hyacinthus, son of Amyclas of Sparta. Apollo laments his death saying (206):

> Flosque novus scripto gemitus imitabere nostros.

And while he laments,

> Ecce cruor, qui fusus humi signaverat herbam,
> Desinit esse cruor; Tyrio nitentior ostro
> Flos oritur . . .
> Non satis hoc Phœbo est, is enim fuit auctor honoris,
> Ipse suos gemitus foliis inscribit; et ai ai
> Flos habet inscriptum; funestaque litera ducta est.
> Nec genuisse pudet Sparten Hyacinthon; honorque
> Durat in hoc ævi, celebrandaque more priorum
> Annua prælata redeunt Hyacinthia pompa.

Cf. Milt. *Nat. non pati Sen.* 62. Apollo's love for the river Eurotas is referred to by Vergil (*Ecl.* 6. 83). Servius says, 'hunc fluvium Hyacinthi causa Apollo dicitur amasse.'

Apollo as the God of Prophecy, Music, and Poetry.—P. L. 1. 517; *P. R.* 1. 458; 4. 260; *V. E.* 37; *C. N.* 176; *Pass.* 23; *Ep. Shak.* 12; *C.* 478; *Lyc.* 77; *Son.* 13. 10.

Such a conception is as old as Homer (*Il.* 1. 603; *Od.* 8. 79), and is common throughout the classics. The most famous oracle of Apollo was that upon 'the steep of Delphos.' In *Hom. Hy. Pyth. Ap.* 103 ff. is a description of the founding of this shrine : 'From hence thou swiftly camest rushing (reading θύων) to the rock, and thou didst reach Crissa below snowy Parnassus . . . but above the rock is suspended aloft, and a rugged hollow cave runs below. Here King Phœbus Apollo resolved to construct a pleasant temple.' *C. N.* 176 ff. is referred by Warton to the general representation in the *Ion* of Euripides. Cf. *Ion* 1–183. The 'hollow shriek' may be reminiscent of the frenzy of the Sibyl in *Æn.* 6. 42 ff.; cf. 98 ff.:

> Cumæa Sibylla
> Horrendas canit ambages, antroque remugit,
> Obscuris vera involvens : ea frena furenti
> Concutit, et stimulos sub pectore vertit Apollo.

Cf. *Ion* 91 ff.:

> On the tripod most holy is seated the Delphian Maiden
> Chanting children of Hellas the wild cries, laden
> With doom, from the lips of Apollo that ring.

The 'pomp and sacrifice' of *P. R.* 1. 457 also are illustrated by the *Ion*.

In the Homeric hymn to Apollo the god is associated with the lyre and song. In *Pyth. Ap.* 10 ff. the Muses sing, while the Graces, the Hours, Harmony, Hebe, and Aphrodite dance, and 'Phœbus Apollo strikes the harp, taking grand and lofty steps.' Cf. *Hy. to Herm.* 476 ff., 500 ff. According to Hes. *Herc. Sh.* 203 his lyre was golden. In *Son.* 13. 10 Milton addresses Lawes as 'priest of Phœbus' quire.' According to *Pyth. Ap.* 338 ff. the Cretans followed Apollo to Delphi as his first choir, chanting Io-Pæan. Plutarch (*De Musica* 3. 1132 A) quotes Heraclides to the effect that Philammon, a Delphian, celebrated in song the births of Leto, Apollo, and Artemis, and established the choruses at Delphi. (Cf. *Schol. Od.* 19. 432; Milton's *Ad Salsil.* 26.) The passage in *V. E.* 37, where the gods listen to Apollo's song, may be referred to *Il.* 1. 603 ff. The epithet 'unshorn' is used of Apollo in Homer *Il.* 20. 39; cf. *Hom. Hy. Ap. Del.* 134. It occurs in later writers, as Pindar, *P.* 3. 20; *Isth.* 1. 8; Ov. *Met.* 12. 585.

In *P. R.* 4. 260 Phœbus is spoken of as challenging the song of Homer for his own, 'alluding,' says Newton, 'to a Greek epigram in the first book of the *Anthologia :*

> ψευδόμ' μὲν ἐγών ἐχάραυσι δὲ θεῖος Ὅμηρος.'

This appears on p. 91 of the *Anthology* of Stephanus, and again in *Anth. Pal.* 9. 455. It is preceded by the line

> τίνας ἂν εἴποι λόγους 'Απόλλων περὶ 'Ομήρου;

Phœbus appears twice as the patron god of the poet (*Pass.* 23; *Lyc.* 77). Odysseus says to the bard of Alcinous, 'Demodocus, I praise thee far above all mortal men, whether it be the Muse . . . that taught thee, or even Apollo' (*Od.* 8. 487). *Lyc.* 77 has been referred by Todd to the familiar 'Cynthius aurem Vellit, et admonuit' of Verg. *Ecl.* 6. 3.

Apollo as the Sun-god.—*P. L.* 5. 423; *C. N.* 19, 36, 79; *C.* 51, 66, 95, 141, 190; *Lyc.* 168; *Son.* 12. 7.

Phœbus is supposed to have been a sun-god from earliest times, although his identification with Helios, the chariot-driver, is peculiar to the Latin writers.

In *C.* 141 the Sun is called 'tell-tale.' This epithet is commonly referred to Hom. *Od.* 8. 270 ff. where Helios told Hephæstus of the secret amour of Aphrodite and Ares. He is called ἄγγελος. In *Od.* 11. 109 Helios is the god 'who overseeth all, and overheareth all things.' He tells Demeter of the rape of Persephone in *Hom. Hy. to Dem.* 74 ff.

Milton mentions the sun's 'bright throne' and 'burning axle-tree' (*C. N.* 84), and again he speaks of 'the gilded car of day' and 'his glowing axle' (*C.* 95, 96). Ovid says in *Met.* 1. 776; 2. 1 ff. that Phaethon, wishing to drive his father's chariot, went to his palace in the east, where

> sedebat
> In solio Phœbus, claris lucente zmaragdis.

The chariot is described in 107 ff.:

> Aureus axis erat, temo aureus, aurea summæ
> Curvatura rotæ; radiorum argenteus ordo.
> Per juga chrysolithi, positæque ex ordine gemmæ
> Clara repercusso reddebant lumina Phœbo.

To speak of Apollo as holding 'the sun in fee' (*Son.* 12. 7), does not seem classical, though his character is regal in the foregoing citations from Ovid.

It is related that Hyperion's chariot hissed as it met the waters of the western ocean at sunset (Stat. *Silv.* 2. 7. 25; Juv. 14. 280). Milton may have reference to this idea in *C.* 96, 97. Ovid (*Met.* 4. 632 ff.) says it was the sea, 'qui Solis anhelis Æquora subdit equis, et fessos excipit axes.' Cf. Milt. *Eleg.* 3. 32 ff.

Though the sun at setting is represented by ancient writers as sinking into Ocean (*Il.* 8. 485), yet he never 'sups with Ocean' as in *P. L.* 5. 423. Statius (*Theb.* 3. 407 ff.) describes the sunset as follows:

> Solverat Hesperii devexo margine ponti
> Flagrantes Sol pronus equos, rutilamque lavabat
> Oceani sub fonte comam.

The Hours and Nereids feed the horses, which in Ovid (*Met.* 4. 214) are refreshed with ambrosia. Cf. *Lyc.* 168 ff. Athenæus quotes different poets to show the manner in which Helios at sun-down returned to his chamber in the East (11. 469, 470). Stesichorus says that he embarked in a golden boat, and sped to the depths of dark night, to his mother, wife, and children. According to Mimnermus he was borne in a golden, winged bed to the Æthiopians where his horses and chariot await him. The 'other goal' of *C.* 100 may have been suggested by Homer's τροπαὶ ἠελίοιο (*Od.* 15. 404).

In the *Ion* (82 ff.) we again find a representation of the sun-god not dissimilar to Milton's (cf. *Lyc.* 168 ff.; *C. N.* 79), though more elaborate:

> Lo, yonder the Sun-god is turning to earthward his splendor-blazing
>   Chariot of light
> And the crests of Parnassus untrodden are flaming and flushed, as with yearning
> Of welcome to far-flashing wheels with glory of daylight returning
>   To mortal sight.

With *C.* 190 compare the description of the Delphic tapestry (*Ion* 1148 ff.):

> His steeds the Sun drave to their goal of fire,
> After him drawing the bright Evening Star,
> And sable-vestured Night with team of twain
> Up floated: and the stars companioned her.

C. N. 31 ff. refers to the Sun as Nature's 'lusty paramour.' This suggests the story of the new creation after the flood by the coöperation of Earth and Sun (Ov. *Met.* 1. 416 ff.; cf. Milt. *Eleg.* 5. 55 f.).

AQUILO.—D. F. I. 8. See **Winds.**

STAR OF ARCADY.—C. 341. See **Calisto.**

ARETHUSA.—Arc. 31; Lyc. 85, 133. See **Alpheus.**

ARGESTES.—P. L. 10. 699. See **Winds.**

ARGO.—P. L. 2. 1017.

The story of Jason's voyage in the Argo in search of the golden fleece is told by Apollonius and by Apollodorus 1. 9. Both relate the incident of the 'justling rocks' (Ap. Rh. 2. 537 ff.; Apollod. 1. 9. 22). These were at the end of the Bosporus where the Argo entered the Black Sea. 'Justling' may be Milton's translation of 'Symplegades,' which is really an adjective (συμπληγάς), but Pind. *Pyth.* 4. 207 should also be considered: 'Then as they set forth toward an exceeding peril they prayed the lord of ships that they might shun the terrible shock of the jarring (συνδρόμων) rocks: for they were twain that had life, and plunged (κυλινδέσκοντο) along more swiftly than the legions of the bellowing winds.' Juvenal (*Sat.* 15. 19) speaks of the 'concurrentia saxa.'

ARGUS.—P. L. 11. 131.

Michael, the archangel, is sent to dispossess Adam and Eve of Eden with a cohort of Cherubim whose bodies are all

> Spangled with eyes more numerous than those
> Of Argus, and more wakeful than to drowse,
> Charmed with Arcadian pipe, the pastoral reed
> Of Hermes, or his opiate rod.

Io, a priestess of Hera, was beloved by Zeus (Apollod. 2. 1. 2). When Hera discovered their relation, Zeus changed Io into a white heifer, and Hera, in jealousy and mistrust of his oath, set Argus to guard her. Apollodorus calls Argus Panoptes because he had eyes all over his body. Hermes was sent by Zeus to steal Io, and killed the all-seeing one with a stone. Ovid (*Met.* 1. 601 ff.) tells the story with pretty elaboration. Of the many eyes of Argus not more than two sleep at one time. Hermes, seating himself in the shade, sings a gentle pastoral of Syrinx until Argus falls asleep. Then he makes sure of his victim, 'Languida permulcens medicata lumina virga,' and kills him with his sword.   Cf. *Il.* 24. 343.

ARIMASPIANS.—P. L. 2. 945.

Herodotus (3. 116) speaks of the one-eyed Arimaspians who are said to steal gold from the 'gold-guarding' griffins (4. 13) in the north. Pausanias (1. 24) quotes Aristeas the Proconnesian to the effect that 'the griffins are like lions, but have the wings and beak of an eagle.' Pliny (*N. H.* 7. 2) says: 'haud procul ab ipso aquilonis exortu, spe-cuque ejus dicto . . . produntur Arimaspi . . . quibus assi-due bellum esse circa metalla cum Gryphis, ferarum volucri genere, quale vulgo traditur, eruente ex cuniculis aurum, mira cupiditate et feris custodientibus, et Arimaspis rapientibus, multi sed maxime illustres Herodotus et Aristeas Proconnesius scribunt.'

ASSYRIAN QUEEN.—C. 1002.   See **Adonis.**

ATLAS.—P. L. 2. 306; 4. 987; 10. 674.

In the *Prometheus* of Æschylus, 348 ff., Prometheus grieves for his kinsman Atlas,

> who doth stand
> In the far West, supporting on his shoulders
> The pillars of the earth and heaven.

Cf. Hom. *Od.* 1. 52 ff; Verg. *Æn.* 4. 481 ff.; Ov. *Met.* 4. 631 ff.   In this last passage Ovid tells the story of Atlas' transformation into a mountain by the Gorgon's head in the hands of Perseus.   Cf. *Pleiades.*

ATROPOS.—E. M. W. 28.   See **Fates.**

ATTIC BOY.—Pens. 124.   See **Cephalus.**

AURORA.—P. L. 5. 1, 6, 124; 6. 2, 12; 7. 373; 11. 173; P. R. 4. 426; L'Al. 19, 54; Pens. 122; C. 139; Lyc. 26.

The dawn is often personified in Milton, and in many cases the accompanying description bears a distinct reference to the Eos or Aurora of classical writers.   The adjective 'rosy' in connection with the morn occurs three times (*P. L.* 5. 1; 6. 3; 11. 175; cf. *P.   R.* 4. 428).   It is common   among   the ancients.   In Homer's stock description we find 'the rosy-fingered Dawn' (*Il.* 1. 477; 6. 175; *Od.* 2. 1; 5. 121 etc.; cf. *Hom. Hy. to Helios* 6; Verg. *Æn.* 6. 535).   In *Il.* 8. 1. she is 'saffron-robed'; cf. Verg. *Georg.* 1. 4. 47.   Purple is also her color (Ov. *Met.* 2. 113).   With 'gold empyreal' of *P. L.* 6. 13 cf. *Od.* 15. 250.   Similar coloring is seen in Milton's *In Quint. Nov.* 133 f.   The 'tricked and frounced' of *Pens.* 123 may be an elaboration of 'lutea' in the story of Cephalus (Ov. *Met.* 7. 703), including however, a reminiscence of similar conventional epithets and de-scriptions.   In *L'Al.* 54 'the slumbering Morn' is 'roused,' with possible reference to Homer, who represents the Dawn as rising from the bed of Tithonus (*Il.* 11. 1; *Od.* 5. 1; cf. Verg. *Georg.* 1. 447).

In *P. L.* 5. 5. Milton speaks of the sleep of Adam as

> temperate vapours bland, which the only sound
> Of leaves and fuming rills, Aurora's fan,
> Lightly dispersed.

'Aurora's fan' suggests the gentle breezes of morning which took personified forms with the ancients. According to Hes. *Theog.* 378 Aurora (Eos) was the mother of Boreas, Notus, and Zephyrus. Milton departs from classical tradition in making Zephyrus instead of Tithonus the paramour of Aurora.

In *P. L.* 6. 2 we read that

> Morn,
> Waked by the circling Hours, with rosy hand
> Unbarred the gates of Light.

This may be referred to two passages, the one in Hom. *Il.* 5. 749, where 'self-moving groaned upon their hinges the gates of heaven whereof the Hours are warders, to whom is committed great heaven and Olympus, whether to throw open the thick cloud or set it to.' The other passage here to be considered is Ov. *Met.* 2. 112: 'ecce vigil rutilo patefecit ab ortu Purpureas Aurora fores et plena rosarum Atria.' One office of the Hours was to attend the Sun (cf. *Apollo*).

The conception of the Dawn as routing the Night and her shades is expressed in *P. L.* 6. 13 and *P. R.* 4. 426. With these lines compare *Orph. Hy.* 77. 4, where Dawn is addressed as the goddess 'who drivest the dark and gloomy progress of Night beneath the earth with thy rising.' In Ov. *Met.* 2. 114, 'Diffugiunt stellæ, quarum agmina cogit Lucifer.' Cf. 144; Eurip. *Ion* 84; also Milton's *Epist.* 18. 111. In his comment on a similar passage in Dante (*Purg.* 2. 56) Cary refers *P. L.* 6. 15 to Sophocles, *Trach.* 94, where Night is represented as slain or despoiled by the flaming Sun whom she brings forth. As the Orphic Hymn speaks of Night's 'gloomy progress,' so Milton (*P. L.* 11. 175) speaks of the 'rosy progress' of the Morning. In *Orph. Hy.* 78. 2 the Dawn is described as ἐρυθαινομένη κατὰ κόσμον. This may have suggested Milton's epithet 'nice' (*C.* 139), though the latter conveys a somewhat different sense.

The fifth book of *Paradise Lost* opens:

> Now Morn, her rosy steps in the eastern clime
> Advancing, sowed the earth with orient pearl.

The passage evidently refers to the legend mentioned by Ovid (*Met.* 13. 621). Memnon, the son of Aurora, was slain by Achilles at Troy. His mother gives herself up to her grief, 'piasque Nunc quoque dat lacrimas et toto rorat in orbe.' A similar idea appears in the 'lumine conserit arva' of Lucretius 2. 211. See also *Leucothea* and *Cephalus*.

BACCHUS.—P. L. 4. 279; 7. 33; L'Al. 16; C. 46, 522.

Bacchus is represented by Milton as the son of Amalthea (*P. L.*

4. 279; see *Rhea*), and the father of Euphrosyne (*L.'Al.* 16; see *Graces*).

In the passage last cited he is 'ivy-crowned.' The ivy was one of his best known symbols. Euripides in the *Phœnissæ* 650 ff., says that in the Aonian plains Bacchus was born, 'whom the wreathed ivy twining around him (περιστεφής) instantly, while yet a babe, blessed and covered with its verdant shady branches.' The worshipper of Bacchus was 'crowned with ivy' (*Bacchæ* 81), as is the god himself in fr. 46 of Pindar (Bergk).

Bacchus was a wine-god only in post-Homeric times. Plato in the *Laws* (2. 672 A) speaks of him as the giver of wine, and a scholium on *Od.* 9. 198 calls him the discoverer of wine.

The story of the transformed mariners in *C.* 46 ff. is told by Ovid (*Met.* 3. 583 ff.). Some Tyrrhene pirates, 'qui postea Tusci sunt dicti' (Hyg. *Fab.* 134), engaged to carry Bacchus to Naxos, but as they turned aside to sell him into slavery, their ship became wreathed with ivy, their oars became serpents, and the sailors dolphins (cf. *Hom. Hy.* 7; Apollod. 3. 5. 3). The classics recount no adventure of Bacchus with Circe. The supposed location of the Æan isle of Circe in the Tyrrhene sea may have been Milton's cue to his invention. A scholium on *Od.* 10. 135 says that some identified it with Circæum off Italy. This is Vergil's location (*Æn.* 7. 10 ff.). Compare also Diod. Sic. 4. 45.

The *Bacchæ* of Euripides is a representation of 'the barbarous dissonance of Bacchus and his revellers,' especially in the following passages : 64-162; 680-764; 977-1022. The story of the fate of Orpheus referred to in *P. L.* 7. 33 ff. (see *Orpheus*), is told by Ovid in *Met.* 11. 1-66, who describes the wild rout of the Mænads:

>   ingens
> Clamor, et inflato Berecynthia tibia cornu,
> Tympanaque, plaususque, et Bacchei ululatus
> Obstrepuere sono citharæ.

BELLEROPHON.—P. L. 7. 18.

In the sixth book of *P. L.* the Heavenly Muse has led the poet in his flight upon Pegasus. At the opening of the seventh book he prays that she may bring him down to earth in safety:

> Lest, from this flying steed unreigned (as once
> Bellerophon, though from a lower clime)
> Dismounted, on the Aleian field I fall,
> Erroneous there to wander and forlorn.

Bellerophon, son of Glaucus, was loved by Anteia, the wife of Prœtus, but when he did not return her love she openly accused him of attempted violation. He was sent with a letter to the king of Lycia, to the end that he might be killed. The Lycian king sent him on dangerous expeditions in the course of which he slew the Chimæra, 'trusting in the signs of the gods' (*Il.* 6. 155 ff.). Pindar (*Ol.* 13. 63 ff.) tells how Athene helped Bellerophon subdue the winged horse, Pegasus, which carried him in the flight. The rest of the story is suggested by Pindar (*Isth.* 6. 45). On the back of Pegasus Bellerophon aspired to reach the assembly of Zeus, but Pegasus threw him. Milton infers that he fell into the Aleian plain, probably from Homer's conclusion of the story (*Il.* 6.200): ' But when even he became hated of all the gods, he went wandering alone through the Aleian plain, consuming his heart, shunning the path of men.'

BELLONA.—P. L. 2. 922.

The Romans worshipped Bellona as a goddess of war. See *Æn.* 8. 703. According to Statius, *Theb.* 7. 72,

> regit atra jugales
> Sanguinea Bellona manu, longaque fatigat
> Cuspide.

BOREAS.—P. L. 10. 699. See Winds.

BRIAREOS.—P. L. 1. 199; V. E. 93.

Briareos, also called Ægæon (*Il.* 1. 404), was a son of Ge and Uranus, and a brother of Cottus and Gyges. The brothers had each one hundred arms and fifty heads and were of invincible strength (Hes. *Theog.* 147). In Homer (*Il.* 1. 396) Briareos helped Thetis to free Zeus from the bonds imposed by the other gods, and again in Hesiod (*Theog.* 617 ff.) Briareos and his brothers assisted the Olympian gods against the Titans. But Vergil (*Æn.* 10. 565) makes him the enemy of Zeus: 'As was Ægæon who, they say, had one hundred arms and one hundred hands and fire flashed from a hundred mouths and a hundred chests when he strove against the thunder-bolts of Jove.' See *Earth.*

BUSIRIS.—P. L. 1. 307.

Busiris is the name given by Apollodorus (2. 1. 5) to one of the sons of Ægyptus who were slain by the daughters of Danaus. Diodorus Siculus uses the name as that of an Egyptian king (1. 45; 4. 27) and son of Poseidon, who, in order to drive off a famine, sacrificed strangers, but was slain by Heracles. Milton gives the name to the oppressor of Israel as does Ralegh in his *History of the World* (2. 2. 7): ' Now that Orus the II. or Busiris, was the king that first oppressed Israel, . . . it is a common opinion of many great and most learned writers, who also think that hereupon grew the fable of Busiris sacrificing strangers.' Ralegh says, however, that Chencres was the Pharaoh who perished in the Red Sea (2. 2. 8).

CADMUS.—P. L. 9. 506.

Cadmus and Harmonia (rather than Hermione) reigned in Thebes. After an eventful life Cadmus retired to Illyria where he

2

prayed that he might be transformed to a serpent (Ov. *Met.* 4. 562 ff.):

> ut serpens, in longam tenditur alvum ;
> Durataeque cuti squamas increscere sentit,
> Nigraque caeruleis variari corpora guttis.

Following his example Harmonia was transformed in the same manner. The story is cited to illustrate the loveliness of the serpent of Eden. None was lovelier, 'not those that in Illyria changed Hermione and Cadmus.' The meaning of 'changed' in this passage has been disputed, but no unusual interpretation seems necessary if we consider Milton's source to be in Nonnus (*Dion.* 44. 107–118). Agaue, daughter of Cadmus, in a prophetic dream saw a gentle serpent approach Cadmus, and, winding fondly about his temples like a fillet, it caressed him. In the same manner a female serpent encircled the head of Harmonia. 'And the son of Cronus changed to stone the limbs of the two serpents, because by the mouth of the serpent-nourishing Illyrian sea Harmonia and Cadmus, with altered countenance, were about to assume the stony form of serpents.' Milton seems to refer to these serpents as effecting the change of Cadmus.

CAECIAS.—P. L. 10. 699. See Winds.

CALISTO.—P. R. 2. 186; C. 341.

The love of Zeus for Callisto is told by Apollodorus (3. 8. 2) and Hyginus (*Fab.* 176, 177; *Astron.* 2. 1), both of whom quote Hesiod, and is again to be found in Ovid (*Met.* 2. 401–530). Callisto was a daughter of Lycaon, king of Arcadia. She followed Artemis in the hunt, but was approached and violated by Zeus in the form of the goddess. Callisto was changed to a bear by the angry Diana, says Ovid, or by Juno or, according to Apollodorus, by Zeus, who carried her to heaven, where she appears as the Great Bear. Hence Milton's 'Star of Arcady' (*C.* 341).

The poet's mention of the 'Tyrian Cynosure' (*C.* 342) refers to another story concerning the constellations of the bears. Hyginus (*Astron.* 2. 2) says that according to the belief of some, Helice and Cynosura, two of the Cretan nurses of Jove, were honored with places in heaven, where Helice appears as the Great Bear and Cynosura as the Little Bear. Aratus (*Phoen.* 36–39) adds that in navigation the Greeks were guided by the former and the Phoenicians by the latter. In this connection Newton cites two passages, Ov. *Fast.* 3. 107, 108, and Val. Flacc. *Arg.* 1. 17:

> neque enim in Tyrias Cynosura carinas
> Certior, aut Graiis Helice servanda magistris.

CAPITOLINE JOVE.—P. L. 9. 508. See Jove.

CAR OF DAY.—C. 95. See Apollo.

CARPATHIAN WIZARD.—C. 872. See **Proteus** under **Sea-gods.**

CASSIOPEIA.—Pens. 19.

Cassiopeia was the wife of Cepheus, king of Æthiopia. Apollodorus (2. 4. 3) tells us that she contended with the Nereids, setting the beauty of her daughter Andromeda above theirs. Poseidon in revenge sent a sea-monster to afflict the land, which would retire only at the sacrifice of Andromeda. Hyginus (*Astron.* 2. 10) says that Cassiopeia was placed among the stars as a penalty for her boast.

CEPHALUS.—Pens. 124.

In the legend of Cephalus there is some confusion. Apollodorus (3. 14. 1) says that Cecrops, an autochthon, was the first king of Attica. One of his daughters was Herse, the mother, by Hermes (Apollod. 3. 14. 3), of Cephalus. To him Milton refers as 'the Attic boy'. Another Cephalus is mentioned by Apollodorus (1. 9. 4) as the son of Deion, and husband of Procris. He relates (3. 14. 1; 1. 9. 4) that both of these men were stolen by Eos (Aurora), who was enamored of them. Ovid (*Met.* 7. 690 ff.) says that the husband of Procris on the morning after his wedding was engaged in the chase on Mount Hymettus, when Aurora stole him away against his will. To end his pining, she restored him to Procris. Servius (on *Æn.* 6. 445) says that Cephalus had the habit of hunting on Hymettus, and implies that Aurora 'was wont' to see him there.

CERBERUS.—P. L. 2. 655; L'Al. 2.

In his description of Sin the poet says:

> About her middle round
> A cry of Hell-hounds never-ceasing barked
> With wide Cerberean mouths full loud, and rung
> A hideous peal.

Cerberus is first mentioned by Hesiod (*Theog.* 311) as the dog of Hell with fifty heads, shameless and strong. According to later tradition he had only three heads (Verg. *Æn.* 6. 417; *Georg.* 4. 483). The expression 'Cerberean mouths' suggests Ovid's 'Cerbereos rictus' in his description of Scylla (*Met.* 14. 65). Milton rather curiously describes the barking of Hell-hounds as ringing 'a hideous peal.' The figure may be a development from Hesiod, who calls Cerberus 'brazen-voiced' (*Theog.* 311).

The genealogy of Melancholy (*L.'Al.* 2) is Milton's own. The wife and sister of Erebus was Night (*Theog.* 123 ff.). Cf. *Saturn.*

CERES.—P. L. 4. 271, 981; 9. 395.

Ceres, to the Greeks Demeter, was the daughter of Cronus and Rhea (Hes. *Theog.* 453) and the mother by Zeus of Persephone, the Roman Proserpina (*Theog.* 912). She is generally mentioned as the goddess of agriculture and nourishment, and is thus characterized by the epithets of Callimachus (*Hy. to Dem.* 2), and in *Hom. Hy. to Dem.* 4.

The best-known incidents in connection with Ceres are the rape of her daughter and the mother's weary search through the world, both suggested by Milton in *P.L.* 4. 268 ff. Ovid thus describes the 'fair field of Enna' (*Met.* 5. 385 ff.):

> Haud procul Hennæis lacus est a mœnibus altæ,
> Nomine Pergus: non illo plura Caystros
> Carmina cycnorum labentibus audit in undis.
> Silva coronat aquas, cingens latus omne; suisque
> Frondibus, ut velo, Phœbos submovet ictus.
> Frigora dant rami, Tyrios humus humida flores,
> Perpetuum ver est.

Here Proserpina was gathering lilies and violets when Dis ('mœstus,' 396) stole her away to be his wife and queen of the Lower World. Cf. *Hom. Hy.* 417–430. *Hom. Hy. to Dem.* 47 says: 'Nine days then through earth did revered Deo wander about with flaming torches in her hands, nor did she once taste of ambrosia or sweet nectar in her grief, nor refresh her body with the bath.' Incidents of her wandering are related by Ovid in *Met.* 5. 438 ff. and *Fast.* 4. 421 ff.

CHALYBEAN.—S. A. 133.

Samson's strength made useless all armor and 'Chalybean-tempered steel.' The Chalybeans, according to Apollonius (2. 375), 'are workmen, and busy themselves with the working of iron.' A scholium on the passage says that they were a Scythian people. Æschylus in the *Prometheus* 740 calls them σιδηροτέκτονες.

CHAM.—P. L. 4. 276. See Ammon.

CHANCE.—P. L. 2. 233; 551, 910, 965; 7. 172; C. 588.

How much of Milton's use of Chance may be referred to the Tyche of Greek mythology and the Latin Fortuna, is uncertain. Where so varied a conception is possible, the line between mythology and philosophy often cannot be clearly determined, and in most of the instances which may have been Milton's antecedents we find little or no suggestion of personification. The poet speaks without personification of Fate and Chance as treated by the Greek tragedians (*P. R.* 4. 265). A fragment of Æschylus is quoted by Stobæus (1. 6. 16) to the effect that πάντων τύραννος ἡ τύχη 'στι τῶν θεῶν. In Euripides (*Phœn.* 1202) are the words, καλῶς τὰ τῶν θεῶν καὶ τὰ τῆς τύχης ἔχει. Milton's conception of Chance as a malignant divinity is not in harmony with the earlier poets, but she is associated by him with malice and sorcery (*C.* 588); with Orcus, Demogorgon, and Discord (*P. L.* 2. 233, 910, 965). With this last association may be compared a passage in Plato (*Laws* 4. 709), where the Athenian says, 'I was going to say that man never legislates, but that destinies and accidents happening in all sorts of ways, legislate in all sorts of ways. Either the violence of war has overthrown governments and changed laws, or the hard necessity of poverty. . . . Any one who sees all this, naturally rushes to the conclusion . . . that no mortal legislates in anything, but that in human affairs chance is almost everything.' A contest between Chance and Fate or other divinities, such as we find in *P. L.* 2. 232, is only hinted at in fr. 38 of Pindar: ἐν ἐργμασιν δὲ νικᾷ τύχα οὐ σθένος. Pausanias (7. 26. 8) quotes Pindar as his authority that ' Tyche is one of the Mœræ (Fates) and is somewhat stronger than her sisters.' In 4. 30. 3 he speaks as though it were common belief that ' this goddess is the greatest of divinities in the affairs of men, and shows the greatest strength.' Plutarch (*De Fort. Rom.* 1, 2) speaks of the contest between Virtue and Tyche, but believes that they work together.

As to her fickleness, Pindar addresses Tyche in *Ol.* 12 saying, ' Up and down the hopes of men are tossed as they cleave the waves of baffling falsity: and a sure token of what shall come to pass hath never any man on the earth received from God.' Pliny (*N. H.* 2. 5. 7) says that in his time Fortuna was believed to be ' cæca, vaga, inconstans, incerta, varia, indignorum fautrix.'

On *P. L.* 2. 551 Todd quotes Bentley to the effect that ' this is taken from the famous distich of Euripides, which Brutus used when he slew himself:

ὦ τλῆμον 'Αρετὴ, λόγος ἄρ' ἦσθ', ἐγὼ δὲ σε
ὡς ἔργον ἤσκουν σὺ δ' ἄρ' ἐδούλευες τύχῃ.

In some places for βίᾳ *force*, it is quoted τύχῃ *fortune*. Milton has well comprehended both.' The poet has shown the same conservatism in *C.* 586:

> Against the threats
> Of malice or of sorcery, or that power
> Which erring men call Chance, this hold I firm:
> Virtue may be assailed, but never hurt,
> Surprised by unjust Force, but not enthralled.

Dion Cassius, from whom Bentley's story of Brutus is taken (47. 49), does not say that the distich is from Euripides, but calls the saying τοῦτο τὸ 'Ηράκλειον. In Nauck's *Trag. Græc. Frag.* the fragment is given among the *Adespota* (305). Milton has discussed the relation between Chance and Causes in his *Artis Log. plen. Instit.* 1. 5, ed. Symmons 6. 208 ff.

CHAOS.—P. L. 1. 10, 543; 2. 233, 895, 907, 960, 970, 1038; 3. 18, 421; 6. 871; 7. 221; 7. 272; 10. 416, 477; C. 334.

Milton's use and representation of Chaos have something in common with classical tradition, but his conception is much more definite and elaborate, and seems to bear some reference to the word's etymological meaning of chasm or abyss. (Cf. χαίνειν, χάσκειν, to yawn.)   In *P. L.* 2. 891 the realm or region of Chaos is 'the hoary Deep—a dark Illimitable Ocean.'   Again it is 'the wasteful Deep' (*P. L.* 2. 961), the 'nethermost' and 'intractable Abyss' (*P. L.* 2 969; 10. 476).   In *The Doctrine and Discipline of Divorce, P. W.* 3. 224, Milton speaks of 'that uttermost and bottomless gulf of chaos, deeper from holy bliss than the world's diameter multiplied.'   This is founded also on Homer's Tartarus (*Il.* 8. 13).

The first mention of Chaos is made by Hesiod (*Theog.* 116), who says that of all things Chaos was (born?) first.   His statement, how-ever, may be a mere personification in order to reconcile speculation with popular belief, and after his times Chaos became associated rather with philosophical discussion than with pure mythology. There is therefore little or no classical authority for Chaos as a dis-tinct divinity ruling and maintaining the great region of anarchy and confusion above Hell.   (Cf. *P. L.* 1. 543; 2. 894, 960; 7. 272; 10. 477.) Plutarch (*De Is. et Os.* 57) says that Hesiod seems to make Chaos a kind of region or place and the foundation of all.   Milton's general conception as well as his description of the elements warring in Chaos (*P. L.* 2. 884–906) seem to refer to Ovid, *Met.* 1. 5 ff.:

> Ante, mare et tellus et quod tegit omnia cælum,
> Unus erat toto Naturæ vultus in orbe,
> Quem dixere Chaos, rudis indigestaque moles;
> Nec quidquam, nisi pondus iners; congestaque eodem
> Non bene junctarum discordia semina rerum.
>
> .   .   .   .   .   .
>
> Sic erat instabilis tellus, innabilis unda,
> Lucis egens aer; nulli sua forma manebat,
> Obstabatque aliis aliud: quia corpore in uno
> Frigida pugnabant calidis, humentia siccis
> Mollia cum duris, sine pondere habentia pondus.

Ovid (*Met.* 10. 30) speaks of Chaos as synonymous with Hell, and in 14. 404 as a divinity of the Lower World; cf. Verg. *Æn.* 4. 510. Though in Milton the old personal conception has been elaborated generally into a ruling divinity, yet Chaos occasionally may denote both ruler and realm, as in *P. L.* 7. 221 ; 10. 416.

There is no classical authority for Night as the consort of Chaos. According to the Orphic cosmogony (*Orph. Hy. to Night* 2), Night is the ancestress of gods and men, in fact, the γένεσις πάντων.   Milton apparently attempts a reconciliation of the two cosmogonies in making 'unoriginal Night and Chaos wild' co-rulers and 'ancestors of Nature.'

In one of his early writings (*Prolusions*) Milton identifies Chaos with Demogorgon.   Cf. *Demogorgon*.   Discussions of Chaos may be found in Schoemann's edition of the *Theogony*, pp. 83–85, and on pp. 10–23 of H. Flach's *Das System der Hes. Kosmogonie.*

CHARYBDIS.—P. L. 2. 1020; C. 259. See Scylla.

CHIMÆRA.—P. L. 2. 628; C. 517.

Of the Chimæra Homer tells us (*Il*. 6. 180) that 'she was of the generation of gods and not of men, in front a lion, and behind a serpent, and in her middle a she-goat, breathing forth the terrible strength of flaming fire.'

The enumeration in *P. L*. 2. 628, of 'Gorgons, and Hydras, and Chimæras dire' is drawn from Vergil's enumeration of the monsters whose abode is at the entrance of Hades (*Æn*. 6. 287):

> bellua Lernæ
> Horrendum stridens, flammisque armata Chimæra
> Gorgones, Harpyiæque.

This location of the Chimæra may account for the connection in C. 57:

> dire Chimeras and enchanted isles,
> And rifted rocks whose entrance leads to Hell.

Vergil describes the place 237–241:

> Spelunca alta fuit, vastoque immanis hiatu,
> Scrupea, tuta lacu nigro nemorumque tenebris.

But the mention of 'enchanted isles' in such close connection with the entrance to Hell is strongly reminiscent of the *Odyssey*, for it was directly from Circe's enchanted isle, and in following out her commands that Odysseus made his visit to the Lower World. The story is found in Odysseus' narrative, *Od*. 10. 503–11. 50. Cf. *Bellerophon*.

CIMMERIAN.—L'Al. 10; cf. Prolusions, ed. Symmons 6. 152.

Homer (*Od*. 11. 13) tells how the ship of Odysseus 'came to the bounds of deep-flowing Ocean. There are the land and city of the Cimmerians, hidden in gloom and mist; and never does the beaming sun look down upon them with his rays, neither when he mounts up in the starry heaven, nor when he turns back toward the earth from heaven, but malignant night is outstretched over unhappy mortals.' In connection with *L'Al*. 8 we may consider Ovid, *Met*. 11. 592:

> Est prope Cimmerios longo spelunca recessu
> Mons cavus, ignavi domus et penetralia Somni.

The abode of the Cimmerians was a matter of dispute among the ancients. Herodotus (4. 12) locates the historic Cimmerians in Scythia, and Strabo (5. 244) mentions the belief that the mythical Cimmerians lived in Italy near Lake Avernus.

CIRCE.—P. L. 9. 522; C. 50, 153, 253, 522.

In the *Odyssey* 10. 136 Circe is an 'awful goddess of mortal speech . . . begotten of Helios'; and again (276), 'the enchantress' (πολυφάρμακος). As Eurylochus and his companions approached her palace they heard her singing so sweet a song as she was weav-

ing at the loom, that Polites wondered whether it was the voice of
goddess or woman. Cf. *C.* 244 ff. About them thronged the wolves
and lions which Circe had bewitched 'with evil drugs.' With a
magic drug and a touch of her wand she turned the companions of
Odysseus into swine. But the hero with the aid of Hermes restored
them. Cf. Verg. *Æn.* 7. 11–20. See *Hermes*.

Milton remembers Ovid's account also (*Met.* 14. 248 ff.). When
the heroes reached the palace of Circe they found her with the
Nereids and Nymphs about her (267 ff.):

> Gramina disponunt, sparsosque sine ordíne flores
> Secernunt calathis, variasque coloribus herbas.
> Ipsa, quod hæ faciunt, opus exigit.

Cf. *C.* 253 and see *Naiads*. It will be seen that in *C.* 244–257 Milton,
with his usual sensitiveness to sound, has taken his cue from Homer,
and greatly surpassed Ovid in this particular representation. As
the charm took effect the victims began (280),

> pro verbis edere raucum
> Murmur, et in terram toto procumbere vultu.

Cf. *C.* 50 ff. See also *Bacchus* and *Sirens*.

CLYMENE.—P. R. 2. 186. See **Apollo.**

COCYTUS.—P. L. 2. 579. See **Rivers of Hell.**

COMUS.—See **Bacchus** and **Circe.**

CORYDON AND THYRSIS.—L'Al. 83.

Lines 81–90 of *L'Allegro* form an idyll of Milton's own making,
but the names, Corydon, Thyrsis, Phillis, Thestylis, as well as some of
the details of the picture, show the influence of Vergil. Corydon (Theoc.
4; Verg. *Ecl.* 2 and 7) and Thyrsis (Theoc. 1; Verg. *Ecl.* 7) are
shepherds, and Phyllis (*Ecl.* 7. 14) and Thestylis (Theoc. 2. 95;
Ecl. 2. 10) are attendants. With Milton's description compare
also *Ecl.* 1. 81:

> Et jam summa procul villarum culmina fumant.

and *Ecl.* 2. 10, 11:

> Thestylis et rapido fessis messoribus æstu
> Allia serpyllumque herbas contundit olentes.

COTYTTO.—C. 129.

Cotytto or Cotys was originally a goddess of the Thracian tribe
Edoni, and was worshipped with noisy rites similar to those used in
the celebration of the Phrygian Rhea or Cybele (Strabo 10. 470).
According to Suidas (θιασώτης, Κότυς) and Hesychius (Κοτυττώ) her
worship in a licentious form was to be found in Corinth. Whether
it actually existed in Athens is disputed. Juvenal at any rate would
imply that it did (*Sat.* 2. 91, 92):

> Talia secreta coluerunt Orgia tæda
> Cecropiam soliti Baptæ lassare Cotytto.

The scholium on this passage says: '*Baptæ*, titulus libri, quo impudici describuntur ab *Epolide*, qui inducit viros Athenienses ad imitationem fœminarum saltantes, lassare psaltriam. *Baptæ*, ergo molles,' etc. It is evident that Milton had this passage and its scholium in mind in *C.* 129:

> Dark-veiled Cotytto, to whom the secret flame
> Of midnight torches burns!

Compare also 143, 144:

> Come, knit hands, and beat the ground
> In a light fantastic round.

The 'secret flame' may be referred to 'secreta tæda' (Juv. 2. 91), and 'thy vowed priests' (136) to the Baptæ, a word which, according to conjecture, derives its significance from some form of lustral rite at initiation. That Cotytto was worshipped at night is implied most directly in 'secreta tæda,' though the few cases in which the goddess is mentioned would seem by their association to point to nocturnal rites. In Strabo (10. 470, 471) Cotytto is mentioned in connection with such gods of nocturnal worship as the Thracian Bendis (cf. Plat. *Rep.* 1. 327), and the Phrygian Sabazius (cf. Cicero, *De Leg*. 2. 15). The same conception appears in the *Defensio contra Alex. Mor.* ed. Symmons 5. 291: 'Nunc non Deus te, sed tua illa Dea audit Cotytto . . . labra tacite moventem:

> Da mihi fallere; da justo sanctoque videri:
> *Noctem peccatis*, et stupris objice nubem.'

From the subject of Juvenal's second satire, and from Horace (*Epod.* 17. 56):

> Inultus ut tu riseris Cotyttia
> Volgata, sacrum liberi Cupidinis,—

it is to be inferred that Cotytto was also worshipped at Rome with great license.

In making Cotytto appear in a 'cloudy ebon chair' Milton follows the tradition of Latin poets, who are fond of this accessory; cf. Ov. *Met.* 2. 531; 5. 645; Verg. *Æn.* 1. 147; Senec. *Med.* 787; see *Hecate.*

A discussion of Cotytto may be found in Buttmann's *Mythologus* 2. 159 ff.

CUPID.—P. L. 4. 763; 11. 589; C. 124, 445, 1004; Son. 1. 13.

In the infrequent use which Milton makes of this divinity he follows the later conception of Love as a sportive, winged boy, armed with the bow, arrows, and firebrands. This is especially true of his Latin poems, in which distinct marks of Ovid's influence are evident. (Cf. *Eleg.* 5. 97; 6. 52; 7. 3, 4; *Ep. Dam.* 191 ff.) In *Met.* 1. 468 ff. Cupid carries two arrows, one of gold, to excite love, and the other of lead, to repel it. Venus depends upon her son for the strength of her own influence. Cf. *Met.* 5. 365 ff.: Verg. *Æn.* 664 ff.; *C.* 124. Speaking of ideal marriage in *P. L.* 4. 763, the poet says,

> Here Love his golden shafts employs, here lights
> His constant lamp, and waves his purple wings.

These lines seem to be the very reverse of a passage in Ovid (*Am.* 3. 9. 7–9):

> Ecce puer Veneris fert eversamque pharetram,
>   Et fractos arcus, et sine luce facem.
> Aspice, demissis ut eat miserabilis alis.

Ovid also mentions Love's ' purpureas alas ' in the *Remedia Amoris* 701. All these accoutrements of Cupid appear in Milton's Latin poems (*Eleg.* 5. 98; 7–17; 47). See *Hesperus*.

The story of Cupid and Psyche to which Milton refers in *C.* 1003 ff. was late in origin. It is related in detail as an allegory by Apuleius in his *Metamorphoses* 4. 28–6. 24. Psyche was the youngest and most beautiful of three sisters. Venus was jealous of her beauty, and the oracle commanded her father to expose her upon the mountains. There, in a splendid palace, she became the wife of Cupid, who warned her not to reveal his name to her sisters. But Psyche could not resist their questions, and Cupid left her. She wandered alone over the earth pursued by the implacable Venus, who imposed many labors upon her. These she accomplished by miraculous means. At length Cupid besought Jove for her restoration. A council of the gods assembled to consider the matter, and Jove decreed that Cupid and Psyche should be united in eternal marriage, at which all the gods assisted. Psyche became the mother of Voluptas. Milton, however, with greater delicacy says that her children are Youth and Joy.

CYBELE.—Arc. 21. See **Rhea**.

CYNTHIA.—C. N. 103; Pens. 59. See **Diana**.

CYTHEREA.—P. L. 9. 19. See **Venus**.

DAMŒTAS.—Lyc. 36.

Damœtas is a name associated with pastoral poetry, and occurs in the sixth idyll of Theocritus, from which it is derived by Vergil in his third eclogue. In both cases Damœtas is a young shepherd who engages in a song contest, of which the chief subject is love.

DAPHNE.—P. L. 4. 273; P. R. 2. 187. C. 661. See **Apollo**.

DARKNESS.—P. L. 3. 421; P. R. 4. 397; L'Al. 2, 6. See **Erebus** and **Night**.

DEATH.—P. L. 2. 789; 10. 230; P. R. 3. 85; Son. 23. 4.

If Milton's Death as represented in *P. L.* 2. 666–703, 785–848, is compared with Thanatos in the *Alcestis* of Euripides (cf. *Son.* 23. 4), certain points of resemblance and difference are to be noticed. In *Alc.* 843 he is ' the sable-vested king of the departed.' In Milton he is also a king (673, 698). As Thanatos rebukes Apollo for unjustly interfering with the Fates and saving the life of Admetus (*Alc.* 29–37), so with even greater vehemence Death defies Satan (689–703). Death is armed with a dart (672), while Thanatos carries a sword (*Alc.* 74, 76.), which, however, serves another end than to smite his victims.

According to Hesiod (*Theog.* 212) Death was born of Night without a father. Hyginus (*Pref. to Fab.*) names Erebus as the father. Homer makes Death the brother of Sleep (*Il.* 4. 231), and to Sleep he ascribes a characteristic which Milton gives Death (cf. *P. L.* 2. 698; *P.R.* 3. 85). He is addressed as 'lord of all gods and of all men.'

DELIA.—P. L. 9. 387. See **Diana.**

DELOS.—P. L. 10. 296. See **Apollo.**

DELPHI.—P. L. 1. 517; P. R. 1. 458; C. N. 178; Shak. 12. See **Apollo.**

DEMOGORGON.—P. L. 2. 965.

Near the throne of Chaos and Night stood

> Orcus and Ades, and the dreaded name
> Of Demogorgon.

It may be well to consider in this connection a passage in the *Prolusions* of Milton (*Utrum Dies an Nox præst.*, ed. Symmons 6. 146), where he says: 'Apud vetustissimos itaque mythologiæ scriptores memoriæ datum reperio *Demogorgonem* deorum omnium atavum (quem eundem et Chaos ab antiquis nuncupatum hariolor) inter alios liberos, quos suceperat plurimos, Terram genuisse, hac, incerto patre Noctem fuisse prognatam.' That Demogorgon and Chaos were the same is not the classical idea. We find it in Boccaccio, who devotes the first book of his *De Genealogia Deorum* to Demogorgon and his progeny, and calls him (1. 1) 'veternosus ille deorum omnium gentilium proavus . . . nomine ipso horribilis'; cf. *P. L.* 2. 964. One of Milton's 'vetustissimi scriptores' appears to be Hesiod. See *Chaos.*

A passage in the *Thebaid* of Statius may throw light upon Milton's use of Demogorgon. Tiresias in calling forth the shade of Laius, urges the other divinities of Hades, but one name he dares not mention (4. 516).

> Et triplicis mundi summum, quem scire nefastum est;
> Illum sed taceo; prohibet tranquilla senectus.

In commenting upon the adjuration Lactantius says: 'dicit deum demogorgona summum, cujus nomen scire non licet.'

DEUCALION.—P. L. 11. 12.

In his reference to the Greek story of the flood and the restoration of man through Deucalion and Pyrrha, Milton has followed the account of Ovid (*Met.* 1. 260–415), who is authority for the statement that 'the ancient pair' consulted the oracle of Themis, as to the right course of action (321; cf. 375). Milton's citation of the legend may have indirect connection with the statement of Apollodorus that Pyrrha was the first mortal woman (1. 7. 2; cf. *P. L.* 11. 11).

DIANA.—P. L. 1. 784; 3. 728; 9. 387; P. R. 2. 355; C. N. 103; Pens. 59; C. 135, 441, 535; Son. 12. 7.

In Homer Artemis (Diana) is especially characterized by her chastity (*Od.* 18. 202; 20. 71) and her stately beauty. Helen and Penelope are compared with her (*Od.* 4. 122; 17. 37). In *Od.* 6. 102 ff. Nausicaa among her handmaids comes forth 'even as Artemis, the archer, moveth down the mountain, either along the ridges of lofty Taygetus or Erymanthus, taking her pastime in the chase of boars and swift deer, and with her the wild wood-nymphs disport them,   .   .   . while high over all she rears her head and brows, and easily may she be known,—but all are fair.' Compare Vergil's imitation (*Æn.* 1. 499):

> Exercet Diana choros; quam mille secutæ
> Hinc atque hinc glomerantur Oreades.

The description occurs frequently. See *Hom. Hy.* 26; Callim. *Hy. to Art.; P. L.* 9. 386 ff.; *P. R.* 2. 355.

In *C.* 442 Diana is called 'the silver-shafted queen.' According to *Il.* 20. 70 her shafts are golden. Milton's alteration may have been considered more in harmony with his idea of womanly purity and beauty (cf. *Arc.* 16, 33), and there seems also to be a remote reference to the moonbeams, since her brother Apollo's golden shafts were supposed to represent the sun's rays (Macrobius 1. 17. 57). But in Homer he is the god of the silver bow (*Il.* 2. 766; 5. 449).

Milton (*C.* 445) represents Diana as also setting at nought

> The frivolous bolt of Cupid; gods and men
> Feared her stern frown, and she was queen o' the woods.

The poet evidently refers to such stories as those of Actæon (Ov. *Met.* 3. 131 ff.) and of Callisto. In *Met.* 5. 365 ff. Venus commands Cupid to defend her with his all-powerful arrows:

> Spernimur; ac mecum vires tenuantur Amoris.
> Pallada nonne vides, jaculatricemque Dianam
> Abscessisse mihi?

Diana is called 'queen of wild beasts' by Homer (*Il.* 21. 470).

The *Moon-goddess* became identified with Artemis later than Homer. In Æsch. fr. 171 (ed. Wecklein) the moon is called 'bright eye of the daughter of Leto.' She is named Cynthia (*Pens.* 59; *C. N.* 103), as her brother was called Cynthius, from Mount Cynthus of Delos, their birth-place.

In *Pens.* 59 (cf. In *Obit. Eliens.* 56) she drives a yoke of dragons. This conception seems to be without classical authority. The car of Selene, the moon-goddess, was drawn by foals (*Hom. Hy.* 31), or, according to a quotation in Fulgentius (*Mythol.* 1. ed. Staveren p. 618), she rode behind bulls as in Claudian (*Rapt. Proserp.* 3. 403). Diana drives either horses (*Hom. Hy.* 8), or deer (Ap. Rh. 3. 879). Cf. Paus. 5. 11. But it is worthy of notice that in Ov. *Met.* 7. 192–221 Medea's prayer to the moon and other divinities is answered by the descent of a chariot drawn by dragons, though in 398 it appears that these belonged to the sun. Dragons pull the chariot of Ceres in 5. 642.

The regal character of the moon, as represented in *P. L.* 4. 606–609; 5. 41; 7. 381, is not common in the classics. The brightness of her golden crown is mentioned in *Hom. Hy.* 32. 5, and Horace calls her 'siderum regina bicornis' (*C. Sæc.* 35). The queenly nature of Diana is easily transferable to the moon. In *P. L.* 4. 609 the moon 'o'er the dark her silver mantle threw.' According to *Hom. Hy.* 32. 8 she begins her progress, 'having put on her far-shining garments.'

Hecate was originally a moon-goddess, but Milton follows the later conception and makes her the malignant divinity of sorcery and the Lower World. Vergil (*Æn.* 6. 247) represents her as 'Cæloque Ereboque potentem' and as 'Tergeminamque Hecaten, tria virginis ora Dianæ' (4. 511). In a note on this line Servius says that some explain 'tergeminam' by the three phases of the moon, quarter, half, and full, or it may have reference to the three forms, Luna, Diana, and Proserpina (Hecate?), as regents of Heaven, Earth, and Hell. Cf. *P. L.* 3. 730.

In *C.* 135 Hecate is associated with Cotytto, and rides with her in 'a cloudy ebon chair,' facts which Masson explains by their common origin in Thrace. But Hecate appears frequently in company with the different gods of darkness, as in Ov. *Met.* 14. 403, where in Circe's enchantment

> Illa nocens spargit, virus succosque veneni:
> Et Noctem, Noctisque Deos Ereboque Chaoque
> Convocat, et longis Hecaten ululatibus orat.

This passage may throw the necessary light on *C.* 532-535. It also suggests the howl of Medea in *Met.* 7. 190. The general character of *C.* 130–135 is not dissimilar to Ovid's description of Medea's nocturnal journey in the chariot drawn by dragons (7. 220–237). Compare also the chariot of *Night.*

For the solitudes suggested by the name of Hecate instances are to be found in Theoc. 2. 12 and in the enchantments of Medea, *Met.* 7. 179–190, who performs the 'abhorred rites' in 240 ff.; cf. Theoc. 2. 1–16. Other examples of these rites may be found in Verg. *Æn.* 6. 257; Sen. *Œd.* 548 ff.; Tibull. 1. 2. 52; Lucan 6. 685.

DIS.—P. L. 4. 270. See Ceres, Pluto.

DISCORD.—P. L. 2. 967; 10.707.

In the light of classical tradition Milton's treatment of Discord is rather indefinite. He makes her the daughter of Sin (*P. L.* 10. 708), while Hyginus (*Pref. to Fab.*) says that she was the daughter of Nox and Erebus, apparently identifying her with Eris (Hes. *Theog.* 225).

The ancients did not give Discord 'a thousand various mouths.' Among the horrors at the mouth of Hades Vergil names 'Discordia demens Vipereum crinem vittis innexa cruentis' (*Æn.* 6. 280). Milton may have referred to 'vipereum crinem,' or he may have adapted Vergil's description of Fama (*Æn.* 4. 181), which in part is based upon Homer's Eris (*Il.* 4. 440–43): 'quot sunt corpore plumæ . . . Tot linguæ, totidem ora sonant.' Cf. also *Il.* 11. 3 with *P. L.* 10. 708–710.

DODONA.—P. L. 1. 518. See **Jove.**

DRYADS.—P. L. 9. 387; C. 963. See **Nymphs.**

EARTH.—P. L. 1. 198, 509, 687, 778; 5. 338; 7. 453; 9. 1000; P. R. 4. 563, 566; D. F. I. 47.

Earth is frequently and naturally represented as the 'all-bearing Mother' as in *P. L.* 5. 338; cf. 1. 687; 9. 1000. In Hesiod *Theog.* 117 ff. Gaia or Ge (Earth) is the first child of Chaos, and from her is born Uranus (Heaven). Ge and Uranus become the parents of the line of Olympian gods. Cf. *P. L.* 1. 509. Pindar seems to refer to Earth when in *Nem.* 6. 1 ff. he says that there is one race of gods and one of men, 'and it is from one mother that we both draw the breath of life.' Cf. Ov. *Met.* 1. 78 ff. After the flood, when Deucalion and Pyrrha could not at first interpret the command to begin the new creation by throwing behind them the bones of their mother, Deucalion at last exclaimed (*Met.* 1. 393),

> Magna parens Terra est: lapides in corpore terræ
> Ossa reor dici.

Then the Earth, pregnant with the rays of the sun, brought forth many different creatures. (Cf. 'viscera terræ' of *Met.* 1. 138 with *P. L.* 1. 687 ff.; see *P. L.* 7. 453.) Milton speaks of Earth as the mother of the hundred-handed giants, *Briareos* and his brothers, of *Typhon* and the *Giants* (*P. L.* 1. 198, 778); of *Antæus* (*P. R.* 4. 563 ff.); of the *Titans* (*P. L.* 1. 198; *D. F. I.* 47). A discussion of each will be found in its place. In *P. L.* 1. 199 'Briareos or Typhon' explain 'Earth-born,' in the previous line, and could not be called Titanian. 'Earth-born' also suggests the Giants proper, as in *P. L.* 1. 778. The 'Giant-angels' of *P. L.* 7. 605 is evidently a reference to Titans rather than the Giants, since their leader, like the angels, was fighting to maintain his place in Heaven. The 'Earth-born giant' mentioned in *V. E.* 93 is Briareos or one of his brothers, as the context shows. See also *Nature.*

ECHO.—C. 230-243; 275.

In his treatment of the legend of Echo, Milton has been very free. But the ancients seem to have differed widely in their conception of the nymph. For example, with some writers as Euripides (*Hec.* 1109 ff.), she is a mountain-nymph. Cf. Ov. *Met.* 3. 363. In later writers she is a water-nymph as in *Anth. Pal.* 9. 825. But the poet has some authority for making her a wood-nymph whose haunts are the 'violet-embroidered vale,' a 'flowery cave,' or 'mossy couch' (275). In *Anth. Pal.* 9. 382, 383 she dwells 'on the border of the land where trees grow tall.' The description of Echo's retreat in *C.* 230–233, 276 may be an expansion of Ov. *Met.* 3. 393:

> Spreta latet silvis, pudibundaque frondibus ora
> Protegit; et solis ex illo vivit in antris.

The nymph is frequently represented as living in a cave; cf. Lucian, *De Domo* 3; Senec. *Troad.* 109 ff. There seems to be no classical authority, however, for her dwelling

> By slow Meander's margent green.

The story of how Juno deprived Echo of the power of voluntary speech, and how she pined away in her love for the fair Narcissus, until she became nothing but an echoing voice, may be found in Ov. *Met.* 3. 351 ff.; cf. *Nat. non pati Sen.* 61.

ELYSIUM.—P. L. 3. 359, 472; D. F. I. 40; L'Al. 147; C. 257, 996.

The words Elysium and Elysian are in a general way used by the poets of that which is free from care. They are as old as Homer, who sang of Elysium as the place where worthy men continued their earthly life without having seen death. In *Od.* 4. 563 Proteus says to Menelaus, 'The deathless gods will convey thee to the Elysian plain and the world's end . . . where life is easiest for men. No snow is there nor yet great storm, nor any rain; but always ocean sendeth forth the breeze of the shrill West to blow cool on men.' It must be noticed, however, that the idea of Elysium is closely associated in the mind of Milton with that of flowers, as the following citations show.

> Iris there with humid bow
> Waters the odorous banks, that blow
> Flowers of more mingled hue
> Than her purfled scarf can shew,
> And drenches with Elysian dew
>
> .   .   .   .   .
>
> Beds of hyacinth and roses.
>
> *C.* 992–998.

> I have oft heard
> My mother Circe with the Sirens three,
> Amidst the flowery-kirtled Naiades,
> Culling their potent herbs and baneful drugs,
> Who, as they sung, would take the prisoned soul,
> And lap it in Elysium.—*C.* 252–257.

And where the River of Bliss through midst of Heaven
Rolls o'er Elysian flowers her amber stream !
P. L. 3. 358, 359.

That Orpheus' self may heave his head
From golden slumber on a bed
Of heaped Elysian flowers.
L'Al. 145-147.

To refer this association to some particular passage or poet would be impossible. Mention may be made, however, of instances where it occurs among the ancients, which make it appear that Milton has borrowed from descriptions of the Blessed Isles. In the *Odyssey* 'the mead of asphodel' is the place 'where dwell the souls, the phantoms of men outworn.' (24. 13; cf. 11. 539). Pindar, however, gives the best example. In *Ol.* 2 he describes the place of reward of the good, saying: 'There round the islands of the blest the Ocean-breezes blow, and golden flowers are glowing, some from the land on trees of splendor, and some the water feedeth, with wreaths whereof they entwine their hands' (78 ff.). Plutarch in the *Consol. ad Apollon.* 120 C saves a fragment of the *Threnoi* of Pindar, which, he says, describes the happy reward of the good: 'And the space of crimson-flowered meadows before their city is full of the shade of frankincense-trees, and of fruits of gold, . . .   and among them thriveth all fair-flowering bliss.' Among the Latin poets may be cited Ovid, who makes Chloris, the goddess of flowers, appear as 'a Nymph of the blessed plains, where, as thou hast heard, was formerly the abode of blessed men' (*Fast.* 5. 195 ff.). Mention should also be made of the description which immediately follows this passage. See also *Naiads* and *Circe*.

EPIDAURUS.—P. L. 9. 507.

Milton speaks of Æsculapius, the divinity of medicine, as 'the god in Epidaurus,' illustrating by this citation the beauty and gentleness of the serpent of Eden. He is evidently thinking of a story in Roman history as told by Valerius Maximus (1. 2). In the early days, during a pestilence, the city of Rome, by the advice of the Sibylline books sent an embassy to Epidaurus, that they might seek the help of Æsculapius in his temple there. Their prayers were answered by the god himself in the form of a serpent. 'Siquidem is anguis, quem Epidauri raro, sed numquam sine magno ipsorum bono visum in modum Æsculapii venerati fuerunt, per urbis celeberrimas partes mitibus oculis et leni tractu labi cœpit, triduoque inter religiosam omnium admirationem conspectus, haud dubiam præ se adpetitæ clarioris sedis alacritatem ferens, ad triremem Romanam perrexit, paventibusque inusitato spectaculo nautis eo conscendit, ubi Q. Ogulni legati tabernaculum erat, inque multiplicem orbem per summam quietem est convolutus.' At Antium the serpent left the ship, but the sailors waited for it to return. On their arrival at Rome it swam to an island in the Tiber, where a temple was erected to it, since the plague had subsided. The same story is told by Livy (*Epit.* 11; cf. Paus. 3. 23).

EREBUS.—P. L. 2. 883; C. 804.

In Homer Erebus is used indefinitely of the abode of the dead. In *Od.* 11. 37. 'the spirits of the dead that be departed gathered them from out of Erebus.' But Erebus was also the personified Darkness of the Depths (Hes. *Theog.* 123). Plutarch (*De Prim. Frig.* 953 A) says: καὶ τὸ ἐρεβος τοῦτο ἦν ἄρα τὸ χθόνιον καὶ ἐγγαιον σκότος. Milton, however, makes no distinction between Erebus and Tartarus in the light of his apparent sources.

The mention of thunder and chains (*C.* 804) points to the story of the battle with the Titans, as told by Hesiod (*Theog.* 664 ff.). See *Titans.* In *P. L.* 2. 883 the infernal doors

> on their hinges grate
> Harsh thunder, that the lowest bottom shook
> Of Erebus.

This is reminiscent of Vergil's description of Tartarus *Æn.* 6. 573 ff., beginning,

> Tum demum horrisono stridentes cardine sacræ
> Panduntur portæ.

Milton's personified treatment of Darkness has reference at times to classical myth. In *P. L.* 3. 421 Darkness seems to be identical with Night as the latter is represented elsewhere. In two places, however, (*P. R.* 4. 397; *L'Al.* 6) there is a suggestion of Erebus, though Night was not his offspring but his sister and wife (Hes. *Theog.* 123 ff.; *In Quint. Nov.* 69). In *L'Al.* 2 there may some allusion to the cave of Scylla, 'a dim cave, turned to Erebus, towards the place of darkness.' Compare also the description of the mouth of Hell, the abode of Scylla and other monsters, Verg. *Æn.* 6. 273 ff. See *Rivers of Hell.* The cave of Darkness is described in *P. L.* 6. 4–11, a passage whose principal antecedent is Hes. *Theog.* 748–757. In the west is the place 'where Night and Day, going about meet one another, passing over the great bronze threshold. While the one shall go in, the other cometh forth out of doors, and never doth the house confine them both within, but ever doth one being without the house wander over the earth, while the other abiding within, awaits the hour of her journey, until it come. The one goeth with far-seeing light for mortals, the other, deadly Night, concealed in a dark cloud, goeth bearing Sleep, the brother of Death, in her arms.'

ERYMANTH.—Arc. 100. See Pan.

ETHIOP QUEEN.—Pens. 19. See Cassiopeia.

EUPHROSYNE.—L'Al. 12, 25, 38. See Graces.

3

EURUS.—P. L. 10. 705. See **Winds.**

EUYRYDICE.—L'Al. 150; Pens. 107. See **Orpheus.**

EURYNOME.—P. L. 10. 581.

The story of Eurynome and Ophion is told by Apollonius of Rhodes (*Arg*. 1. 503 ff.), where Orpheus sings 'how once Ophion and Eurynome, daughter of Ocean, held the rule of snowy Olympus, and how he, struggling with mighty arms, yielded honor to Cronus, and she to Rhea, and they fell into the waves of Ocean, . . . while Zeus still a boy, and still with boyish thoughts in mind was living within the Dictæan cave.' There seems to be no distinct statement of the ancients to the effect that this revolution in Olympus took place 'ere yet Dictæan Jove was born,' though Hesiod implies that Cronus deposed Uranus before the birth of Zeus (*Theog*. 176 ff., 453–465; cf. Paus. 5. 7. 4). Tzetzes also has told the story in the scholia on Lycophron 1191, but Milton's mention of Olympus and the epithet 'Dictæan' would seem to indicate Apollonius as the source. In introducing the story the poet suggests an etymological connection between Ophion and ὄφις, serpent.

EVEN.—C. 188. See **Apollo.**

FATES.—E. M. W. 28; Arc. 65; Lyc. 75.

The part played by the Fates or Mœræ in classical mythology seems to have been rather indefinite, and it varied from century to century. In Homer as a rule they are not clearly personified, and are associated with birth and death, but their number is uncertain, as in *Od.* 3. 236–238; 7. 197; *Il.* 24. 49. In *Od.* 7. 196 ff. we first find the spindle of life's thread associated with Fate: 'But thereafter he (Odysseus) shall endure such things as Fate and the stern spinning women drew off the spindles for him at his birth.' Hesiod (*Theog*. 217) first speaks of Clotho, Lachesis, and Atropos, but does not assign to them their respective functions, though Clotho by etymology, would be the spinner, Lachesis the assigner of fate, and Atropos the implacable one. In all times the Mœræ were associated with birth as well as death, a fact which is suggested by Milton's mention of Atropos in *E. M. W.* 28 ff. In the first part of the seventh Nemean ode Pindar addresses Eileithyia, 'that sittest beside the deep-counselling Mœræ, child of mighty Hera, thou who bringest babes to the birth.' The Roman Lucina performed a similar office, though her association with Atropos seems to be of Greek origin.

In *Lyc.* 75 Milton calls Atropos 'the blind Fury.' Though the Fates were not regarded as identical with the Furies they were sometimes associated with them, especially in tragedy. The *Prometheus* of Æschylus (516) furnishes perhaps the best example. 'Who guides the helm, then, of Necessity?' inquires the chorus, and Prometheus answers, 'Fates triple formed, Erinnyes unforgetting.'

The shears which cut the thread of life are a common accessory of Atropos in modern literature, but rarely appear in classical literature, and seem to be of late Roman origin. In the *Latin Anthology* 1. 792, ed. Riese (Teub.) occur the lines:

> Tres sunt fatales quæ ducunt fila sorores:
> Clotho colum baiulat, Lachesis trahit, Atropos occat.

The passage in *Arcades* (62 ff.) which describes the subduing of the Fates by the music of the Spheres is clearly drawn from Plato's story of the journey of Er after death (*Rep.* 10. 616, 617). The spirits saw the line of light which binds together the circle of the universe (616 C), 'and there in the midst of the light, they saw reaching from heaven the extremities of the chains of it. . . . And from the extremities of the chains is extended the spindle of Necessity, on which all the revolutions turn. The shaft and hook of this spindle are made of steel (ἐξ ἀδάμαντος, Milton's adamantine spindle, 66). And again in 617 B: 'The spindle turns on the knees of Necessity; and on the upper surface of each circle is a siren, who goes round with them, hymning a single sound and note. The eight together form one harmony; and round about, at equal intervals, there is another band, three in number, each sitting upon her throne: these are the Fates, daughters of Necessity, who are clothed in white raiment and garlands upon their heads, Lachesis, and Clotho, and Atropos, who accompany with their voices the harmony of the sirens —Lachesis singing of the past, Clotho of the present, Atropos of the future.'

FAUNS, FAUNUS. P. R. 2. 191; Lyc. 34; P. L. 4. 709. See **Wood-gods.**

FAVONIUS.—Son. 20. 6. See **Winds.**

FLEECY STAR.—P. L. 3. 5 8.

Here Milton speaks of Aries as 'the fleecy star that bears Andromeda far off Atlantic seas.' Aratus says that this constellation is obscure, but that one may locate it by the girdle of Andromeda, 'for it is situated not far beneath her' (*Phæn.* 229). Eratosthenes (*Katasterismoi* 19) says that Aries was the ram of the golden fleece, who bore away Phrixus and his sister, Helle, as they were about to be sacrificed by their father, Athamas. Among the stars, according to Milton, he bears Andromeda, as he had borne Helle on earth. The story of Phrixus is told by Apollodorus (1. 9. 1).

FLORA.—P. L. 5. 16; P. R. 2. 365.

The story of Zephyrus and Flora, to which Milton alludes in *P. L.* 5. 16 is really the story of Zephyrus and Chloris (Ov. *Fast.* 5. 195 ff.): 'I, who now am called Flora, was once called Chloris. The Greek spelling of my name became corrupted by the Latin pronunciation.' Thus she begins to tell how Zephyrus stole her away.

> Dum loquitur, vernas efflat ab ore rosas.

At the end of her story (375),

> tenues secessit in auras,
> Mansit odor.

This may have suggested to Milton the expression ' Flora's earliest smells' (*P. R.* 2. 365).

FORCE.—P. L. 2. 551; C. 590. See Chance.

FURIES.—P. L. 2. 596, 671; P. L. 6. 859; 10. 560; P. R. 4. 422; C. 641; Lyc. 75.

From earliest writers the idea of Furies held by the ancients is indefinite and varied. Homer in *Il.* 9. 454 speaks of only one, but elsewhere of a greater number. Among the tragedians the number varies. Apollodorus (1. 1. 4) names three, Alecto, Tisiphone, and Megæra. They are variously represented, with fire-breathing garments (Eurip. *Iph. T.* 288), and with fiery hair (Senec. *Herc. Fur.* 87). Serpents writhed in their hair (Hor. *C.* 2. 13. 35), and Claudian speaks particularly of the snaky locks of Megæra (*In Ruf.* 1. 378, 134; cf. *P. L.* 10. 560). A famous description of the Furies may be found in the *Orestes* of Euripides, 255 ff.

Beginning with Homer (*Il.* 19. 259) the Furies are always the avengers of crime and are associated with the Lower World. The passage in *P. L.* 2. 596 may have some connection with Verg. *Æn.* 6. 570 ff.:

> Continuo sontis ultrix adcincta flagello
> Tisiphone quatit insultans, torvosque sinistra
> Intentans anguis, vocat agmina sæva sororum.

Tisiphone is here presiding over the punishment of the damned.

In *P. L.* 2. 596 Milton speaks of the Furies as 'harpy-footed.' This epithet seems to have no particular forerunner among those used of the Eumenides. However we find the following passage in Æschylus comparing the Furies with the Harpies (*Eumen.* 45 ff.):

> And a troop
> Of women strange to look at sleepeth there,
> Before this wanderer, seated on their stools;
> Not women they, but Gorgons I must call them;
> Nor yet can I to Gorgon forms compare them;
> I have seen painted shapes that bear away
> The feast of Phineus. Wingless though are these,
> And swarth, and every way abominable.

In the *Æneid* Celæno, the Harpy, speaks of herself as ' Furiarum maxima' (3. 252), and Servius in commenting upon 3. 209 says of the Harpies, ' ipsæ furiæ esse dicerentur: unde etiam epulas prohibentur abripere, quod est furiarum.' See *Fates*.

GANYMED.—P. R. 2. 353.

The story of Ganymed was popular in all times. It is first told by Homer in *Il.* 20. 231: ' To Tros three noble sons were born, Ilos and Assarakos and godlike Ganymedes, who became the most beautiful of mortal men. Him the gods caught up to be cupbearer to Zeus. for sake of his beauty, that he might dwell among immortals.' Cf. *Hylas*.

GENIUS.—C. N. 186; Pens. 154; Person in Arcades; Lyc. 183.

The genius-cult of Rome was of Italian origin, though in later times it is colored by the Greek belief in the dæmon. The word is associated with *gignere*, and at first always, and afterward gener- ally is the force which brings human beings into the world. 'In lucem editis hominibus cunctis . . . hujusmodi quædam velut actus rectura numina sociari,' says Ammianus Marcellinus (21. 14. 3). Servius says, by way of comment on Verg. *Georg.* 1. 302, 'Genium autem dicebant antiqui, naturalem deum uniuscujusque loci, vel rei, aut hominis.' The genius of a place was propitious and tutelary (cf. Verg. *Æn.* 5. 84 ff.), and Milton elaborates this conception in assigning specific duties to the genii of the wood and of the shore. Cf. Preller, *Röm. Myth.* pp. 66 ff.

GERYON.—P. L. 11. 410.

Geryon lived in Erytheia, an island of Spain, and his cattle were stolen away by Heracles (Apollod. 2. 5. 10). Milton's lines suggest a passage in Spenser (*F. Q.* 5. 10. 9):

> And sooth they say that he was borne and bred
> Of Gyants race, the sonne of Geryon;
> He that whylome in Spaine so sore was dred
> For his huge power and great oppression.

Servius (on *Æn.* 7. 662) says: 'Geryones rex fuit Hispaniæ, qui ideo trimembris fingitur, quia tribus insulis præfuit, quæ adjacent His- paniæ: Baliaricæ minori et majori et Ebuso . . . hunc Gery- onem alii Tartessiorum regem dicunt fuisse.' Diodorus mentions the fact that Chrysaor, Geryon's father, was named from his wealth of gold (4. 17), and that the inhabitants of the Baleares 'do not make use of gold or silver, rigorously forbidding either to be brought into the island, and giving this reason for it, that Geryon, son of Chry- saor, was killed by Heracles on account of these metals' (5. 17). In calling the Spanish explorers 'Geryon's sons' Milton may have in- tended some reference to the name's connotation of gold.

GIANTS.—P. L. 1. 198, 577, 778.

The giants on the plain of Phlegra are cited by Milton to illus- trate the strength of the legions of Hell. Hesiod describes them as strong and tall, gleaming with armor and holding long spears (*Theog.* 185, 186). Apollodorus (1. 6. 1) says that they were unsurpassed in size of body, and in strength invincible, and their glance was terrible. Pindar is among the first to mention Phlegra as the scene of their battle with the gods (*Nem.* 1. 67), and Apollodorus (1. 6) gives us the oldest story of the fight. The latter says that in her anger at the defeat of the Titans by the gods, Earth brought forth these monsters to oppose the Olympians, who overcame them in single combat. The Giants and Titans are associated by Horace (*C.* 3. 4. 43) and Vergil (*Georg.* 1. 278), as in *P. L.* 1. 198. Cf. *Earth, Briareos, Titans.*

GLAUCUS.—C. 874. See Sea-gods.

GORGON.—P. L. 2. 611, 628; 10. 297, 527; C. 447.

Homer speaks of only one Gorgon. In *Il.* 5. 738 ff. Athena, arming for battle, cast about her shoulders 'the tasselled ægis terrible, . . . and therein is the dreadful monster's Gorgon head, dreadful and grim, portent of ægis-bearing Zeus.' Odysseus in his account of his visit to the Lower World (*Od.* 11. 633) says, 'Pale fear gat hold of me, lest the high goddess Persephone should send me the head of the Gorgon, that dread monster, from out of Hades.' This treatment of the Gorgon as one of the terrors of Hades may account for Milton's use of the monster in *P.L.* 2. 611, 628; see *Chimæra.* Hesiod names three Gorgons, Stheino, Euryale, and Medusa, of whom Medusa alone was mortal. He describes them (*Herac. Sh.* 230) as unapproachable: 'on their belts two serpents hung, thrusting their heads forward. They darted forth their tongues and gnashed their teeth with violence, glancing wildly about.' Apollodorus (2. 4. 2) tells of their 'heads covered with serpents' scales, and great teeth as of hogs, and brazen hands and golden wings with which they flew; and those who looked upon them they turned to stone.' Then follows the story of how Perseus slew Medusa, and how her head was fixed on the shield of Athene, still retaining its awful power; cf. Pind. *P.* 10. 47. Ovid also tells the story in *Met.* 4. 771 ff., and in *C.* 447 ff. Milton follows his account. He says that of three Gorgons, Medusa was the only one with snaky locks. She had once been fair, but as a penalty for sacrilege in the temple of Minerva the goddess changed her hair to snakes, which finally became a part of the divine armor (801, 802):

> Nunc quoque, ut attonitos formidine terreat hostes,
> Pectore in adverso, quos fecit, sustinet angues.

In *Met.* 4. 616 ff. we find a later story, the basis of *P.L.* 10. 525 ff., to the effect that the drops of blood from Medusa's head fell upon Libya, and from them serpents sprang up in the land (619):

> Unde frequens illa est, infestaque terra colubris.

The story is first told by Apollonius of Rhodes (4. 1515).

GRACES.—P. L. 4. 267; L'Al. 12, 15; C. 986.

Homer speaks of an indefinite number of Graces (*Il.* 14. 267). Hesiod, however, says that to Zeus 'Eurynome, daughter of Oceanus, bore three fair-cheeked Graces, . . . Aglaia, and Euphrosyne, and the lovely Thalia.' This genealogy was the commonest though many others are to be found. Milton himself says in *L'Al.* 14 that Venus bore the Graces to Bacchus, for which Servius (on *Æn.* 1. 724) is his authority: 'Acidalia Venus dicitur. . . . a fonte Acidalio . . . in quo se Gratiæ abluunt, quas Veneri constat esse sacratas. Ipsius enim et Liberi filiæ sunt, nec immerito.' The other genealogy of the Graces, as daughters of Zephyr and Aurora (*L'Al.* 19), is without classical authority except that it seems more in harmony with the early and more elevated conception of the Graces as exemplified in Pindar. Milton seems to favor it especially in *L'Allegro*, for his Euphrosyne is distinctly tuneful, as she is in the fourteenth Olympian of Pindar, where she is addressed as 'lover of song.' Thalia too, appears 'delighting in sweet sounds,' while all the Graces are called 'queens renowned in song.' Pindar sings this light and beautiful ode "in Lydian mood of melody'; cf. *L'Al.* 136.

The Graces are associated with most of the principal divinities, and very frequently with the Hours, as in Paus. 2. 17. 4; 5. 11. 7. In the Homeric hymn to Pythian Apollo (16 ff.) occurs this description: 'But the fair-tressed Graces, and the wise Hours, and Harmony, and Hebe, and Venus, the daughter of Jove, dance, holding each others' hands by the wrist.' Beyond such association as this the Graces have nothing to do with the coming of Spring, though their name often suggested flowers, especially roses (*Anacreont.* 44; 56, Bergk; Apul. *Met.* 6. 24; see *Hours*). The association of the Graces with Pan (*P. L.* 4. 266) seems to be Pindaric. In fr. 62 (Bergk) the poet calls Pan 'delightful darling of the Graces,' perhaps because he also speaks of him as χορευτὴν τελεώτατον θεῶν (Aristides 1. 49).

HAMMON.—C. N. 208. See **Ammon.**

HÆMONY.—C. 638.

Milton's use of this name may have reference not only to Thessaly or Hæmonia as the land of magic, but to Ovid's description of Æson's renewal of youth by means of Medea's incantation (*Met.* 7. 159 ff.). Among the countries which the sorceress visited in search of ingredients was Thessaly (264, 265):

> Illic Hæmonia radices valle resectas,
> Seminaque, floresque, et succos incoquit acres.

Compare Milton's second elegy 7, 8:

> O dignus tamen Hæmonio juvenescere succo,
> Dignus in Æsonios vivere posse dies.

HARPIES.—P. R. 2. 403, 596; C. 605.

In *P. R.* 2. 403 the feast of Satan vanishes 'With sound of harpies' wings and talons heard.' As this passage contains no definite evidence of a particular source, it may best be referred to the 'locus classicus,' Verg. *Æn.* 3. 216 ff.:

> Virginei volucrum vultus, fœdissima ventris
> Proluvies, uncæque manus, et pallida semper
> Orá fame.

The comrades of Æneas had spread their feast upon the shore of the Strophades (225–227):

> At subitæ horrifico lapsu de montibus adsunt
> Harpiæ, et magnis quatiunt clangoribus alas,
> Diripiunt dapes.

Cf. 233:

> Turba sonans prædam pedibus circumvolat uncis.

In *C.* 605 Harpies and Hydras are closely associated with 'the griesly legions that troop Under the sooty flag of Acheron.' One is reminded of *Æn.* 6. 287, where, among the crowd of monsters at the gate of Hell, are the Harpies. See *Chimæra, Rivers of Hell, Furies.*

HEAVEN.—P. L. 1. 509. See Earth.

HEBE.—V. E. 38; L'Al. 29; C. 290.

Hebe is mentioned by Homer (*Od.* 11. 604) as the daughter of Zeus and Hera, and in *Il.* 4. 2 she serves wine to her father and the other gods. The scene in which she appears in *V. E.* 35 ff. is evidently suggested by *Il.* 1. 584 ff., though Hebe herself is not present in the latter case, and the only reference to her is the burlesque of Hephæstus acting in her capacity. See *Apollo.*

Hebe is the Greek personification of youth, and is identified with the Roman Juventas. In Ov. *Met.* 9. 397 Iolaus is restored to his youth, having his cheeks covered with an almost imperceptible down, and his visage changed to that of the first years of manhood. Hebe had granted this favor. Cf. *C.* 289, 290. Homer (*Od.* 11. 603) speaks of 'Hebe of the fair ankles,' and T'.eocritus repeats the epithet (17. ?2). Pindar calls her θαλερά (*Nem.* 1. 71) and καλλίστα θεῶν (*Nem.* 10. 19), and Propertius adds the epithet 'cælestis' (1. 13. 23).

HECATE.—C. 135, 534. See Diana.

HELENA.—C. 676.

This passage is founded upon Hom. *Od.* 4. 219–230. Telemachus is entertained in the house of Menelaus. 'Then Helen, daughter of Zeus, turned to new thoughts. Presently she cast a drug into the wine whereof they drank, a drug to lull all pain (νηπενθές, Milton's Nepenthes) and anger, and bring forgetfulness of every sorrow. Whoso should drink a draught thereof, when it is mingled in the bowl, on that day he would let no tear fall down his cheeks, not though his mother and his father died, not though men slew his brother or dear son with the sword before his face, and his own eyes beheld it. Medicines of such virtue and so helpful had the daughter of Zeus, which Polydamna, the wife of Thon, had

given her, a woman of Egypt.' Menelaus and Helen returned from
Troy by way of Egypt (3. 300; 4. 83, 125). The epithets 'born of
Zeus' and 'daughter of Zeus' are common in connection with Helen,
as illustrated by the above passage and *Il.* 3. 199, 418, 426.

HELICON.—E. M. W. 56. See Muses.

HERALD OF THE SEA.—Lyc. 89. See Triton under Sea-gods.

HERCULES.—P. L. 2. 542; 9. 1060; P. R. 4. 565; Pass. 14; Son. 23. 3.

In *Pass.* 14 the reference to Hercules is evident. The story of
his labors is told by Apollodorus (2. 4. 8), but the many stories about
the hero were popular with classical writers of all ages. The Latin
poets commonly call him Alcides from his grandfather Alceus, father
of Amphitryon. But in *Son.* 23. 3 Milton follows another tradition,
and calls him Jove's son according to Homer (*Il.* 14. 324) and others.

The poet has compared the wild uproar of Hell to the dying
agony of Hercules (*P. L.* 2. 541–546):

> As when Alcides, from Œchalia crowned
> With conquest, felt the envenomed robe, and tore
> Through pain up by the roots Thessalian pines,
> And Lichas from the top of Œta threw
> Into the Euboïc sea.

The source of this passage is in Ovid (*Met.* 9. 134 ff.), as is shown
by its adaptation of the following expressions: 'Victor ab Œchalia
Cenæo sacra parabat Vota Jovi'(136; cf. Soph. *Trach.* 751); 'Ster
nentemque trabes' (209); 'Mittit (Lichas) in Euboïcas, tormento
fortius, undas' (218). There is some obscurity in Ovid's story. The
other accounts (Soph. *Trach.* 753; Senec. *Herc. Œt.* 783) show clearly
that these incidents took place in Cenæum, a promontory of Eubœa,
but Ovid, though he mentions the sacrifice to Cenæan Jupiter, and
speaks of the Euboïc waves, twice afterward speaks of Mount Œta
in Thessaly as the scene (165, 204). Milton follows this version.
There is evident reference to the Ovidian account in Milton's *Prolusions* (ed. Symmons 6. 145); cf. *In Ob. Procan.* 10.

See also *Antæus, Alcestis, Hylas, Hydra.*

HERMES.—P. L. 3. 603; 4. 717; 5. 285; 11. 133; C. 637, 962.

In *P. L.* 3. 603 Milton speaks of 'volatile Hermes' in poetic desig-
nation of the metal, mercury. Hermes, as a messenger, was a
winged god with all the ancients, and the adjective 'volatile' seems
to bear reference to this fact, in addition to its chemical meaning. In
Vergil's famous introduction of Mercury (*Æn.* 4. 222 ff.), the verb
volare is a favorite (cf. 246, 255, 256). This same passage is suggested
by Milton's description of Raphael's descent from heaven (*P. L.* 5.
277–287). Vergil (4. 239) and Homer (*Il.* 24. 341) both speak of the
god's golden sandals, the former calling them winged; but Milton's
gorgeous coloring of the wings is wanting among the ancients,
and Raphael's equipment is more complete than that of Hermes.

In *C.* 959 Hermes is associated in the dance with the Dryades. While there is no one passage to which Milton's rather specific mention may be referred, yet we find good authority for it in several places. In the Homeric hymn to Aphrodite (262) the nymphs in company with the immortals moved in the fair dance. 'And with them the Sileni and the sharp scout, the slayer of Argus, were mingled in love, in a recess of the pleasant caves. *But together with them at their birth were born either fir-trees or high-crested oaks.*' In the hymn to Hermes the god is a patron of music and the dance, and the chorus of Aristophanes' *Thesmophoriazusæ* invoke the pastoral Hermes and the nymphs to smile favorably upon their dance (977). Aristides says that the poets call Hermes the choregus of the nymphs (vol. 2, p. 708, ed. Dindorf). Milton's whole description is in tune with *Hom. Hy.* 18.

In Hom. *Od.* 10. 275–306 Odysseus himself tells how Hermes gave him a φάρμακον ἐσθλόν, an herb which the gods call moly, as a safeguard against the charms of Circe.

See *Argus, Pandora.*

HERMIONE.—P. L. 9. 506. See Cadmus.

HESPERIDES.—See Hesperus.

HESPERUS.—P. L. 1. 520; 3. 568; 4. 250, 605; 8. 632; 9. 49; 11. 582; P. R. 2. 357; C. 393, 982.

Among the ancients Hesperus is at first the evening star, and generally this conception is preserved. See *Lucifer.* Homer says (*Il.* 22. 317, 318) that the light gleamed from the spear of Achilles 'as a star goeth among stars in the darkness of night, Hesperos, fairest of all stars set in heaven.' Cf. *P. L.* 4. 605. In a similar manner Milton speaks of Lucifer in *P. L.* 7. 133.

Milton speaks of Hesperus as the star 'whose office is to bring Twilight upon the Earth' (*P. L.* 9. 49). The idea appears in Catull. 62; Claud. 14. 1, 2; and in Senec. *Hip.* 749–751:

> Qualis est primas referens tenebras
> Nuntius noctis, modo lotus undis
> Hesperus.

In the citations from Catullus and Claudian Hesperus is hailed more than once as the bringer of Hymen and the wedding-night, and is thus 'Love's harbinger,' as he is represented in *P. L.* 11. 589. Cf. Claud. *De Rapt. Proserp.* 2. 361. See also *Hymen.*

The epithet 'short arbiter twixt day and night' (50) may be based ultimately upon Hesiod. He says that Atlas stands at the meeting-place of day and night (746 ff.), and that this was in the bounds of the earth, that is, the west, near the Hesperides (518), whom Milton closely relates to Hesperus. While the ancients generally speak of the gardens of the Hesperides, he prefers the adjective Hesperian in three references to the gardens and their fruit (*P. L.* 3. 568; 4. 250; *C.*

393), and makes the Hesperides daughters of Hesperus (*C.* 982). Their genealogy varies from Hesiod down (*Theog.* 215; cf. Diod. Sic. 4. 27), but Milton follows Servius, who adds that there were but three daughters (on *Æn.* 4. 484; cf. Apollon. Rh. 4. 1427; *C.* 982). That they were famous for their songs appears in several places. Hesiod calls them λιγύφωνοι (*Theog.* 518), Euripides says that they were musical (*Hip.* 743; *Herac. Fur.* 394), and Apollonius that they sang delightfully (4. 1399). Milton follows Ovid in speaking of the golden tree (*Met.* 4. 636 f.):

> Arboreæ frondes, auro radiante virentes,
> Ex auro ramos, ex auro poma tegebant.

The beauty of the Hesperides themselves seems to have been little 'feigned of old' (*P. R.* 2. 358). The same might also be said of the gardens, though Pliny (*N. H.* 19. 4) says, 'Antiquitas nihil prius mirata est, quam Hesperidum hortos.' Cf. Mart. 4. 64:

> Juli jugera pauca Martialis
> Hortis Hesperidum beatiora.

But Milton, as appears by *P. L.* 3. 568 ff. (cf. 8. 631), has identified these with Homer's Elysium, the πείρατα γαίης, and the Islands of the Blest (cf. Hes. *Theog.* 334, 518; see *Elysium*). Authorities from Hesiod to Servius speak of the dragon who guarded the golden apples.

In *P. L.* 1. 520 Hesperian is used as Vergil and others use it, as applied to the western lands, that is, Italy or Spain (*Æn.* 2. 781; cf. Milt. *Eleg.* 3. 46).

HIPPOTADES.—Lyc. 98.

Æolus, god of the winds, is called Hippotades (son of Hippotas) by Homer (*Od.* 10. 2, 36). The name appears again in Ov. *Met.* 14. 86. His home, where Odysseus found him, was a rocky island in which the winds lived with him. But Milton is here indebted to two later traditions. First, he mentions a dungeon, after the manner of Vergil, who says that in such a place Æolus confined the winds,— 'vinclis et carcere frenat' (*Æn.* 1. 50 ff., 84, 141; Ov. *Met.* 14. 224). Furthermore the epithet 'sage' seems to go back to a passage in Diodorus, who speaks of Æolus as reverent and just. 'He also taught the use of the sails to the seamen, and by close observation of the omen of fire he gave his countrymen a correct forecast of the winds: therefore fable represents him as dispenser of the winds, and for his unusual reverence he is called friend of the gods' (5. 7).

HORROR.—P. L. 4. 989.

Warton, in a note on *In Quint. Nov.* 148, quoted by Todd, refers this passage to Spenser, *F. Q.* 2. 7. 23, where Horror with 'his yron wings' soars above the hideous shapes about the cave of Mammon.

But Milton's association of Horror with the onset of battle is distinctly similar to the Greek treatment of Φόβος. In the description of Agamemnon's preparation for battle (*Il.* 11. 15 ff.) Homer says that on his shield 'was embossed the Gorgon fell of aspect glaring terribly, and about her were Dread and Terror (Φόβος).' His helmet bore 'a plume of horse-hair, and terribly the crest nodded from above.' In the preparations in 13. 299 ff. Φόβος is called 'stark and fearless, that terrifies even the hardy warrior.' In the form of a lion's head he adorns a shield of Agamemnon on the chest of Cypselus in Pausanias 5. 19. 4.

HOURS.—P. L. 4. 267; 6. 3; T. 2; C. 986; Son. 1. 4.

According to Hes. *Theog.* 901 Themis bore to Zeus the Hours, Eunomia, Dike, and Eirene. The description of the dawn which occurs in *P. L.* 6. 2–4 is discussed under *Aurora.* The epithet 'circling' is a translation of κυκλάδες, which occurs frequently in this connection (cf. *Orph. Hy.* 60. 10; Eurip. *Alc.* 449). 'The lazy leaden-stepping Hours' of *T.* 2 suggests at once Theocritus, who calls them 'slowest of the Blest' (15. 104).

The Hours stand for all the seasons as early as Homer (*Od.* 10. 469), but Milton, with later classical writers, associates them with Spring and the flowers. Pindar says (fr. 75. 13–16, Bergk), 'with the opening of the chamber of the Hours, the nectareous plants perceive the fragrant Spring. Then are strewn over the face of the eternal earth the lovely violet-tufts, then are roses twined in hair.' (Compare also Call. *Hy. to Ap.* 81 ff.; Theoc. 15. 102–105.)

The Hours are often associated with the Graces as in *C.* 986 ff., where both bring their bounties to the garden of Hesperus. The passage is suggestive of one in Ovid (*Fast.* 5. 200 ff.) about the garden of Flora, whither (217),

> Conveniunt pictis incinctæ vestibus Horæ;
> Inque leves calathos munera nostra legunt.
> Protinus arripiunt Charites; nectuntque coronas,
> Sertaque cælestes implicitura comas.

The epithet 'rosy-bosomed' of *C.* 986 offers some difficulty. Verity is reminded of ῥοδόπαχυς, applied to Adonis in Theoc. 15. 128. It would thus seem to describe the glow of the flesh, and to carry out Milton's association of the Hours with the Dawn in *P. L.* 6. 3. Cf. *Aurora.* On the other hand roses were often mentioned in connection with the Hours (*Anacreont.* 4, Bergk; Apul. *Met.* 6. 24), and these were represented as clothed in long garments either dyed in the bright colors of flowers, or actually woven of them (see quotations under *Naiads*). 'Rosy-bosomed' may be intended to suggest this fact.

HYACINTH.—D. F. I. 25; Lyc. 106, 148. See Apollo.

HYDRA.—P. L. 2. 6?8; C. 605; Son. 15. 7.

In *P. L.* 2. 627 f. Hell is represented as the breeding place of monsters

worse
Than fables yet have feigned or fear conceived,
Gorgons, and Hydras, and Chimæras dire.

Thus Vergil stations at the mouth of Hades (*Æn.* 6. 286 ff.)

bellua Lernæ
Horrendum stridens, flammisque armata Chimæra,
Gorgones, Harpyæque.

Cf. *Harpies.*

The story of Heracles' fight with the Hydra is told by Apollodorus (2. 5. 2). He says that she had nine heads, eight of them mortal, but the middle one immortal, and for every mortal one that Heracles struck off, two grew in its place. There may be a slight reminiscence of this story in *Son.* 15. 7. In *Æn.* 8. 300 the Hydra has a 'turba capitum,' and elsewhere fifty heads (6. 576). Euripides (*Herac. Fur.* 1190) calls her ἑκατογκέφαλος and μυριόκρανος (419). Verity in his note on *P. L.* 2. 628 cites the phrase in Milton's *Of Reformation*, *P. W.* 2. 411, 'a continual hydra of mischief and molestation.' With this may be compared *Eikonoklastes*, *P. W.* 1. 395, where he quotes the king's epithet of Parliament: a 'manyheaded hydra of government, full of factious distractions, and not more eyes than mouths.' He adds, 'Yet surely not more mouths, or not so wide, as the dissolute rabble of all his courtiers had.'

Son. 15. 8 mentions the Hydra's 'serpent wings.' Todd cites πτανὸν πυρίφλεκτον of Euripides (*Ion.* 195) as the only authority. The reading πτανόν, controverted then, has been abandoned.

HYLAS.—P. R. 2. 353.

Hylas was beloved of Heracles, but was stolen away by the Naiads as he went to draw water at a spring (*Theoc.* 13; cf. Apollon. Rh. 1. 1207 ff.). His beauty was famous. Apollonius represents him κάλλεϊ καὶ γλυκερῇσιν ἐρευθόμενον χαρίτεσσι. Theocritus calls him ξανθός (13.36) and κάλλιστος (72), and Valerius Flaccus mentions his 'niveos artus' (1. 219). Milton's lines may be founded upon Martial 9. 26. The poet wishes that he may look at fair Hyllus:

Trux erat Alcides; sed Hylam spectare licebat.
Ludere Mercurio cum Ganymede licet.

In the same way in *Eleg.* 7. 21–24 Milton illustrates the beauty of Cupid by referring to Hylas and Ganymed.

HYMEN.—P. L. 11. 591; L'Al. 125; E. M. W. 18.

Hymen or Hymenæus is a conception of the later classical mythology of not infrequent occurrence in the Latin poets. Servius (on *Æn.* 1. 651) says that some call him the god of marriage, but that

rather he was a young Athenian whom brides invoke, because he had
saved the Athenian maidens in time of war.   Again (on *Æn.* 4.
127) he says, 'Alii hunc Veneris et Liberi filium dicunt primum nuptiis
prospere usum, ob quod in nuptiis vocatur: unde nuptiale carmen
Hymenæus.'   In the note to *Ecl.* 8. 30 he says that Hesperus, the
evening-star, loved the fair youth Hymen.   Cf. *P. L.* 11. 588 ff.
The torch and garland are often associated with Hymen, whose
presence is the signal for glad music and revelry.   At the wedding of Perseus and Andromeda (Ov. *Met.* 4. 757 ff.) ' Hymen
and Cupid wave their torches before them . . . Garlands, too,
are hanging from the houses; flageolets, and lyres, and pipes, and
songs resound, the happy tokens of a joyous mind.'   Cf. Seneca,
Med. 67 ff.; Claudian, *Epithal. Pall. et Cel.* 34 ff. esp. 96, 97.
The invocation by Catullus (61. 1 ff.) may be compared with *L'Al.* 125.

> Cinge tempora floribus
> Suaveolentis amaraci.
> Flammeum cape: laetus huc
> Huc veni, niveo gerens
> Luteum pede soccum;
>   Excitusque hilari die,
> Nuptialia concinens
> Voce carmina tinnula,
> Pelle humum pedibus, manu
> Pineam quate tædam.

According to Todd, Jortin first noted the parallel between *E. M. W.*
18 ff. and Ov. *Met.* 10. 1 ff.   Hymen was invoked at the marriage of
Orpheus and Eurydice, and came, ' croceo velatus amictu'; but he
brought 'neither auspicious words, nor joyful looks, nor happy
omen,' nor did his torch burn with a steady flame, but blinded the
eyes with smoke, for Eurydice, soon after her marriage, perished of
a serpent's sting.   The ' croceo velatus amictu' of verse 1 seems to
be the original of ' saffron robe,' *L'Al.* 126.   Warton cites the stage-
direction at the beginning of Jonson's *Masque of Hymen*, where
Hymen appears ' in a saffron-colored robe.'   Cf. Milton, *Eleg.* 5.
105 ff.

IAPETUS.—P. L. 4. 717.

Iapetus, whom Milton identifies with Japhet, was one of the
Titans, and the father of Prometheus and Epimetheus (Hes. *Theog.*
507 ff.).   See *Pandora.*   According to Jerome (*Hebr. Quæst. in Gen.*
10. 2), from Javan, the son of Japhet, are sprung the 'Iones, qui et
Græci.'   Cf. *P. L.* 1. 508; *S. A.* 716.   The fact is mentioned by
Ralegh in his *History of the World* 1. 8. 7.

IDA.—P. L. 1. 515; 5. 382; Pens. 29.   See Venus and Saturn.

ILIUM.—P. L. 1. 578; 9. 16; Pens. 100.

In this passage Milton refers to the war of Troy, which is the
background of the story of the *Iliad.*   The catalogue of the heroes

is found in 2. 484–877. Poseidon, Pallas, and Hera sided with the Greeks, while Apollo, Ares, and Aphrodite took the part of the Trojans, and Zeus turned the tide of battle this way and that for the glory of Achilles. The sack of Troy is described in Verg. *Æn.* 2. The story of Troy was a favorite subject with tragic poets (*Pens.* 100). It was treated by Sophocles in the *Ajax*, by Euripides in the *Andromache*, the *Helena*, the *Hecuba*, the *Trojan Women*, and the *Rhesus*, and by Seneca in the *Troades.* 'Troy divine' of *Pens.* 100 suggests Homer's 'sacred Ilios' (*Od.* 11. 86; 17. 293). See *Achilles.*

IRIS.—P. L. 11. 244; C. 83, 992.

Iris was the daughter of Thaumas (Hes. *Theog.* 780; cf. *Eleg.* 3. 41) and messenger of the gods (*Il.* 15. 158). As the personified rainbow, Iris is suggestive of brilliant colors of raiment in Milton. With this application may be compared Ov. *Met.* 11. 589, where Iris 'induitur velamina mille colorum.' In Verg. *Æn.* 4. 700 she descends,

croceis per cœlum roscida pennis,
Mille trahens varios adverso Sole colores ;

and in 5. 609, 'viam celerans per mille coloribus arcum.' The idea that Iris is clothed in bright-colored raiment is found again in *Met.* 1. 270, where it is joined with the conception that through the rain bow, water is drawn up into the clouds, which afterwards falls as dew or rain:

Nuntia Junonis varios induta colores,
Concipit Iris aquas, alimentaque nubibus adfert.

These two conceptions are adapted by Milton in *C.* 992 ff.:

Iris there with humid bow
Waters the odorous banks, that blow
Flowers of more mingled hue
Than her purpled scarf can show,
And drenches with Elysian dew

. . . . . .

Beds of hyacinth and roses.

Reference to the agency of Iris in bringing the rain occurs in Senec. *Œd.* 314; Tibull. 1. 4. 44; Stat. *Theb.* 9. 404; Verg. *Georg.* 1. 380, and in his comment on this last citation Servius says that this conception was the vulgar one. Seneca refers to it in *Nat. Quæst.* 1. 6. 1, and asserts that the rainbow which appears at noon will bring on a heavy rainfall, but if it appears at evening, there will be a fall of dew and light rain. In the above citations from Seneca's *Œdipus*, Tibullus, and Statius, the rainbow bears the epithet 'imbrifer,' which may explain Milton's 'humid bow.'

JANUS.—P. L. 11. 129.

According to Ov. *Fast.* 1. 44 ff. Janus was a Latin divinity, considered as guardian of the universe (119). He is the gate-keeper of heaven, and has two faces, that he may at the same time behold the east and the west, or, according to Macrobius (*Sat.* 1. 9. 4), in token of his knowledge of the past and future. A 'double Janus' of four faces was not unknown (Macr. 1. 9. 13; cf. Serv. on *Æn.* 7. 610).

JAPHET, JAVAN.—P. L. 4. 717; 1. 508; S. A. 716. See Iapetus.

JOVE.—P. L. 1. 198, 512, 514, 741; 2. 1005; 4. 499, 719; 9. 396, 508; 10. 584; 11. 185; P. R. 2. 190, 214; 3. 84; 4. 565; D. F. I. 45; V. E. 39; Pens. 30, 48; Arc. 44; C. 1, 20, 41, 78, 676, 803, 1011; Lyc. 16, 82; Son. 1. 7; 23. 3.

The name of Jove frequently occurs in Milton, but the poet's treatment of the legends of Jove is somewhat fragmentary, and it often happens that the god takes a place incidental and subordinate to another personage, about whom some legend is grouped. Discussion of this subject will therefore be found partly under other heads, to which reference will be made.

Cronus (Saturn) and Rhea were the father and mother of Jove (Hes. *Theog.* 453 ff.), and Milton refers to the fact in *P. L.* 1. 512; 10. 584; *Pens.* 30. See *Eurynome* and *Rhea*. In *Il.* 15. 187 ff. Poseidon tells of drawing lots for his domain with his brothers Zeus and Hades, known also as 'nether Jove' (Ζεὺς καταχθόνιος, *Il.* 9. 457; cf. *C.* 20 and *Neptune*). On the other hand ὕπατος, highest, is a frequent epithet of Zeus, to whom was given 'the wide heaven, in clear air and clouds' (*Il.* 5. 756; 15. 192). After his boyhood in Crete, where he was hidden from his father, Jove took his position on Olympus (*Theog.* 633), and warred with 'Saturn's crew,' the Titans, for ten years. These giants were confined in chains (*Theog.* 717 ff.), and hurled to Tartarus, where they trembled to hear the angry thunder of Jove in his battle with Typhon (*Theog.* 850). Cf. *P. L.* 1. 198, 512; *Pens.* 30; *C.* 803, and see *Titans* and *Typhon*. Milton mentions other contentions of Jove such as the expulsion of Mulciber (*P. L.* 1. 741; see *Vulcan*), and his vengeance on Prometheus (*P. L.* 4. 719; see *Pandora, Tantalus*).

In *P. L.* 2. 1005, 1051, we find the world linked to Heaven with a golden chain. This figure is found first in Hom. *Il.* 8. 18 ff., where Zeus exclaims, 'Fasten ye a rope of gold from heaven, and all ye gods lay hold thereof and all goddesses; yet could ye not drag from heaven to earth Zeus, . . . not though ye toiled sore.'

The origin of the scales as a sign of the Zodiac in *P. L.* 4. 996 is suggested by the well-known passages in the *Iliad.* In 22. 209 ff. 'the Father (Zeus) hung his golden balances, and set therein two lots of dreary death, one of Achilles, one of horse-taming Hector, and held them by the midst and poised. Then Hector's fated day sank down, and fell to the house of Hades.' In the same manner the fate of the Achæans sank to earth in 8. 69. Cf. Verg. *Æn.* 12. 725. Newton shows that in these lines Milton also conforms with Scripture, and he cites such passages as Is. 40.12; *Job* 28.25; 37.16; Dan. 5.27. To what extent he has adapted his sources will be apparent. The identification of the scales of God with the constellation, Libra, is after the manner of stories such as those found under the subjects, *Calisto, Cassiopeia, Fleecy Star, Justice, Twins.*

Among the later classics the eagle is the bird of Jove, as represented in *P. L.* 11. 185. The passage may be referred to *Æn.* 1. 393, where as an omen Venus pointed to a flock of swans,

> Ætheria quos lapsa plaga Jovis ales aperto
> Turbabat cælo.

A similar omen appears in *Æn.* 12. 247 ff. The eagle figures as an ominous bird in *Il.* 12. 200 ff.; *Od.* 15. 160.

The oracle of Jove at Dodona in Epirus, which Milton mentions in *P. L.* 1. 518, was considered the oldest in Greece, according to Herodotus 2. 52. In *Od.* 19. 296 Odysseus says of himself that he had gone 'to Dodona to hear the counsel of Zeus, from the high leafy oak-tree of the god, how he should return to his own dear country.' Æschylus (*Prometh.* 858) speaks of 'the strange portent of the talking oaks' with reverence. Cf. Soph. *Trach.* 1164; *Il.* 16. 233 ff.

Hera (Juno) was the wife of Zeus. Homer tells the story of Hera's beguiling of Zeus in order to withdraw his attention from the Trojans, who with his help were then winning success in battle (*Il.* 14). She first obtained the girdle of Aphrodite (cf. *P. R.* 2. 214; see *Venus*), then having adorned herself she met and charmed her lord; 'and beneath them the divine earth sent forth new grass, and dewy lotus, and crocus, and hyacinth, thick and soft, that raised them aloft from the ground. Therein they lay, and were clad on with a fair golden cloud, whence fell drops of glittering dew' (346–351). But the words of Milton seem to contain a naturalistic sense which is explained in the elaborate allegory set forth by the scholiast in his note on this passage. He believes that Hera typifies the lower air or haze which surrounds the earth, and Zeus the upper air (æther). The mingling of the two produces the spring with its flowers. The golden cloud represents those clouds which in the spring flash back the golden rays of the sun. Cf. Verg. *Georg.* 2. 324 ff.

Several love intrigues of Jove are mentioned by Milton, such as the one with Ceres (*P. L.* 9. 396); with Antiopa, Callisto, and Semele (*P. R.* 2. 190; cf. *Eleg.* 1. 64). Each of these is discussed under its respective head. It was a common thing among the ancients to ascribe superhuman origin to the great warriors, and Milton refers to this fact in *P. L.* 9. 508; *P. R.* 3. 84. For Jove as the father of Alexander see *Ammon.* The story of Scipio's miraculous birth is told by Livy (26. 19; cf. Gellius 7. 1; Silius 13. 615). Capitoline Jove appeared to his mother in the form of a serpent. See also *Cadmus, Epidaurus.*

Among the other children of Jove Milton mentions Proserpina (*P. L.* 9. 396; see *Ceres*), Hercules (*P. R.* 4. 565; *Son.* 23. 3), Hebe

4

(*V. E.* 39), Helena (*C.* 676).   A discussion of each may be found in its respective place.   In connection with *Pens.* 48 and *Lyc.* 16 see *Muses.*

It remains to consider several characteristics of the Miltonic Jove which may be referred to general conceptions held by the ancients. In *D. F. I.* 45 Jove acts 'in nature's true behoof;' cf. *Son.* 1. 7. From earliest times it is evident that he was regarded as a controller of nature.   He is the wielder of thunder and lightning, and Apuleius (*De Mundo* 37) mentions the Latin epithets *Imbricitor* and *Serenator*. He quotes from an Orphic poem to show that Jove is the father of all—of the earth, the heaven, and the sea—and he is the sun and the moon.

With this conception is related the conception of Zeus as the giver of power in *Arc.* 43, where the Genius of the Wood receives his power from Jove.   In this case there seems to be a reference to a tradition that Jove was born in Arcadia (Callim. *Hy. to Jove.* 7; Ov. *Met.* 2. 405 f.).   The mention of the 'oaken bower' in *Arc.* 45 may refer to the fact that the oak was sacred to Jove, as illustrated by the oracle at Dodona.   It is from Zeus that kings in the Homeric poems derive their power (*Il.* 2. 205; 9. 99).   He hates injustice (*Il.* 16. 387), and gives protection and reward to brave men.   Thus Ovid represents the apotheosis of Hercules as coming from Jove (*Met.* 9. 242 ff.; cf. 258).   In *Lyc.* 82–84 Jove is the judge of merit and the giver of fame.   Cf. *C.* 1011 and *Cupid.*   In the *Comus* the Attendant Spirit bears much the same relation to Jove (1, 41, 78) as does the Satyr to Pan in John Fletcher's *Faithful Shepherdess.*   The influence of this play on the *Comus* is well known, and is illustrated in *C.* 1, where the Attendant Spirit descends from his abode, 'Before the starry threshold of Jove's court.'   Thenot, in Act 2. Sc. 2 of the play, addresses the moon as

> whiter than that way
> That leads to Jove's high court.

Cf. *Eleg.* 5. 37, and see *Olympus.*   In connection with *C.* 41, 78 and the general conception of the poem it may be well to consider Verg. *Æn.* 6. 129 ff., where the poet speaks of the difficult return from Hades:

> Pauci, quos æquus amavit
> Juppiter, aut ardens evexit ad æthera virtus,
> Dis geniti potuere.

JUNO.—P. L. 4. 500; 5. 382; 9. 18; Arc. 23; C. 701.

Juno, or Hera, was the daughter of Cronus and Rhea, and the wife and sister of Zeus (see *Jove*).   In *Arc.* 23 she appears with Latona and Cybele as an example of queenly beauty.   No conception of the goddess among the ancients is more in harmony with Milton's comparison than the one found in the *Iliad.*   She is 'Hera of the golden throne' (1. 611; 14. 153), 'the goddess queen' (5. 721; 14.

194), and the epithet πότνια occurs frequently. Especially important is the celebrated description of Hera arrayed to meet Zeus (14. 170-187). Having anointed herself with ambrosial oil and plaited her shining hair, 'she clad her in her fragrant robe that Athene wrought delicately for her, and therein set many things beautifully made, and fastened it over her breast with clasps of gold. And she girdled it with a girdle arrayed with a hundred tassels, and she set earrings in her pierced ears, earrings of three drops, and glistening; therefrom shone grace abundantly. And with a veil over all the peerless goddess veiled herself, a fair new veil, bright as the sun, and beneath her shining feet she bound goodly sandals.' *C.* 701 may best be referred to *Il.* 1. 584 ff., where Hephæstus restored quiet at the banquet of the gods by first offering the cup to Hera.

In *P. L.* 9. 18 Milton refers to Vergil's story of Æneas, Cytherea's son, who was driven abroad 'sævæ memorem Junonis ob iram' (*Æn.* 1. 8). See *Venus* in connection with *P. L.* 5. 382.

JUSTICE.—P. L. 10. 857, 858; D. F. I. 50; C. N. 141.

In these passages Justice is associated with Mercy and Truth. In Hes. *W. and D.* 200 we find that Aidos and Nemesis, after the golden age, clothe their fair bodies in white robes, and ascend to the abode of immortals, leaving men to grievous affliction. In Latin writers it is Pudicitia and Astræa (Justitia) who are the last of the gods to leave earth (Juv. *Sat.* 6. 19. ff.; Ov. *Met.* 1. 149). We find a slightly different grouping in Horace's lament for Quintilius (*C.* 1. 24. 6): 'Pudor et Justitiæ soror, Incorrupta Fides, nudaque Veritas.' Among later poets it is Dike (Justice) who leaves the earth, and Aratus (*Phæn.* 96 ff.) describes her in the form of the constellation Virgo (Astræa, *P. L.* 4. 998), which she assumed in heaven.

Milton's Mercy is a youth, if Heskin emends correctly (see Todd) while Aidos is a goddess. Yet it is worth noticing that Aidos seems to have suggested Pudor to Latin poets (cf. Hor. supra; Ov. *Fast.* 1. 251), and that something like 'mercy' may be contained in the meaning of both. (Cf. Plat. *Laws* 867 E; Soph. *O. C.* 1268.) In Philostratus (*Imagg.*, *Amphiaraus*) Aletheia (Truth) is 'white-robed' as in *D. F. I.* 54. In connection with *C. N.* 141-143 Verity quotes from *Eikonoklastes* 28, *P. W.* 1. 484: 'Either truth and justice are all one (for truth is but justice in our knowledge, and justice is but truth in our practice), . . . or else if there be any odds, that justice, though not stronger than truth, . . . is to put forth and exhibit more strength in the affairs of mankind.'

LADON.—Arc. 97. See Pan.

LAERTES.—P. L. 9. 441. See Ulysses.

LARS AND LEMURES.—C. N. 191.

The Lars, or Lares, and Lemures are peculiar to the Roman mythology. The distinction between them is not quite clear, though St. Augustine (*De Civitate Dei* 9. 11) quotes the neo-Platonic opinion, ' animas hominum dæmones esse, et ex hominibus fieri Lares, si boni meriti sunt; Lemures, si mali.' They were often confounded with the Manes, but St. Augustine adds that the latter were not distinguished by the moral consideration which affected the Lares and the Lemures. Apuleius (*De Deo Soc.* c. 15) says that the bad spirit, ' nullis bonis sedibus, incerta vagatione . . . punitur, inane terriculamentum bonis hominibus, ceterum noxium malis.' The scholium on Hor. *Epist.* 2. 2. 209 explains ' nocturnos Lemures' as ' umbras vagantes hominum ante diem mortuorum, et ideo metuendas.' Ovid (*Fast.* 5. 421 ff.) gives an account of the festival of the Lemures, at which gifts were offered to the ashes of the dead, and at midnight a solemn ceremony was performed to exorcise the ghost from the house, as was first done when the gibbering ghost of Remus visited the living. Pliny (*N. H.* 21. 8) speaks of both public and private Lares, whose office was protective (Ov. *Fast.* 2. 617). Ovid also describes the protective office of the public Lares (præstites) in *Fast.* 5. 129–146. Distinguished members of a family became its Lares after death. Servius says ' omnes in suis domibus sepeliebantur, unde ortum est ut Lares colerentur in domibus' (on *Æn.* 6. 152). The private worship of the Lares is described in Marquardt's *Römische Staatsverwaltung* 3. 119–123. It centered about the hearth, and Pliny speaks of the 'focus Larium, quo familia convenit' (*N. H.* 28. 20. 81). The altar for the offerings of food and prayer was called the 'lararium.' Cf. Ov. *Fast.* 2. 634. It has already been noticed, however, that Lares and Lemures sometimes stood for all departed spirits, and Milton's lines may reflect a passage like Ov. *Fast.* 2. 533–570, where offerings of grain, wine, and flowers are recommended to appease the dead. Once upon a time, says Ovid, when these rites were neglected, ghosts howled ominously through the streets at night, but now they wander about peacefully to receive the offerings.

LATONA.—Arc. 20; Son. 12. 6.

Latona, the Greek Leto, was the mother of Apollo and Diana. (See *Apollo*.) In *Arc.* 20 she is mentioned as an example of queenly majesty. The ancient poets treated Latona with reverence, as the mother of glorious children. In *Hom. Hy. to Del. Ap.* 5 she is throned with Jove, and throughout the first part we meet epithets such as 'revered' (11), and 'far-renowned' (182). In *Orph. Hy.* 34 the same conception is held. Milton's 'wise' seems to have no definite classical original. Plato says (*Cratylus* 406 A): ' Leto is called by this name, because she is such a gentle goddess, and willing to grant our requests; or her name may be Letho, as strangers often call her; they seem to imply in this her slowness to anger, and her readiness to forgive and forget.'

LAVINIA.—P. L. 9. 17. See **Turnus.**

LETHE.—P. L. 2. 583, 604. See **Rivers of Hell.**

LEUCOTHEA.—P. L. 11. 135; C. 875.

Homer (*Od.* 5. 333) speaks of 'Ino of the fair ankles, Leucothea, who in time past was a maiden of mortal speech, but now in the depths of the salt sea she had gotten her share of worship from the gods.' She gave Odysseus the veil which bore him up as he struggled with the waves, and when he reached land he cast it again into the water. It was borne out to sea, 'and lightly Ino caught it in her hands' (χερσὶ φίλησιν, 462; cf. *C.* 875). Ino was the wife of Athamas, but having incurred his anger she fled with Melicertes her son, and plunged into the sea, where they became sea-divinities (Ov. *Met.* 4. 513–541). In *Fast.* 6. 541 ff. she is addressed in these words:

> gaude, defuncta laboribus, Ino,
> Dixit; et huic populo dextera semper ades.
> Numen eris pelagi: natum quoque pontus habebit
> In vestris aliud sumite nomen aquis.
> Leucothee Graiis, Matuta vocabere nostris:
> In portus nato jus erit omne tuo.
> Quem nos Portunum, sua lingua Palæmona dicet.

Cf. Verg. *Æn.* 5. 241. Leucothea (Matuta) is a goddess of the dawn as represented in *P. L.* 11. 135. According to Lucretius 5. 655, 'roseam Matuta per oras Ætheris Auroram defert, et lumina pandit.' Cf. 5. 462 f.

LIBERTY.—L'Al. 36.

In classical mythology Liberty was not a mountain-nymph, but a Roman goddess who appears in art having a Phrygian cap in her right hand and a javelin in her left (Hirt, *Bilderb. für Mythol.*).

LICHAS.—P. L. 2. 545. See **Hercules.**

LIGEA.—C. 880. See **Sirens.**

LOVE.—C. 124; Son. 1. 13. See **Cupid.**

LUCIFER.—P. L. 5. 760; 7. 131; 10. 425; C. N. 74; May Morn. 1.

Milton is true to the ancient distinction between Hesperus and Lucifer. Pliny says (*N. H.* 2. 8), 'Ante matutinum exoriens, Luciferi nomen accipit, . . . contra ab occasu refulgens nuncupatur Vesper.' Cf. Hyg. *Astr.* 2. 42. In *C. N.* 69 ff. Lucifer warns the stars to flee, as in Ovid *Met.* 2. 114:

> diffugiunt stellæ; quarum agmina cogit
> Lucifer, et cæli statione novissimus exit.

As in Hom. *Il.* 23. 226 'the Morning Star goeth forth to herald light upon the earth,' so in the *May Morn.* 1 he is 'Day's harbinger.'

Lucifer becomes a name of Satan through Is. 14. 12, ' How art thou fallen from heaven, O Lucifer, son of the morning' (Authorized Version).   See *P. L.* 5. 760; 7. 131; 10. 425; cf. 1. 745.   Lucifer (Eosphorus) was the son of Eos, the Dawn (Hes. *Theog.* 381).   See *Hesperus*.

LUCINA.—E. M. W. 26, 28.

Lucina is the Latin name of the goddess invoked at childbirth (Hor. *Car. Sæc.* 13 ff.).   To the Greeks she was Eileithyia (*Hom. Hy. to Del. Ap.* 97, 115).   She was sometimes identical with Juno or Diana, as Catullus suggests (34. 13 ff.).   Cf. *Fates*.

LYCÆUS.—Arc. 98. See Pan.

LYCIDAS.

Jerram, in his introduction to *Lycidas*, says, ' The name " Lycidas " was a common one with the ancient bucolic poets, but perhaps the seventh idyll of Theocritus was especially in Milton's mind when he adopted it.'   In this idyll Lycidas is a goatherd, 'a favorite with the Muses' (12; cf. 95; Bion 15).   In Verg. *Ecl.* 7. 67 he is called 'formosus.'   Cf. Hor. *C.* 1. 4. 19.

MÆNALUS.—Arc. 102. See Pan.

MÆONIDES.—P. L. 3. 35.

This is the name which Milton gives Homer, as in *P. R.* 4. 259 he calls him Melesigenes.   Plutarch (*De Vita Hom.* 1. 2) says that he was born near the river Meles, and was therefore called Melesigenes, and that the name Homer was given him because of his blindness.   In 2. 2 Plutarch mentions the belief that he was the son of Mæon.   Ovid (*Am.* 3. 9. 25) calls him Mæonides.

MAIA.—P. L. 5. 285. See Hermes.

MARS.—P. R. 3. 84.

Mars was the Roman god of war, generally identified with the Greek Ares.   He was the father of Romulus, the mythical founder of Rome, and Remus, by the vestal, Rhea Silvia (Liv. 1. 4).   Plutarch (*Rom.* 28) relates that after death Romulus appeared to his friend Proculus, and announced that he was henceforth to be saluted as the god Quirinus.   Ovid (*Fast.* 2. 511, 512) mentions the temples and sacrifices connected with his worship.

MEDUSA.—P. L. 2. 611. See Gorgons.

MEGÆRA.—P. L. 10. 560. See Furies.

MELESIGENES.—P. R. 4. 259. See Mæonides.

MELIBŒUS.—C. 822.

Milton here uses a name which owes its association with pastoral poetry to Vergil.   In *Ecl.* 1 the poor fortune of the goatherd Melibœus is contrasted with the better one of his friend.

MEMNON.—P. L. 10. 308; Pens. 18.

Milton describes the robe of Melancholy as

> Black, but such as in esteem
> Prince Memnon's sister might beseem.

Memnon, king of the Æthiopians, was the son of Eos and Tithonus (Hes. *Theog*. 984). He took part in the Trojan war, and Odysseus afterward said of Eurypylus, 'He truly was the comeliest man that ever I saw, next to goodly Memnon' (*Od*. 11. 522). In *Od*. 4. 188 he is called 'the glorious son of the bright Dawn.' Commentators have said that Memnon's sister is not mentioned in the classics, but that Milton argues her beauty from that of her brother. Verity cites Trench to the effect that Himera, or Hemera, was the sister of Memnon. In the *History of the Trojan War* ascribed to Dictys Cretensis we are told that she was named after her mother, but her beauty is not mentioned. The later writers used Hemera as the name of Eos (Paus. 3. 18. 12), though in Hesiod, Hemera and Eos are distinct (*Theog*. 124, 372).

In *P. L.* 10. 308 the poet speaks of Xerxes' Memnonian palace at Susa. Herodotus (5.53) says that this palace was called Memnonian. Pausanias (10. 31. 7) says that Memnon went from Susa to the aid of Troy, and Strabo (15. 3. p. 728) relates the tradition that the city was founded by Tithonus, the father of Memnon, and its citadel was called Memnonia.

MERCURY. C. 962. See **Hermes.**

MEROE. D. F. I. 50; C. N. 144. See **Justice.**

MIDAS.—Son. 13. 4.

The allusion to Midas' ears is explained by the accounts in Ov. *Met*. 11. 146 ff., and Hyg. *Fab*. 191. Midas is a name proverbial for wealth and asininity. In a contest of song between Apollo and Pan on Mount Tmolus, he would have given the reward to Pan, but for his bad judgment Apollo caused his ears to assume the form of asses' ears.

MIDNIGHT.—L'Al. 2. See **Erebus.**

MINERVA.—P. L. 5. 382; C. 448.

Minerva is the Latin name of Athene, virgin daughter of Zeus. She was a celebrated example of womanly purity. In the Homeric hymn to Athene (27. 3) she is 'the revered virgin, guardian of cities, valiant.' 'Innupta' and 'casta' are Latin epithets (Verg. *Æn*. 2. 31; Ov. *Met*. 4. 798; *Am*. 1. 7. 18). For the Gorgon's head upon the shield of Minerva see *Gorgons*, and in connection with *P. L.* 5. 382 see *Venus*.

MIRTH.—L'Al. See **Graces.**

MOON.—P. L. 1. 784; 3. 726; C. N. 103; Pens. 59; Son. 12. 7. See **Diana.**

MORN.—P. L. 5. 1; 6. 12; 11. 173; P. R. 4. 426; Pens. 122; C. 139. See **Aurora.**

MORPHEUS.—Pens. 10.

The 'locus classicus' concerning Morpheus and the dreams is in Ov. *Met.* 11. 633–652. Somnus (Sleep) was father of the dreams, and they are represented as 'populus natorum mille suorum.' Morpheus is older than the rest, and in his apparitions assumes the forms of men alone. The others may appear as a beast, a bird, or a serpent. Milton's epithet 'fickle' is consistent with the general classical conception of dreams as propitious or baneful (Hom. *Il.* 2. 6 ff.; *Orph. Hy.* 86).

MULCIBER.—P. L. 1. 740. See **Vulcan.**

MUSÆUS.—Pens. 104.

In his journey through Elysium Æneas saw the souls of patriots and priests and bards 'banqueting, and chanting in chorus the joyful Pæan amid the fragrant grove of bay-trees,' with Musæus in their midst, towering above all (*Æn.* 6. 656 ff.). This fragrant grove seems to be the bower mentioned by Milton. Servius, in commenting upon *Æn.* 6. 667, says that there were various opinions about the mythical poet Musæus, some saying that he was a son of Orpheus, 'and it is a fact that he was his pupil.'

MUSES.—P. L. 1. 6, 376; 3. 19, 27; 7. 6, 37; 9. 21; V. E. 53; C. N. 15; Pass. 4; E. M. W. 56; Pens. 47; C. 515; Lyc. 15, 19, 58, 66, 133; Son. 1. 13; 8. 9.

The number and genealogy of the Muses vary among the ancients, but the common tradition is that of Hesiod, who gives the names of nine Muses (*Theog.* 77), the daughters of Zeus and Mnemosyne (52 ff.). In *Il.* 2. 484 Homer invokes the Muses 'that dwell in the mansions of Olympus.' Cf. *P. L.* 7. 7. Hesiod (*Theog.* 2) says that their seat is the 'great and divine' mountain of Helicon. Cf. *E. M. W.* 56. In *P. L.* 1. 15 Milton refers to the 'Aonian mount' as the abode of the Muses. 'Aonian' is a word frequently associated with the Muses by Latin poets, and Vergil (*Georg.* 3. 11) speaks of Helicon as 'Aonius vertex.' The adjective is derived from Aonia, the older name of the mountainous part of Bœotia, especially the region about Thebes.

Milton's reference to Hesiod is marked in three places. In *Pens.* 47 the Muses

in a ring
Aye round about Jove's altar sing.

In *Lyc.* 15 he addresses them as

Sisters of the sacred well,
That from beneath the seat of Jove doth spring.

Hesiod begins his *Theogony* with the Muses of Helicon, ' who dance about the dark spring with tender feet, and about the altar of the mighty son of Cronus, . . . lifting up their fair voices in praise of ægis-bearing Zeus.' Homer also represents them as singing sweetly on Olympus (*Il.* 1. 604). The dark spring is probably Aganippe (*Paus.* 9. 29. 5). The association of the Muses with springs and groves is common among the ancients; cf. *P. L.* 3. 26–32; 1. 10; *Lyc.* 133-151; *Son.* 1. 13; 8. 9. Pausanias (9. 28. 1) describes the beauty of Helicon, and Ovid (*Met.* 5), besides mentioning Hippocrene and Aganippe (312), tells how Pallas beheld there 'the groves of the ancient wood, and the caves and the grass studded with flowers innumerable; and she pronounces the Mnemonian maids happy . . . in their retreat' (265 ff.). *Lyc.* 133-151 is another instance of Milton's flowery elaboration. Cf. Theoc. 1. 133 and *Elysium*.

The third reference to Hesiod is found in *P. L.* 1. 6 ff., where Milton invokes the Muse who on Oreb or Sinai inspired

> That shepherd who first taught the chosen seed
> In the beginning how the heavens and earth
> Rose out of Chaos.

Aside from the direct reference to Moses, there is here a suggestion of Hesiod, whom the Muses inspired to sing the cosmogony, as he tended sheep at the foot of Helicon (*Theog.* 22). Ralegh, an example of the learned enthusiasm of his times for classico-Biblical comparison, says that Moses and Musæus were considered the same (*Hist. of the World* 2. 3. 1).

The relation of the Muse or Muses to the poet, as it appears in Milton (*P. L.* 1. 6, 376; 7. 1–20; 9. 20–41; *C.* 515), is much the same as that in Homer, Hesiod, and the later poets and imitators. Odysseus says that minstrels are honored of men, 'inasmuch as the Muse teacheth them the paths of song, and loveth the tribe of minstrels' (*Od.* 8. 479; cf. 63). At the beginning of both the *Iliad* and the *Odyssey*, the poet appeals to the Muse as the source of his song, and renews his appeal in *Il.* 2. 484. 761; 14. 508; 16. 112; cf. *P. L.* 1. 376 ff. This early example is followed by Vergil, Pindar (*Nem.* 3. 1), Nonnus (*Dionys.* 1. 1), and Statius in the *Thebaid*. In *P. L.* 1. 6 Milton invokes the Heavenly Muse (cf. *P. L.* 1. 376; 3. 19; 7. 1; 9. 21; *C. N.* 15; *Pass.* 4), and implies that she was the Muse who inspired the ancient epic poets (*C.* 515). In *P. L.* 7. 1 he addresses her as Urania, but explains that she is not that one of the nine known as Urania; she is 'heavenly-born,' for it is 'the meaning, not the name' which he calls. The later writers assigned functions to the different Muses, and Urania was appointed to govern the stars and their movements (Ausonius 22. 3. 7. *Id.* 20; Plut. *Quæst. Conv.* 9. 14. 7). Diodorus (4. 7) says that Urania is so called because those who are taught by her are borne aloft by fame and courage to the highest heavens. Cf. *P. L.* 7. 12. In *Lyc.* 133 the 'Sicilian Muse' is invoked in imitation of Vergil (*Ecl.* 4. 1), or of Moschus (*Id.* 3. 8. ff.). The 'Sicilian Muse' stands in each case for pastoral poetry as exemplified by Theocritus. The conception of the Muses as it appears in *Lyc.* 15, 66, 133 is in accord with that of Theocritus (1. 64–145; 16), though in *Lyc.* 66 'Muse' may mean poetry itself as in Verg. *Ecl.* 1. 2.

The association of Pegasus with the Muses, as suggested in *P. L.* 7. 4, 17, is based upon the story told by Strabo (8. p. 379). Near Corinth is the spring Peirene, sacred to the Muses, which Pegasus, the winged horse, had caused to gush forth by the stroke of his hoof. The conception of the poet as borne aloft on the back of Pegasus is referred in Pauly's *Real-Encyc.* 5. 1275 to Boiardo's *Orlando Innamorato.* Cf. *Bellerophon.*

For Calliope as the mother of Orpheus (*P. L.* 7. 37; *Lyc.* 58) see *Orpheus.*

NAIADS.—P. R. 2. 355; C. 254, 833.

The Naiads are generally distinguished by the ancients as the nymphs of springs and rivers. In the description of the landing-place of Odysseus in Ithaca (*Od.* 13. 103 ff.), Homer says, 'Hard by is a pleasant cave and shadowy, sacred to the nymphs that are called Naiads. . . . And there are great looms of stone whereon the nymphs weave a raiment of purple stain, a marvel to behold, and therein are waters welling evermore.'

Milton's use of flowers as an accessory of the Naiads is characteristic, as is seen elsewhere (*Elysium, Hours*). In *P. R.* 2. 355 the Naiads appear

> With fruits and flowers from Amalthea's horn.

In *C.* 254 they are 'flowery-kirtled.' This epithet is in harmony with a common phase of the classical conception of the Naiads and the nymphs in general. In the Homeric hymn to Demeter, Persephone and the nymphs gather 'the beauteous crocus, and the iris, and the hyacinth, and the rosebuds, and the lilies' (417 ff.). Cf. also Apollon. Rh. *Arg.* 4. 1143. Corydon in his love-song to Alexis says (Verg. *Ecl.* 2. 45 ff.):

> tibi lilia plenis
> Ecce ferunt Nymphæ calathis; tibi candida Nais,
> Pallentes violas et summa papavera carpens,
> Narcissum et florem jungit bene olentis anethi.

Cf. Theoc. 13. 39 ff. Ovid, in speaking of the Hours, who in many respects resemble the Naiads, says (*Fast.* 5. 217, 218) that in the spring

> Conveniunt pictis incinctæ vestibus Horæ
> Inque leves calathos munera nostra legunt.

'Pictis' doubtless has reference to flowers, as the context and the classical conception of the Hours show, but 'pictis incinctæ vestibus' and 'flowery-kirtled' are in themselves equally indefinite, nor does the one explain the other. Three interpretations of Ovid are possible, which would likewise apply to Milton. The first and least proba-

ble explanation is that the kirtles or ' vestes ' were embroidered with a
flower-pattern. Examples of *pictus* in this sense are Verg. *Æn.* 1. 708,
711; 9. 582; Ov. *Her.* 12. 30; Mart. 10. 72. 7. A John Gower of Cambridge (1640) renders the passage, ' in broydred gowns.'

A second and more probable explanation is that the robes were
dyed in the bright colors of flowers. In *Ars Am.* 3. 173 ff. Ovid, in
prescribing colors for the dress of women in love, names the color of
the sky, or that of the golden fleece, or the color of the waves. ' I
could imagine that the nymphs are clad in vestments of this color.
. . . Another resembles the Paphian myrtles; another the purple amethysts or the white roses. . . . As many as the flowers
which the new earth produces, when in warm spring the vine puts
forth its buds and sluggish winter retreats, so many, or still more,
shades of dye does the wool imbibe.' The majority of translators in
different languages seem to prefer this meaning, and imply that the
garments of the Hours were of bright and variegated colors. The
most notable supporter of this interpretation is Bentley, who appeals
to a fragment of the *Cypria* given by Athenæus (15. 682): ' Then
were donned garments, which the Graces and the Hours had made
and dyed (ἔβαψαν) in spring flowers, such as the Hours wear (or
bring); in the crocus, and the hyacinth, and in the blooming violet,
and in the fair flower of the rose, sweet and nectareous, in the
ambrosial calixes, . . . the flowers of the narcissus and the lily,
such garments as Aphrodite wears, fragrant with all kinds of odors '
(ὀδμαῖς παντοίαις τεθυωμένα).

This last expression suggests the third and apparently most
probable interpretation of Ovid, namely, that the robes of the Hours
are actually woven of different kinds of flowers. This is the belief
of Heinsius, who cites *Orph. Hy.* 42. 6, where these divinities appear,
' wearing dewy robes of many flowers that grow.' He mentions also
the reading ' pictis floribus,' which occurs in three cases for ' pictis
vestibus.' In addition to this should be considered a fragment of
Hermippus (Kock, *Comicorum Atticorum Fragmenta* 3. 226): 'The
Hours' fresh close-woven robe of flowers. (The breeze) blowing the fine garments full of flowers.' Cf. Plat. *Rep.* 8. 557 C.
Whatever light this evidence may throw upon Ovid and the tradition
which he had in mind, it can hardly be determined whether Milton's
'flowery-kirtled' suggested a definite thing to the poet, or whether he
realized an artistic possibility in leaving it indefinite, as Ovid had
done. That ' kirtle ' was put for a long, flowing garment, implied in
' vestibus,' seems not unlikely, for the kirtle, already becoming an
antiquity at Milton's time, had often been a long garment, as worn
by women. See Planché, *Cycl. of Costume* 1. 320.

For his association of the Naiads with Circe (*C.* 253), Milton has
Homer as his authority (*Od.* 10. 350). Circe's handmaids were ' born
of the wells, and of the woods, and of the holy rivers.'

In the story of the British Sabrina, told in *C.* 24 ff., we find traces
of the classics, as in 833, where the water-nymphs draw the 'guiltless
damsel' into the river. Whether Milton is thinking of Naiads or
Nereids (*C.* 835), the passage is reminiscent of a somewhat similar
experience of Hylas, whom the Naiads stole away into the spring
whence he was drawing water, as related by Theocritus in the
thirteenth idyll. Verity cites Jonson's *Sad Shepherd* 1. 2:

> and those nymphs,
> Those treacherous nymphs pulled in Earine.

See *Amalthea* in connection with *P. R.* 2. 356.

NARCISSUS.—P. L. 4. 453; C. 237.

Eve's story of her discovery of her own beauty, told in *P. L.*
4. 453–469, is based upon Ovid's account of Narcissus (*Met.* 3. 407 ff.):
'There was a clear spring, like silver with its unsullied waters.'
Grass grew roundabout, nourished by the water, and trees shut out
the rays of the sun. Narcissus lay here resting from the hunt, when
he caught sight of his own figure in the water, and fell in love with
it. In vain he tried to embrace it. 'What thou seest,' says the poet,
'the same is but the shadow of a reflected form; it has nothing of its
own. It comes and stays with thee; with thee it will depart.' As
Narcissus started forward, so did the image, ever imitating his
movements. In the course of time he pined away, and in that place
grew the flower which bears his name. See *Echo*.

NATURE.—P. L. 2. 895, 911, 1037; 3. 455; 9. 1001; C. N. 32; V. E. 46.

In their treatment of Nature the ancients get little beyond a
mere personification, and in Milton's representation of the goddess we
find much that is borrowed from the classical conception of Earth
(Tellus or Ge; see *Earth*). Among the Orphic hymns is one addressed to Nature (9), in which the poet employs such epithets as
'mother of all,' 'ancient,' (cf. *V. E.* 46). She is also 'the ruler,' 'the
guardian in air, under earth, and in the sea' (14), 'the vanquisher,
the unsubdued' (3; cf. *P. L.* 2. 1037).

In *P. L.* 2. 895 Chaos and Night are 'ancestors of Nature.' As
shown elsewhere, Milton has here reconciled the cosmogonies of
Hesiod and of Orpheus (see *Chaos*). Earth was the eldest child of
Chaos, and the mother of gods and men, according to Hesiod, but in
this passage Nature seems to include not only Earth but all that
sprang from her. The sources of such passages as *P. L.* 2. 911;
9. 1001; *V. E.* 46 must be found in ancient philosophy, from which
the poet has derived mythology by increasing the vividness of personification. Before the world was created all was Chaos: 'conges-
taque eodem Non bene junctarum discordia semina rerum' (Ov. *Met.*
1. 8). Diodorus (1. 7) describes the

> secret things that came to pass
> When beldam Nature in her cradle was.

The world (κόσμος) gathered the elements within itself, where they they became impregnated, increasing by the night mists, until they burst forth in the forms of all created things. According to Ovid *Met.* 1. 416 ff.), this order of creation followed the flood: 'fecundaque semina rerum, Vivaci nutrita solo, ceu matris in alvo Creverunt.' Cf. *P. L.* 2. 911; 9. 1001. For the allusion in *C. N.* 32 see *Apollo.* In connection with *P. L.* 2. 911 editors cite Lucretius 5. 260: 'Earth, the universal mother, is found at the same time to be the general tomb of things.'

At the fall of man (*P. L.* 9. 1001) Earth trembled, 'and Nature gave a second groan.' This seems to be a reference to the theory of creation just given. It is related by Hesiod, however, that Earth groaned deeply when Heaven banished her children from her sight (*Theog.* 159).

NEÆRA.—Lyc. 69.

Neæra is a name common among Latin erotic poets and their imitators. Since Warton, *Lyc.* 69 has generally been referred to Buchanan (*Elegies* and *Epigrams*). See also Trent's edition of *Lycidas.* In Hor. *C.* 3. 14. 21 we find the lines

> Dic et argutæ properet Neæræ
> Murrhenum nodo cohibere crinem.

Cf. Tibull. 3. 2. 11; Verg. *Ecl.* 3. 3.

NECESSITY.—S. A. 1666; Arc. 69.

Milton's 'dire Necessity' in *S. A.* 1666 is adapted from the 'dira Necessitas' of Hor. *C.* 3. 24. 6, as Todd suggests. Such personification of Necessity (Ananke) was especially common among the Greek dramatists. According to a fragment of Sophocles (236, Nauck, *Trag. Græc. Frag.*) not even Ares can withstand Necessity, and Æschylus speaks of 'the resistless might of Necessity' (*Prom.* 105). On *Arc.* 69 see *Fates.*

NECTAR.—See Ambrosia.

NEPTUNE.—P. L. 9. 18; P. R. 2. 190; V. E. 43; C. 18, 869; Lyc. 90.

C. 18 ff. refers to the division of the world among the gods. Poseidon (Neptune) himself tells the story in *Il.* 15. 187 ff.: 'For three brethren are we, and sons of Cronus, whom Rhea bare, Zeus, and myself, and Hades is the third. . . . And in three lots are all things divided, and each drew a domain of his own, and to me fell the hoary sea, to be my habitation forever, when we shook the lots: and Hades drew the murky darkness, and Zeus the wide heaven, in clear air and clouds.' Milton speaks of Neptune's rule as extended over each ebbing stream and 'all the sea-girt isles.' Servius, in a note on Verg. *Georg.* 1. 12, says that Neptune presides over the rivers, the springs, and all waters. Plato in the *Critias,*

113 C, relates that in the distribution of territory among the gods, Poseidon obtained the rich island of Atlantis, where he reared his children. Plato enumerates these and the realms which Neptune appointed them, and says (114 C): ' All these and their descendants (for many generations) were the inhabitants and rulers of divers islands in the open sea.'

The Homeric Poseidon is mighty and warlike, driving his chariot up from his palace in the sea, and rushing fiercely into battle (*Il.* 13. 13, 10–65). He is frequently called the Earth-shaker by Homer (ἐνοσίχθων, ἐννοσίγαιος, 13. 10, 59; cf. *C.* 869). In *Il.* 12. 27 he appears wielding his 'mace,' the trident, against the Greek wall. With his trident he also stirred up storms against Odysseus, as the hero was returning home from Calypso's isle (*Od.* 5. 291 ff.). In one case (*Il.* 13. 59) Poseidon carried a sceptre or staff, whose stroke inspired strong courage.

Among the great epic subjects referred to in *P. L.* 9. 14 ff. occurs ' Neptune's ire . . . that so long Perplexed the Greek.' Milton means the *Odyssey*. Homer begins his narrative with the year ordained by the gods for the return of Odysseus to Ithaca; ' not even there was he quit of his labors, not even among his own; but all the gods had pity on him save Poseidon, who raged continually against godlike Odysseus, till he came to his own country ' (*Od.* 1. 16–21). Poseidon was angry because Odysseus had blinded the one eye of his son Polyphemus. ' From that day forth Poseidon the Earth-shaker doth not indeed slay Odysseus, but driveth him wandering from his own country ' (74).

V. E. 42 ff. may be a remote reference to strife between Zeus and Poseidon. It was Poseidon who conspired against Zeus in *Il.* 1. 399. They are enemies again in *Il.* 15. 162 ff., and finally we see them engaging in battle on opposite sides (20. 54 ff.): ' And terribly thundered the father of gods and men from heaven above; and from beneath Poseidon made the vast earth shake and the steep mountain tops.'

The epithet ' green-eyed ' (*V. E.* 43) may be referred to Pausanias or Cicero. The former (1. 14. 5) says that Poseidon's eyes were γλαυκοί, that is, the color of the sea (blue or gray). Cicero (*N. D.* 1. 30) calls them ' cærulei ' (dark-green or dark blue). The word is often used of the sea.

For Neptune and Triton (*Lyc.* 90) see *Sea-gods*. For Neptune and Amymone (*P. R.* 2. 190) see *Amymone*.

NEREUS.—C. 835-871. See Sea-gods.

NIGHT.—P. L. 1. 543; 2. 150, 439, 894, 962, 970, 986, 1002, 1036; 3. 18, 71, 421, 424; 4. 776; 5. 685; 6. 14, 406; 7. 105; 9. 65; 10. 477; P. R. 4. 398; Pass. 29; Pens. 58, 121; C. 195; L'Al. 2.

Milton's treatment of Night presents some difficulty in distinguishing between personification and mythology, nor is the line clearly drawn by the ancients, especially the later writers.

In *P. L.* Night is represented as the wife of Chaos, and co-ruler with him in the confused abyss between Heaven and Hell. See *Chaos*. Many of the epithets used by Milton such as 'old' (*P. L.* 1. 543; 2. 1002; 3. 421), 'ancient' (2. 970, 986), 'eldest' (2.894), seem to be derived from the place of Night in the Orphic cosmogony. In 3. 18 she is 'eternal,' as in Orph. *Arg.* 15 she is called ἀειγνήτης and αιανή in Æsch. *Eum.* 408. The epithets 'uncreated' (*P. L.* 2. 150) and 'unoriginal' (10. 477) cannot be referred directly to classical originals. As 'ancestor of nature' and 'eldest of things' (2. 894, 962) she may be considered as without origin, since 'the beginning is unbegotten' (ἀγένητον, Plat. *Phædr.* 245 D). In *P. L.* 2. 439 Night is 'unessential,' where the word refers rather to the dark realm than to the goddess herself. She is called 'unsubstantial' in *P. R.* 4. 399, where Milton makes her the offspring of Darkness. This, however, is contrary to classical tradition, according to which her parent, if she had one, was Chaos (Hes. *Theog.* 123), or Phanes (Proclus on *Tim.* 5. 291). Georgius Cedrenus (*Hist. Comp.* 57 C) says that according to Orpheus æther was first created, and 'on either side were Chaos and gloomy Night, wherein all things beneath æther were concealed, showing that Night was the oldest.' Of the other epithets of Night used by Milton, 'thievish' (*C.* 197) may be compared with 'furtivæ noctis' of Ov. *Eleg.* 1. 11. 3. 'Sable-vested (*P. L.* 2. 962) has been referred to Eur. *Ion* 1150 (see *Apollo*).

In *P. L.* 2. 434–441, 877–883 there seems to be some suggestion of Hesiod's description of the gates and walls of Tartarus (*Theog.* 721 ff.). They were of bronze, and night lay about them threefold. There was the terrible abode of dark Night, concealed in murky clouds, whence Day and Night go forth to mortals, each in turn, the one bearing light, the other concealed in a dark cloud (cf. *P. L.* 5. 685; 6. 409). The figure of Night's thick mantle (*Pass.* 30; cf. *P. L.* 6. 407) is similar to *Il.* 8. 485, where the sun set 'drawing black night across Earth.' Cf. Juvencus 2. 2: 'furvamque super Nox cærula pallam . . . per inane trahebat.' Night's mantle is mentioned in *Orph. Hy.* 6. 10.

The 'car of Night' is mentioned in *P. L.* 9. 65 (cf. *Pens.* 121). Æschylus speaks of the 'dusky car of Night' in *Choeph.* 646. In Theoc. *Id.* 2. 166 Simaitha bids farewell to the bright Moon and 'ye other stars, attendants on the chariot of stilly Night.' This suggests Milton's 'pale career' (*Pens.* 121). It was common among the Latin poets to represent Night as driving a chariot; (cf. Verg. *Æn.* 5. 721; Tibull. 2. 1. 87; Claud. 15. 213).

As in *Pass.* 29 Night is the 'best patroness of grief,' so Ovid calls her 'curarum maxima nutrix' (*Met.* 8. 81). In the *Orestes* of Euripides (174) the Chorus calls upon Night: 'venerable Night, thou that dispensest sleep to languid mortals, come from Erebus, . . . for by our griefs and by our sufferings we are quite undone.'

The royal and warlike character of Night as exemplified in *P. L.* 2. 986; 1002; 3. 421 is almost without classical antecedent. Homer calls Night 'the subduer of gods and men,' and Proclus (on *Tim.* 5. 291) says that after Phanes, Night held the rule.

See *Erebus* and *Sleep*. In connection with *P. L.* 2. 1036; 6. 14 see *Aurora*.

NOTUS. P. L. 10. 702. See **Winds.**

NYMPHS.—P. L. 4. 707; 5. 381; 9. 386; P. R. 2. 184-189, 297, 355, 374; C. N. 188; L'Al. 25, 36; Pens. 21, 137; Arc. 1. 33, 96; C. 54, 120, 230, 254, 275, 422, 824, 833, 883, 963; Lyc. 50, 99.

Of the different classes of nymphs Milton distinguishes the Oreads and Dryads (*P. L.* 9. 387; *C.* 963), the Naiads, and the Nereids (*Pens.* 21), though the first two may be included under the name 'wood-nymph' (*P. L.* 5. 381; 9. 386; *P. R.* 2. 297; *C.* 120), and 'water-nymph' may apply to either Naiads or Nereids (*C.* 833). Servius says (on *Æn.* 1. 500): 'nymphæ montium Oreades dicuntur, silvarum Dryades, . . . fontium Napeæ vel Naides, maris vero Nereides.' (See *Naiads, Diana, Cassiopeia, Echo.*) The Nereids, daughters of Nereus and Doris, are mentioned by Homer (*Il.* 18. 35 ff.), and Hesiod gives the names of fifty (*Theog.* 240–264). Both of them mention Panope. The epithet 'sleek' (*Lyc.* 99) seems to have no distinct original in this connection, though Hesiod, in a conventional way, speaks of her sisters as 'charming,' 'lovely,' 'smiling,' 'fair-ankled,' 'fair-haired.' In the light of *C.* 882, the last epithet may have suggested 'sleek.' In Verg. *Æn.* 5. 825 it is 'Panopea virgo' and her sisters who sport upon the calm surface of the sea after the storm.

Milton dwells often upon the beauty of places haunted by the nymphs (*P. L.* 4. 705–708; *P. R.* 2. 184 f., 289–297, 354; *Pens.* 133–146; *Arc.; C.* 119–121, 230–243, 423, 964). Homer speaks of the nymphs 'that haunt fair thickets, and springs of rivers, and grassy water-meadows' (*Il.* 20. 8; cf. *Od.* 6. 123). Theocritus describes a place where he lay under the poplars and elms, 'while close at hand the sacred water from the nymphs' own cave welled forth with murmurs musical' (7. 135 ff.). The bathing place of Diana and her nymphs is thus described by Ovid (*Met.* 3. 155 ff.): 'There was a valley, thick set with pitch-trees and the sharp-pointed cypress; by name Gargaphie, sacred to the active Diana (cf. *P. L.* 4. 706). In the extreme recess of this, there was a grotto in a grove, formed by no art . . . A limpid fountain ran murmuring on the right hand with its little stream, having its spreading channels edged with a border of grass.' In Arcadia was another bathing place of Diana, 'a cool grove, out of which a stream ran, flowing with its murmurming noise, and borne along the sand worn fine by its action.' Hither came the nymphs with their mistress, to rest from the chase. In the *Arcades* Milton has represented his Arcadian nymphs as silver-buskined (33), and in

Comus they are armed with quiver and arrows (422). The followers
of Diana were dressed and armed for hunting (*Met.* 2. 411–421; 1. 695).
The association of the nymphs with Arcadia may be traced to their
association with Artemis or Diana, or with the wood-divinities (see
Wood-gods). This association is common in pastoral poetry, and
examples may be found in Theocritus (1; 5) and in Vergil's *Eclogues*.
As in *Arcades* Milton represents the nymphs and shepherds dancing
together, so Vergil (*Ecl.* 5. 58) says, ' sprightly pleasure charms the
woods and all the fields beside, and Pan, and shepherd swains, and
Dryad girls.' For the localities mentioned in *Arc.* 97 ff. see *Pan*.

As the nymphs are considered the protectors of Lycidas (*Lyc.*
50), so in *Id.* 1. 66 Theocritus appeals to the nymphs who failed
Daphnis in his distress. Jerram suggests that Milton follows Vergil's imitation of Theocritus (*Ecl.* 10. 9) in identifying the Muses with
the nymphs. The latter poet calls the Muses ' Castalian nymphs'
(7. 148; cf. Milt. *Ep. Dam.* 1).

Examples of the fondness of nymphs for the dance are of frequent occurrence (see *Diana* and *Hermes*). In *Orphic Hymn* 50
they are addressed as ' dancing with Pan upon the mountains.' In
Hor. *C.* 1. 1. 34 they are thus associated with the satyrs, and in 4. 7.
5 with the Graces.

Occasionally we find among the classics a suggestion of their
' flower-inwoven tresses ' (*C. N.* 187). In Hes. *Theog.* 255 Alimede, a
Nereid, is εὐστέφανος. Cf. *C.* 120, 862. Claudian (22. 345) speaks of
the nymphs as ' redimitæ tempora.' Offerings of wreaths were made
to them (Hor. *C.* 3. 27. 30; Ov. *Met.* 9. 377).

Milton seems to use the word nymph in the more inclusive sense
of maiden in *L'Al.* 25; cf. Ov. *Ep.* 16. 126; 9. 50. In *C.* 54 he calls
Circe a nymph, as does Homer in *Od.* 10. 543.

OCEANUS.—C. 868. See Sea-gods.

OLYMPIAS.—P. L. 9. 509. See Ammon.

OLYMPUS.—P. L. 1. 516; 7. 7 10. 583; D. F. I. 44.

Milton illustrates the earlier conception of Olympus as a
mountain, distinguished from heaven itself, in *P. L.* 1. 516; 7. 7;
10. 583; cf. *Il.* 15. 192; 5. 750; *Od.* 6. 42–46. In two cases he uses
Homeric epithets. Olympus is ' high ', ' snowy' (*P. L.* 10. 583; 1. 515;
cf. *Eleg.* 5. 117), as in Homer it is frequently μακρός, ἀγάννιφος, νιφόεις
(*Il.* 1. 532, 420; 18. 186, 616). The later conception of Olympus as
heaven itself appears in *D. F. I.* 44; cf. *C.* 1. This is especially common among the Latin poets (cf. Verg. *Ecl.* 5. 56). Olympus is
called ' stelliger' in Seneca, *Herc. Œt.* 1907. See *Saturn, Muses,
Jove, Eurynome.*

OPHION.—P. L. 10. 581. See Eurynome.

OPS.—P. L. 10. 584. See Rhea.

5

ORCUS.—P. L. 2. 964.

Though by later writers Orcus is confounded with Pluto (Ades), Milton here observes a distinction. Hesiod (*W. and D.* 804) calls him 'avenging Orcus, whom Strife bore as a bane to men forsworn.' Hesiod and Vergil (*Georg.* 1. 277) associate Orcus with the Eumenides (Furies).

OREADS.—P. L. 9. 387. See Nymphs.

ORPHEUS.—P. L. 3. 17; 7. 33; L'Al. 145; Pens. 105; Lyc. 58.

Orpheus is the name of a mythic singer 'of lyrics to whom was assigned a body of poetry, including the story of the Argonauts and a number of hymns. Milton seems to refer to the Orphic hymn to Night (2) in *P. L.* 3. 17, though the passage has been interpreted in several ways. At any rate, the Miltonic representation of the divinity of Night differs almost entirely from the Orphic Night, who is addressed as gentle and much beloved by mortals for her benefits.

The story of Eurydice, the wife of Orpheus, whom her husband half regained from Hades by his sweet song, but lost by looking back, is related by Ovid in *Met.* 10. 11–77. As his plaintive music was heard in Hades, the punishment of evil-doers ceased, tears moistened the cheeks of the Eumenides, and Proserpina and Pluto were moved to grant his request. According to Seneca (*Herc. Fur.* 578), whose account is similar to Ovid's, 'Deflent et lacrymis difficiles dei.' Cf. *Herc. Œt.* 1031–1089; *Ad Pat.* 21.

The Muse referred to in *P. L.* 7. 37 and *Lyc.* 58, as the mother of Orpheus, is Calliope, the Muse of epic poetry (Auson. *Id.* 22. 3, ed. Peiper). In the *Rhesus* of Euripides (947) there is evident reference to this story of his parentage, which, according to Pausanias (9. 30), was a common belief. Cf. schol. on *Rhesus* 895.

The story of the fate of Orpheus at the hands of the angry Mænads is told by Ovid (*Met.* 11. 1-66). Though both of Milton's accounts are rather general, they present distinct correspondence with certain details given by Ovid. *Met.* 10. 90–105 is an elaborate list of the trees which assembled on Rhodope to hear the song of the Thracian bard. The expression, 'had ears to rapture' (*P. L.* 7. 35), suggests the 'auritas quercus' of Hor. *C.* 1. 12. 11. The 'hideous roar' and 'savage clamor' are described in *Met.* 11. 15-18. Cf. *Bacchus*. The sweet music at first prevailed, but was at length overcome.

> Te, mœstæ volucres, Orpheu, te turba ferarum,
> Te, rigidæ silices, tua carmina sæpe secutæ
> Fleverunt silvæ: positis te frondibus arbos,
> Tonsa comam, luxit: lacrymis quoque flumina dicunt
> Increvisse suis; obscuraque carbasa pullo
> Naiades et Dryades, passosque habuere capillos.

The poet was torn in pieces, and his head and lyre were rolled down the Hebrus,

> Et Methymnææ potiuntur litore Lesbi.

His spirit passed to Elysium and,

> quærens per arva piorum
> Invenit Eurydicen, cupidisque amplectitur ulnis.

Cf. *L'Al*. 145–150. Vergil (*Æn*. 6. 645) represents Orpheus singing among the shades in Elysium. Milton refers again to Ovid in this connection in the *Prolusions*, ed. Symmons, 6. 173. Cf. *Tractate on Education*, *P. W*. 3. 466 f.

PALES.—P. L. 9. 393.

Pales was a Roman goddess of the pastures (Serv. on Verg. *Georg*. 3. 1; Ov. *Fast*. 4. 721 ff.). In Ovid she is 'alma' (722), 'rustica,' 'silvicola' (744, 746). Cf. *Ep. Dam*. 32.

PAN.—P. L. 4. 266, 707; P. R. 2. 190; C. N. 89; Arc. 106; C. 175, 268.

Pan was the 'goat-footed, two-horned god of shepherds' (*Hom. Hy*. 19. 2, 5). We find him going 'hither and thither through the dense thickets, sometimes allured by the gentle streams, but sometimes again he passes over the sun-traversed mountains . . . and oftentimes he runs over the long hoary mountain ranges. . . . And with him then the mountain-nymphs of sweet song, coming frequently on foot to the dark-watered fountain, raise the song, and the echo sounds around the height of the mountain' (*Hom. Hy*. 19. 8–21). In 19. 24 he appears 'delighting his mind with sweet lays in the soft meadow, where the crocus and fragrant hyacinth flourishing are mingled with abundant grass.' With this description compare *P. L*. 4. 266 and Milton's more elaborate description of Eden preceding; see also 705 ff ; *C*. 268; *P. R*. 2. 184 ff.

The story of Pan's love for Syrinx (*P. R*. 2. 188; *Arc*. 106) is told by Ovid (*Met*. 1. 689–706) in Mercury's song to Argus.

> Arcadiæ gelidis sub montibus, inquit,
> Inter Hamadryadas celeberrima Nonacrinas
> Naias una fuit. Nymphæ Syringa vocabant.

In purity she emulated Diana, whom she followed in the chase. Often had she escaped the satyrs, but Pan, meeting her as she was returning from Lycæus, pursued and overtook her 'arenosi placidum Ladonis ad amnem' (702). With the last quotation, and the 'calamos palustres' of 706, compare 'sandy Ladon's lilied banks' of *Arc*. 97. The localities of Arcadia here mentioned, were all associated with Pan, and so with the nymphs. Lycæus (98) and Mænalus (102) are mentioned by Theocritus (1. 123, 124) as haunts of Pan. At least a part of Mount Erymanthus was sacred to the god (Paus. 8. 24. 3), and 'Cyllene hoar' was sacred to Pan's father, Hermes (*Hom. Hy*. 3. 2). Vergil (*Æn*. 8. 139) speaks of the 'gelido vertice' of Cyllene; cf. 'Arcadiæ gelidis sub montibus' of Ov. *Met*. 1. 689.

In *P. L*. 4. 266; *C*. 175; *C. N*. 89 we find suggestions of the conception of Pan which appears in *Orph. Hy*. 10, where he is called 'the

god of shepherds' (1), and 'the giver of increase, of light, and of
fruits' (11). In 1 ff. he is addressed as 'mighty Pan . . . entire
substance of the universe, the heaven, and the sea, and the earth,
queen of all, and immortal fire.' He is also 'the father of all' (10),
'the ruler of the world' (11), 'for in thee the boundless soil of the
earth is established, and to thee yield both the deep-sown water of
the untiring sea, and Ocean, circling in waters about the earth'; cf.
Serv. on Verg. *Ecl*. 2. 31. In each of these cases there is evident
reference to the etymology of Pan, as suggested in Milton's epithet
'universal' (*P. L.* 4. 66). Isidorus, in *Etymol*. 8. 11. 81, says, '*Pan*
dictus est, id est, *omne*. Fingunt enim eum ex universali elemen-
torum specie.' Cf. *C. N*. 89.

In *Orph. Hy*. 10. 4 Pan is 'enthroned with the Hours'; cf. *P. L.*
4. 267; see *Hours* and *Graces*. As Milton speaks of Pan asleep in *P.
L.* 4. 707; *Ep. Dam.* 52, so in Theocritus (1. 16) the goatherd fears to
disturb the god while he rests at noon, weary of the chase.

PANDORA.—P. L. 4. 714.

In revenge for the theft of the fire of Zeus for mortals by Prometheus, or Forethought, Zeus ordered Hephæstus and the other immortals to fashion a woman, godlike in mind and body. She was called
Pandora, and was conducted by Hermes to Epimetheus, or After-
thought (called ἀμαρτίνοος in Hes. *Theog*. 511), 'unwiser son' of
Iapetus. He received her, and thus were engendered all the ills
that flesh is heir to. The story is told by Hesiod in *W. and D*. 50 ff.

PANOPE.—Lyc. 99. See Nymphs.

PARTHENOPE.—C. 879. See Sirens.

PEGASUS.—P. L. 7. 4, 17. See Bellerophon and Muses.

PELOPS.—Pens. 99.

Milton here refers to Pelops' line as the subject of ancient tragedy. The line of descent in this Argive family ran thus: Tantalus,
Pelops, Atreus, Agamemnon, the last being the father of Orestes,
Electra, and Iphigenia, and the brother of Menelaus (Eur. *Or*. 5–26).
Three of the remaining tragedies of Æschylus, two of Sophocles,
and five of Euripides deal with the stories of this house. Of these
the most celebrated are the *Agamemnon*, the *Choephoræ*, and the
Eumenides of Æschylus, the *Electra* of Sophocles, and the *Orestes*,
the *Iphigenia at Tauris*, and the *Iphigenia at Aulis* by Euripides.
The family frequently went by the patronymic name Pelopidæ (Soph.
El. 10). Plato mentions the sufferings of the Pelopidæ and the
events of the Trojan war as subjects of tragedy (*Rep*. 2. 380 A).

To one of their calamities Milton refers in *P. L.* 10. 688. The
story of the Thyestean banquet is as follows: Atreus contended with
his brother Thyestes for the throne of their father, but Thyestes
seduced the wife of Atreus, and gained the power by dishonest means.

In revenge Atreus slew the children of his brother, and served them before him at a banquet. The Sun could not endure this transgression, and turned his course for one day from west to east. A reference to the story is to be found in Eur. *El.* 714 ff. It appears in detail in the scholium on Eur. *Or.* 812, and in Hyg. *Fab.* 88.

PHILLIS.—*L'Al.* 86. See **Corydon.**

PHILOMEL.—*Pens.* 56.

The name Philomel, meaning the nightingale, is a reference to the story of Tereus, the husband of Procne, who, preferring Procne's sister Philomela, violated the latter and cut out her tongue. According to the usual account, Philomela was changed to a swallow (Apollod. 3. 14. 8), but Hyginus says that she became a nightingale (*Fab.* 45; cf. Ov. *Met.* 6. 668).

PHINEUS.—*P. L.* 3. 36.

Phineus was a 'prophet old' who dwelt at Salmydessos in Thrace, and was visited by the Argonauts (Apollod. 1. 9. 21; Apollon. Rh. 2. 178 ff.). Because he prophesied, he was visited by the gods with blindness. He is described by Ovid as 'Perpetuaque trahens inopem sub nocte senectam' (*Met.* 7. 2).

PHLEGETON.—*P. L.* 2. 580. See **Rivers of Hell.**

PHLEGRA.—*P. L.* 1. 577. See **Giants.**

PHŒBUS.—*P. R.* 4. 260; Pass. 28; *C.* 66, 190, *Lyc.* 77; *Son.* 13. 10. See **Apollo.**

PHŒNIX.—*P. L.* 5. 272; *S. A.* 1699.

For his two accounts of the phœnix Milton draws upon several sources. According to Herodotus (2. 73) there lived but one phœnix at a time. It resembled the eagle, and had wings of gold and ruby. Once in five hundred years it flew from its home in Arabia to the temple of the Sun in Egypt, bearing the remains of the parent bird enclosed in myrrh. Milton's authority for saying that the phœnix flew to Thebes is not in the classical writers. These all agree that the bird visited Heliopolis. Ovid (*Met.* 15. 391 ff.) describes the pyre of incense which the phœnix erects for itself. From the ashes of the old bird the young one is born. In *S. A.* 1703 the new phœnix is not represented as a young bird, but as the old one rejuvenated by the fire. Pomponius Mela tells the legend in the same way (*De Situ Orbis* 3. 8).

As Raphael descends to earth (*P. L.* 5. 269 ff.), 'to all the fowls he seems A phœnix' as it flies to Egypt. This may have some relation to the narrative found in Achilles Tatius 3. 25, who says that a company of other birds flies with the phœnix toward Egypt as a bodyguard, 'and he is like a king departing from his own country.'

The brilliant plumage suggested by Herodotus, and elaborated by Pliny (*N. H.* 10. 2. 2), helps to establish the connection between Milton's figure and Raphael.

S. A. 1707 is an adaptation of *Met.* 15. 395: 'Hæc ubi quinque suæ complevit secula vitæ.' As Milton speaks of the 'sole bird' (*P. L.* 5. 272), so Ovid says 'unica avis' (*Am.* 2. 6. 54).   Cf. *Ep. Dam.* 187 ff.   The adjective occurs also in Claud. 22. 417 and Lactantius, *De Ave Phœn.* 31, 32.

PLEIADES.—P. L. 7. 374; 10. 674.

The Pleiades are mentioned as daughters of Atlas in Hesiod (*W. and D.* 383; cf. *P. L.* 10. 674), who adds that their rising was the sign of the beginning of summer.   The fact is repeated in Aratus, *Phœn.* 254–267, and their genealogy and number are discussed by Athenæus (11. 489, 490), who mentions the story that they were transferred to heaven to save them from Orion.   Cf. Hyg. *Astr.* 2. 21.   They were originally seven in number.

PLUTO.—P. L. 4. 270; 10. 444; L'Al. 149; Pens. 107.

Plato says, 'Pluto is concerned with πλοῦτος, and means the giver of wealth, because wealth comes out of the earth beneath. People in general use the term as a euphemism for Hades' (*Crat.* 403 A).   The adjective 'Plutonian' in *P. L.* 10. 444 is used in a general sense of that which belongs to the Lower World.   'Plutonian hall' suggests the 'domus Plutonia' of Horace (*C.* 1. 4. 17).   See *Ades.*   In connection with *P. L.* 4. 270 see *Ceres*, and on *L'Al.* 149 and *Pens.* 107 see *Orpheus.*

POMONA.—P. L. 5. 378; 9. 393.

In both cases Milton's representation of Pomona is drawn from Ovid (*Met.* 14. 623 ff.).   She was a beautiful maiden, more skillful than any of the Hamadryads of Latium in caring for the trees and vines.   She enclosed her little orchard with a wall to shut out her many suitors, but the god Vertumnus often found his way to her in disguise, unsuccessfully pleading his own cause, until at length he captivated her by appearing in his own splendor.   Pomona is mentioned by Servius (on Verg. *Æn.* 7. 190) as 'pomorum dea,' the goddess of fruits.

PROMETHEUS.—S. A. 500.   See Pandora, Tantalus.

PROSERPINA.—P. L. 4. 269; 9. 396.   See Ceres.

PROTEUS.—P. L. 3. 604.   See Sea-gods.

PSYCHE.—C. 1005.   See Cupid.

PYGMIES.—P. L. 1. 576, 780.

Homer speaks of the pygmies in *Il.* 3. 6 as meeting the cranes in battle, but does not name their dwelling-place.   In placing them ' be-

yond the Indian mount' Milton follows Pliny (*N. H.* 7. 2. 2), who
also describes them as 'ternas spithamas longitudine, hoc est, ternos
dodrantes non excedentes,' the equivalent of twenty-seven inches
in length, and says that they live 'extrema in parte montium.' Just
what mountains Pliny meant is uncertain, though he intimates
that they were 'ad extremos fines Indiæ ab oriente circa fontem
Gangis.' This seems to indicate the range of Imaus. In 6. 19. 22
he speaks of a report that the pygmies live in Maleus, a mountain of
the interior.

PYRRHA.—P. L. 11. 12. See Deucalion.

PYTHON.—P. L. 10. 531.

According to Ovid the Python was engendered during the new
creation which followed the flood. The story runs as follows (*Met.*
1. 434-440): 'When therefore the Earth, covered with mud by the
late deluge, was thoroughly heated by the ethereal sunshine and a
penetrating warmth, she produced species of creatures innumerable.
. . . She indeed might have been unwilling, but then she produced thee as well, thou enormous Python; and thou, unheard-of
serpent, wast a source of terror to this new race of men, so vast a part
of a mountain didst thou occupy'. Accounts do not say that this
took place in the Pythian vale, as Milton says, though it was there
that Apollo slew the Python with arrows soon after. The story is
first told in *Hom. Hy. to Pyth. Ap.* 122 ff. Ovid and others say that
in memory of this deed Apollo established the Pythian games, which
in historic times were celebrated near Delphi in his honor. Cf. Hyg.
Fab. 140; *P. L.* 2. 530.

In the *Reason of Church Government*, *P. W.* 2. 505, the story is
worked into a simile of the pestiferous contagion of prelaty, with
evident reference to the interpretation given in Macrobius (1. 17. 57),
who says that the myth typifies the sun dispelling the mists, and his
rays are the arrows. Cf. *Prolusions*, ed. Symmons, 6. 152.

RHEA.—P. L. 1. 513; 4. 279; 10. 584; Arc. 21.

Cybele is the Phrygian name of Rhea, the revered mother of
gods, according to Strabo 10. 469, 470. As an illustration of stately
divinity Milton speaks of 'the towered Cybele, Mother of a hundred
gods' (*Arc.* 21). His words seem to be based principally on Verg.
Æn. 6. 785-788:

> qualis Berecynthia mater
> Invehitur curru Phrygias turrita per urbes
> Læta deum partu, centum complexa nepotes,
> Omnes cælicolas, omnes supera alta tenentes.

Servius makes the following comment on this passage: 'Berecynthia
mater . . . Nam Berecynthos castellum est Phrygiæ juxta
Sangarium fluvium: ubi mater deum colitur. Turrita. Vel quia ipsa

est terra, quæ urbes sustinet.' Ovid says, however, that she wears a crown of towers, because she gave towers to the Phrygian cities. That this was also Vergil's idea seems probable in the light of *Æn.* 10. 252:

> Alma parens Idæa Deum, cui Dindyma cordi,
> Turrigeræque urbes, bijugique ad frena leones.

Cf. *Eleg.* 1. 65, 74; 5. 62. To Rhea is applied the ephithet πυργοφόρος (Suidas). Hesiod (*Theog.* 453 ff.) says that Rhea was the mother of Istia, Demeter, Hera, Hades, Poseidon, and Zeus. She was well known as 'the mother of gods and mortal men,' or simply as the mother.' Cf. *Orph. Hy.* 13. 9; 40. 1; 26. 1; Ov. *Fast.* 4. 202, 250, 259, 263; *Anth. Pal.* 6. 220.

The story of the jealous Rhea, as related in *P. L.* 4. 275 ff., is taken from Diodorus Siculus (3. 68–70), the only ancient authority for this version of the Dionysus myth. Diodorus cites Thymœtes, 'a contemporary of Orpheus,' as his authority, and says that Ammon first took Rhea to wife, but afterward met the beautiful Amalthea, who bore him a son, 'a wonder of beauty and strength.' Milton calls the boy 'florid.' In fear of Rhea's jealousy Ammon sent the child Dionysus to the distant Nysa, which lies in an island 'girt with the river Triton' (*P. L.* 4. 276). Here, safe from the wiles of Rhea, the boy was reared in a cave under the guardianship of Athene. μητρυιά (Diod. 3. 70) may have suggested the epithet 'stepdame' (*P. L.* 4. 279). The Latin goddess Ops was identified with Rhea, as in Macrobius (*Sat.* 1. 10. 19). Thus Milton speaks of Rhea and Cronus as Ops and Saturn in *P. L.* 10. 584. See *Eurynome*.

RIVERS OF HELL.—P. L. 1. 239; 2. 506, 574-586, 604, 875; 3. 14; 10. 453; L'Al. 3; C. 132, 604.

In the passage *P. L.* 2. 574–586 Milton names and describes the five rivers of the Lower World as they were known to the ancients. He assigns to them the attributes which classical tradition generally gave them, and which it connected with their etymology. A good illustration is Porphyry's quotation of Apollodorus, cited by Stobæus (*Ecl. Phys.* 1. 52. 46), where Styx is connected with the root στυγ, to hate; Acheron with ἄχος, sorrow, pain; Cocytus with κωκύειν, to lament; and Phlegethon with φλέγεσθαι, to burn with a flame. Milton speaks of 'fierce Phlegeton' and its 'waves of torrent fire.' So in Vergil, round about Tartarus 'rapidus flammis ambit torrentibus amnis' (*Æn.* 6. 550). Lethe is so called because it is the river of forgetfulness. The fact is mentioned by Lucian (*De Luctu* 5). Cf. *P. L.* 2. 604 ff.; Plat. *Rep.* 10. 621; Verg. *Æn.* 6. 714. In this last passage the souls of the blessed drink the 'securos latices et longa oblivia.' Cf. also Ov. *Met.* 11. 602 ff.

In *C.* 603 mention is made of

> the griesly legions that troop
> Under the sooty flag of Acheron.

The figure is referred by Todd to Phineas Fletcher's *Locusts:* ' All Hell run out, and sooty flagges display.' The context seems to show that by 'griesly legions' Milton referred to monsters which were found about the entrance to Hell, as in Vergil (see *Harpies, Hydra*). Compare Hesiod's description of the region about Tartarus in *Theog.* 725–817, which passage also contains a suggestion of the illimitable Deep of Chaos (*P. L.* 2. 879 ff.). *C.* 603, 604 in some measure resembles *P. L.* 2. 898–906, where the elements contend in Chaos,

> and to battle bring
> Their embryon atoms: they around the flag
> Of each his faction, in their several clans,
> Light-armed or heavy, sharp, smooth, swift or slow,
> Swarm populous.

This passage may be referred to Ovid's description of Chaos (*Met.* 1. 18–20; see *Chaos*).

The topography of the infernal rivers is rather indefinite and varied in classical writers. Lethe is generally removed from the rivers of horror as in Milton. Plato gives an elaborate, but obscure, description of these waters in *Phœdo* 112 ff. He says that Phlegethon passes through a lake of fire into Tartarus, which is also the mouth of Cooytus. Along the different rivers are borne the souls of wicked men to their destinies; cf. *P. L.* 2. 570–576.

Milton's use of the word Stygian, in the general sense of that which belongs to the Lower World, is classical. Thus we have 'Stygius lacus' (*Æn.* 6. 134; cf. *P. L.* 3. 14); 'Stygiæ tenebræ' (*Verg. Georg.* 3. 551; cf. *C.* 132); 'Stygius rex' (*Æn.* 6. 252; cf. *P. L.* 2. 506, 875 etc.). The 'Stygian cave' haunted by Cerberus and Midnight in *L'Al.* 3, 4, or the 'uncouth cell' (5), may owe something to the cave of Sleep, described by Ovid (*Met.* 11. 592 ff.) as lying near the Cimmerians, and covered with eternal darkness. It has been noted by Hales, however, that the 'Stygian cave' may have been suggested by Vergil's cave of Cerberus (*Æn.* 6. 418–423), near the bank of the Styx. See also *Morpheus* and *Erebus*.

RUMOR.—P. L. 2. 965.

Rumor is named among the monsters which stand about the throne of Chaos. She is hardly a divinity, since Vergil's Fama, which seems to be her antecedent, and which is in turn based on Homer's Eris (*Il.* 4. 440; see *Discord*), is only a personification. Fama is described in *Æn.* 4. 174–188 as 'surpassed in swiftness by nothing else that is bad; she grows by her restless motion, and gathers vigor as she speeds along; small through fear at first, presently she exalts herself towards heaven, and stalks along the ground, and hides her head amid the clouds.' She was born 'with nimble feet and rapid wings, a monster frightful, huge; who, for every feather on her body, had as many wakeful eyes beneath, (wondrous to tell) as many

loud tongues and mouths, as many ears that she pricks up to listen.
By night she flies between heaven and earth, through the gloom,
with buzzing wings, nor droops her eyelids in soothing sleep; by day
she keeps watch, perched either on the very top of a house, or on
high towers, and continually terrifies great cities, being as firmly
attached to what is false and wrong as she is a messenger of truth.'

SATURN.—P. L. 1. 512, 519; 10. 583; Pens. 24; C. 805.

Cronus (Saturn) was the youngest, but most terrible, of the sons
of Earth and Heaven. He unmanned his father, and ruled in his
stead (Hes. *Theog.* 137, 138, 176 ff.). According to the Orphic theogony, however, it was against Ophion and Eurynome that Cronus
rebelled, and Milton makes use of this version in *P. L.* 10. 580–584.
See *Eurynome*. Fearing his own children, Cronus swallowed them
all except Zeus, who was removed by stratagem to Dicte in Crete,
where he grew to manhood. The hundred-handed giants armed him
with the thunderbolt, and he was thus enabled to usurp his father's
throne (Hes. *Theog.* 453–506).

According to Diod. Sic. 5. 70, it was in Mount Ida that the young
Zeus was reared, and in Crete that Cronus held sway. Zeus also
reigned there (71), but afterward took up his seat in Olympus. Vergil,
however, says (*Æn.* 8. 319):

> Primus ab ætherio venit Saturnus Olympo
> Arma Jovis fugiens, et regnis exsul ademtis.

He thus implies that Saturn reigned in Olympus, and was thence
driven to the Hesperian fields. Cf. Ov. *Fast.* 1. 235. Diodorus
relates the tradition of the Cretans (3. 61) that Cronus reigned not
only in Italy, but in Sicily and Africa, and generally in the western
parts of the world. Dionysius of Halicarnassus (1. 38) says that he
was worshipped among the Gauls (cf. *P. L.* 1. 521), and from Plutarch (*De Defectu Oraculorum* 18) we learn that ' of the islands
around Britain, many, scattered about, are deserted. . . . And
there is one there in which Cronus in slumber is held prisoner by
Briareos; for this bond of slumber was invented against him; and
about him are many divinities, his companions and servants.' Cf.
P. L. 1. 519. Again, in *De Facie in Orbe Lunæ* 26, Plutarch says
that these divinities were the ones who had been associated with the
god while he was still the king of gods and men. He is called ' old '
in Verg. *Æn.* 7. 180; cf. Æsch. *Eum.* 638.

The reign of Saturn, to which Milton refers indirectly in *Pens.*
23, was celebrated by ancient writers as the Golden Age (Hes. *W. and
D.* 111–126; Ov. *Met.* 1. 89–112). Men enjoyed themselves without
growing old, and the earth of her own accord yielded all things.
Plato (*Laws* 4. 713 B) says that it furnished a model of political
administration. Milton refers again to the 'pleasing license' of
Saturn's reign in *Doct. and Discip. of Divorce, P. W.* 3. 227.

Vesta, a goddess of the hearth (Cic. *N. D.* 2. 27), was celebrated for her purity (*Hom. Hy. to Aphrod.* 21 ff; Ov. *Fast.* 6. 286 ff.). Vesta never bore any other relation to Saturn than that of daughter (Hes. *Theog.* 454). Milton's reasons for making them the parents of Melancholy (*Pens.* 23) have been a subject of conjecture. Warton's explanation is that the 'bright haired Vesta' signifies Genius, and Saturn is 'the god of Saturnine dispositions, of pensive and gloomy minds.' Browne says that Saturn, the origin of civilization, means Culture, and the virgin-goddess Retirement. Masson interprets Saturn as Solitude, but is uncertain as to Vesta. He says, 'One remembers, however, that Vesta was the goddess of the sacred eternal fire that could be tended only by vowed virginity; and here one is on the track of a peculiarly Miltonic idea.'

Classical writers sometimes praise Cretan Ida for its woods, as in Ovid (*Am.* 3. 10. 39): 'Ipse locus nemorum canebat frugibus Ide;' cf. Claud. 33. 205. Phrygian Ida, however, was the more noted on this account. Euripides (*Hipp.* 1252) speaks of the many pines of Ida, though the scholiast is uncertain which Ida is meant.

For the reference in *C.* 805 see *Titans*.

SATYR.—P. R. 2 191; Id. 94. See Wood-gods.

SCYLLA AND CHARYBDIS.—P. L. 2. 660, 1020; C. 257, 259.

In *Od.* 12. 73 ff. Circe describes to Odysseus the terrors of the cruel monster Scylla and the whirlpool Charybdis, which beset either side of his homeward way. Among later writers a more definite location was assigned to Scylla and Charybdis on the Italian and Sicilian shores, respectively, of the strait separating these lands (Verg. *Æn.* 3. 420; cf. Ov. *Met.* 14. 47 ff.; schol. *Od.* 12. 85). At the same time the island of Circe was located at Circeii on the Italian coast, and the home of the Sirens, whom Odysseus passed just before encountering Scylla, lay somewhere between Circeii and the Sicilian straits. Cf. discussion in Strabo 1. 22, 23. That Milton accepts this location is evident both in *P. L.* 2. 1019 and in *C.* 49 (see *Bacchus*). Thus Odysseus, holding a southward course, 'on the larboard shunned Charybdis.'

In *P. L.* 2. 660 we have a reference to the story of Scylla's transformation, told by Ovid (*Met.* 14. 40–74; cf. Hyg. *Fab.* 199). Circe, jealous of Glaucus' love for the beautiful Scylla, overcame her with enchantments as she was bathing in the Sicilian straits. Scylla was beset with barking dogs:

> Ac primo non credens corporis illas
> Esse sui partes, refugitque, abigitque, timetque
> Ora proterva canum: sed quos fugit, adtrahit una.

In this plight she was changed into a rock, a menace to sailors. The epithet 'fell' of Charybdis (*C.* 259) may be a rendering of Vergil's 'implacata' (*Æn.* 3. 420). The passage in *Comus* has been referred to Silius Italicus 14. 471–474. The music of Daphnis

> Mulcebat silvas, non umquam tempore eodem
> Siren adsuetos effudit in æquore cantus;
> Scyllæi tacuere canes; stetit atra Charybdis.

SEA-GODS.—P. L. 3. 604; C. 24-29, 835, 867-889; Lyc. 89.

The 'tributary gods' of *C.* 24 seem to be distinguished from the 'blue-haired deities' (29), though no such distinction exists in the classics. Strictly speaking, none but Neptune carried a trident, if we except Nereus (Verg. *Æn.* 2. 418). 'Blue-haired' seems to be an adaptation of Poseidon's epithet κυανοχαῖτα (*Il.* 13. 563; 14. 390). The Nereids are κυανοπλόκαμοι in Quintus Smyrnæus 5. 345, and Ovid calls the marine gods 'cærulii' (*Met.* 2. 8; see *Neptune*).

Much of the detailed work of identifying Milton's classical sources under this head has been done by Newton. Neptune, Leucothea, and the sirens are discussed in their respective places. In Homer *Oceanus* is the personification of the streams which encircle the earth. He lives at the ends of the earth, and is called 'father of the gods' (*Il.* 14. 301 f.). Milton's epithet 'great' has an antecedent in 21. 193 ff.: 'Against the son of Cronus it is not possible to fight. For him not even king Acheloïos is a match, nor yet the great strength of deep-flowing Ocean.' Hesiod also calls Oceanus 'great' (*Theog.* 20). In *P. L.* 1. 510 Oceanus is a Titan. See *Titans*.

Tethys was the wife of Oceanus (*Theog.* 337), and both were children of Earth and Heaven (133 ff.). Tethys is called 'lovely' (136), and 'august' or 'revered' (368). Her 'grave majestic pace' (*C.* 870) suggests her appearance at the wedding of the Medway and the Thames (Spenser, *F. Q.* 4. 11. 18):

> Next came the aged Ocean and his Dame
> Old Tethys, th' oldest two of all the rest.

In Homer (*Il.* 18. 141) *Nereus* is called 'the Ancient One of the Sea,' whose house is a bright cave in the depths of the sea (50). Apollonius of Rhodes (4. 772) locates it in the Ægean. Nereus was the oldest son of Pontus, says Hesiod (*Theog.* 234). They call him the Ancient One 'because he is unfailing and gentle, neither does he forget the laws, but knows just and gentle counsel.' Vergil calls him 'grandævus' (*Georg.* 4. 392). Servius (on *Georg.* 4. 402) says that most of the sea-gods are aged: 'Albent enim eorum capita spumis aquarum.'

When Odysseus landed in Egypt he was told that to gain knowledge of his return home he must catch the prophetic sea-god, *Proteus*, when he should come on shore to count his seals. 'And when he has told their tale and beheld them, he will lay him down in the midst, as a shepherd mid the sheep of his flock' (*Od.* 4. 412 ff.). In the light of this figure editors explain Proteus' hook (*C.* 872) as a shepherd's crook. Cf. Verg. *Georg.* 4. 433; Hor. *C.* 1. 2. 7; Milt. *Eleg.* 3. 26; *Ep. Dam.* 99; Spenser, *C. C.* 248. In captivity Proteus would 'take all manner of shapes of things that creep upon the earth, of water likewise, and of fierce fire burning' (*Od.* 4. 417 f.). Thus when Odysseus seized him, he took the shapes of a lion, a snake, a pard, a boar, then of water and of a tree (456 ff.).

Proteus is a 'Carpathian wizard' in Vergil (*Georg.* 4 387): 'Est in Carpathio Neptuni gurgite vates Cæruleus Proteus.' Cf. also 'Carpathius vates' of Ov. *Met.* 11. 249. The Carpathian sea, to which Vergil refers as the home of Proteus, took its name from Carpathos, an island in its midst, between Crete and Rhodes. Servius says that by 'Carpathian' Vergil may mean 'Egyptian' since 'Carpathos is an island of Egypt.' The Homeric tradition was that Proteus dwelt in the depths of the sea around Pharos, a day's journey from Egypt (*Od.* 4. 355, 385).

Triton was a sea-monster whose body, according to Apollonius (4. 1610 ff.), resembled that of the gods, but supported the forked tail of a fish. Pausanias (9. 21. 1) says that the Triton was covered with scales, and Pliny (*N. H.* 9. 4. 5) speaks thus of Triton and the Nereids: 'squamis modo hispido corpore, etiam, qua humanam effigiem habent'; cf. *C.* 873. This divinity appears as Herald of the Sea in Ov. *Met.* 1. 333 ff., where Neptune calls him to give signals to the waves and rivers. Cf. *Lyc.* 89. He sounds them with a shell: 'Cava buccina sumitur illi *Tortilis*, in latum quæ turbine crescit ab imo.'

Glaucus was originally a fisherman of Anthedon, who, having eaten of a certain herb, became immortal, and was changed to a sea-divinity. The scholium on Apollon. Rh. 1. 1310 says that he was an old man when he took his place in the sea. It was said that he afterwards prophesied (Athen. 7. 297; Paus. 9. 22. 6), and Apollonius calls him soothsayer (1. 1310). Spenser mentions 'Glaucus, that wise southsayes understood' (*F. Q.* 4. 11. 13).

Thetis was a Nereid, and the mother of Achilles (*Il.* 18. 35). In *C.* 877 Milton adapts Homer's ἀργυρόπεζα, 'silver-footed,' a frequent epithet of the goddess (*Il.* 18. 127, 146).

SEA-NYMPHS.—Pens. 21. See Nymphs.

SEMELE.—P. R. 2. 187.

Semele was a daughter of Cadmus, king of Thebes, and the mother of Dionysus (Bacchus) by Zeus. Her beauty is mentioned by Diodorus (4. 2), and in the Homeric hymn to Dionysus (6. 58). In *P. R.* 2. 187 Milton seems to refer to Ovid's narrative of the fate of Semele. She resented the disguise and secrecy of Jove in his visit to her, but when he appeared in his glory of thunder and lightning, she was consumed, and Bacchus was born. Cf. *Eleg.* 5. 91.

SILENCE.—P. L. 4. 604; 7. 106; Pens. 56; C. 250, 557. See Sleep.

SIRENS.—S. M. 1; Arc. 63; C. 253, 878.

Circe warned Odysseus against the sirens in *Od.* 12. 39, saying, 'To the sirens first shalt thou come, who bewitch all men, whosoever shall come to them. Whoso draws nigh them unwittingly, and hears the sound of the sirens' voice, never doth he see wife or babes stand by him on his return, . . . but the sirens enchant him with their clear song, sitting in the meadow.' The adventure with the sirens is told in 12. 166–200. According to 167 there were two of them, whom Eustathius, the commentator, calls Aglaopheme and Thelxiepeia (1709). He adds that later writers tell of three sirens, Parthenope, Ligeia, and Leukosia; cf. *C.* 879, 880. Strabo says that the Neapolitans claimed to possess the tomb of Parthenope (1. 23, 26; 5. 246). Later writers, such as Vergil (*Æn.* 5. 864), represent the sirens sitting upon rocks rather than in a meadow (cf. *C.* 881). That these rocks were diamond or adamantine does not seem to be stated in the classics. Strabo says that some located the sirens in Sicily, on the promontory of Pelorus, and others at the Sirenusæ, off the promontory of Minerva, between the bays of Naples and Pæstum. These three small islands are not high, though desert and rocky (1. 22).

The sirens nowhere in the classics are represented as combing their hair, but we do find the following lines in Vergil (*Georg.* 4. 336, 337):

> Drymoque, Xanthoque, Ligeaque, Phyllodoceque.
> Cæsariem effusæ nitidam per candida colla.

See *Fates* in connection with *Arc.* 63.

SLEEP.—P. L. 706; Pens. 146-150; C. 554.

To the early poets Sleep was the brother of Death, and a subduer of men (*Il.* 14. 231 ff.; Hes. *Theog.* 756 ff.). The epithet 'dewy-feathered' of *Pens.* 146 is evidently the equivalent for 'humentibus alis,' in Stat. *Theb.* 10. 148, which is in turn explained by 'Rore madens Stygio' of *Theb.* 198. As early as Homer the idea of moisture is connected with sleep and its influence. In *Il.* 2. 19 the dream found Agamemnon sleeping, with 'ambrosial slumber poured over him,' and the expression is varied in 14. 165; *Od.* 2. 395. Among the Latin poets the figure occurs frequently. It is suggested in Vergil's 'Fessos sopor irrigat artus' (*Æn.* 3. 511; cf. 5. 854), and is elaborated in Stat. *Theb.* 5. 199; 2. 143, where the god Somnus pours his influence upon mortals from a horn. Milton uses it without mythological significance in *P. L.* 4. 614:

> The timely dew of sleep,
> Now falling with soft slumberous weight, inclines
> Our eye-lids.

Cf. *P. L.* 9. 1044. On the other hand, Sleep is winged, as appears by Hom. *Il.* 14. 287, and by Ovid's epithet 'plumeus' (*Met.* 11. 611). Cf. Senec. *Herc. Fur.* 1068; Stat. *Theb.* 10. 137; Tibull. 2. 1. 89.

Following the poet's petition for Sleep (*Pens.* 139–146), is another petition:

> And let some strange mysterious dream
> Wave at his wings, in airy stream
> Of lively portraiture displayed,
> Softly on my eyelids laid.

The meaning of these lines has been much disputed. The passage among the classics which approaches it most closely is in the *Punici* of Silius Italicus (10. 337–371), where Juno urges Sleep to visit Hannibal with his dreams. As the god approaches the warrior,

> quatit inde soporas
> Devexo capiti pennas, oculisque quietem
> Irrorat, tangens Lethæa tempora virga.

Then follow baneful dreams in order. In his vision Hannibal now girds the Tiber with his army, now stands before the very walls of Rome, and now in triumph ascends the Tarpeian rock, whence he sees the smoking plains about the city. The passage just cited would seem to support the explanation of Milton, that in airy stream the order of visions follows the movement of the wings of Sleep, as he waves them over the sleeping mortal. But withal, our poet shows greater delicacy than his original, and is appropriately indefinite. Compare the description of dreams in *Met.* 11. 592–649, *Morpheus*.

The Attendant Spirit in *Comus* says (552) that when the uproar of the revellers ceased, the sudden silence

> Gave respite to the drowsy-flighted steeds
> That draw the litter of close-curtained Sleep.

Macbeth 2. 1. 51 and *Romeo and Juliet* 3. 2. 5 have been cited as originals of 'close-curtained,' and 2 *Henry VI* 4. 1. 3–6 as an original of 'drowsy-flighted.' To this last may be added the 'drowsy race of night' of *King John* 3. 3. 39. Many editors, however, prefer the reading 'drowsy frighted.' Warton cited the fact that Sleep drives the horses of Night in Claudian, *De Bello Gildonico* 213: 'Humentes jam Noctis equos, Lethæaque Somnus Frena regens, tacito volvebat sidera curru.' He also cites Stat. *Theb.* 2. 59. To these may be added Tibull. 2. 1. 89, where Night's chariot is followed by the stars; 'Postque venit tacitus fuscis circumdatus alis Somnus.' Sleep sometimes drove the chariot of the moon, as in *Theb.* 12. 307, where Juno meeting Cynthia, says: 'Hunc quoque, qui curru madidas tibi pronus habenas Ducit, in Aonios vigiles demitte Soporem.' The epithet 'lenti,' used of Night's team in Valerius Flaccus 3. 211, and the 'Lethea frena' of Claudian may be compared with 'drowsy-flighted.'

Milton associates Sleep with Night and Silence in personification (*P. L.* 7. 105; *C.* 557), but without well-defined reference to the classics. Ovid's grouping is not dissimilar, when in *Met.* 11. 602, 606 he says that in the cave of Sleep 'mute Rest (Quies) has her abode,' and from the juice of the poppies growing there 'humid Night gathers sleep, and spreads it over the darkened earth.' We find 'mute Silence' mentioned in *Pens.* 56. According to Statius, at the door of Sleep stands 'opaca Quies,' and there sit the Silentia with folded wings (*Theb.* 10. 89). In *C.* 249 the wings of Silence are distended.

STYX, STYGIAN.—P. L. 1. 239; 2. 506, 577, 875; 3. 14; 10. 453; L'Al. 3; C. 132. See **Rivers of Hell.**

SUN.—See **Apollo.**

SYLVAN.—P. L. 4. 707; P. R. 2. 191; Pens. 134; C. 268. See **Wood-gods.**

SYRINX.—P. R. 2. 188; Arc. 106. See **Pan.**

TANTALUS.—P. L. 2. 614; S. A. 500.

'Now if any man ever had honor of the guardians of Olympus, Tantalus was that man; but his high fortune he could not digest, and by excess thereof won him an overwhelming woe, in that the Father hath hung above him a mighty stone that he would fain ward from his head' (Pind. *Ol.* 1. 55 ff.). Pindar adds that his crime was the theft of ambrosia and nectar from the table of the gods, at which he was a favored guest. The stories of Tantalus vary, but in *S. A.* 500 Milton seems to refer to the version that the crime of Tantalus was the revelation of divine secrets. This is implied in Eur. *Or.* 10, and asserted by Tzetzes (*Chiliades Histor. Variarum* 471). The punishment of Tantalus, as related in *P. L.* 2. 614, follows the version found in the scholium on Eur. *Or.* 7. He was afflicted with terrible thirst in the abyss of Hades, and compelled to stand in water up to his chin, but, as he attempted to drink, the water receded. Classical writers do not place him in Lethe, as does Milton with greater effectiveness. The suffering of Tantalus was frequently cited by Latin writers (cf. Hor. *Sat.* 1. 1. 68; Ov. *Met.* 4. 457; Verg. *Æn.* 6. 604; Cic. *Tusc. Disput.* 1. 5).

Beside the reference to Tantalus in *S. A.* 501, Milton seems to refer to the somewhat similar case of Prometheus, who, having stolen fire from the gods, gave it to mortals. For his offence Zeus had him chained to a cliff of the Caucasus, where his liver was torn each day by an eagle, and renewed each night. The story is first told by Hesiod in *Theog.* 521 ff., but the principal source is the *Prometheus Bound* of Æschylus, which deals with the sufferings of the hero; cf. especially 1–35. The account of Hesiod more closely resembles that of Milton in one respect; he differs from Æschylus in his apparent disapproval of Prometheus. Horace associates Tantalus with Prometheus in *Epod.* 17. 66.

TARTARUS.—P. L. 2. 69, 858; 7. 238; 6. 54; S. A. 500.

In *Il.* 8. 10 Zeus addresses the assembly of gods, and threatens any who shall disobey him, saying: 'I will take and cast him into misty Tartarus, right far away, where is the deepest gulf beneath the earth; there are the gate of iron and threshold of bronze, as far beneath Hades as heaven is high above the earth.' Hesiod describes Tartarus in *Theog.* 721 ff. It is surrounded with a brazen wall, and about its neck or mouth night is enfolded in triple thickness. Above it are the foundations of earth and sea. Here, 'in the gloomy gulf' (cf. *P. L.* 2. 858), are confined the vanquished Titans, guarded by Briareos and his brothers. Vergil, in his more elaborate description (*Æn.* 6. 548–627), names the evil-doers who are suffering there. Tartarus proper is not represented as fiery (cf. *P. L.* 6. 55; 2. 69), though such an idea is not strange in view of such general representations of Hades as are found in Verg. *Æn.* 6. 240; Sil. Ital. 13. 570. The fiery river Phlegethon would reinforce this idea (see *Rivers of Hell*). Vergil speaks of 'Tartareus Phlegethon' (*Æn.* 6. 551), using the adjective in the general sense of 'infernal,' which it carries in the 'Tartarean sulphur' of *P. L.* 2. 69; cf. 7. 238.

See *Chaos, Erebus, Titans, Night.*

TETHYS.—C. 870. See **Sea-gods.**

THAMMUZ.—P. L. 1. 446; C. N. 204. See **Adonis.**

THAMYRIS.—P. L. 3. 35.

In *Il.* 2. 594 Homer speaks of Dorion, 'where the Muses met Thamyris, the Thracian, and made an end of his singing, as he was faring from Oichalia, from Eurytos the Oichalian; for he averred with boasting that he would conquer, even did the Muses themselves sing against him, the daughters of ægis-bearing Zeus; but they in their anger maimed him; moreover, they took from him the high gift of song, and made him to forget his harping.' Euripides refers to Thamyris in *Rhesus* 925, and says that he was punished with blindness.

THEBES.—P. L.1. 578; 3. 36; P. R. 4. 572; Pens. 99.

That part of the story of Thebes related by Milton in *P. R.* 4. 572–575 corresponds with the version of Apollodorus (3. 5. 8). The latter describes the Sphinx as having the face of a woman, the breast, gait, and rear of a lion, and the wings of a bird. This monster, sent by the angry Hera, took up her position on the Phician mount. Milton calls it 'the Ismenian steep' (*P. R.* 4. 574). Pausanias speaks of a hill at Thebes called Ismenian, from the river Ismenus, which flows by. It was the seat of Ismenian Apollo (9. 10. 2), but is nowhere spoken of as the hill of the Sphinx, and Pausanias also says that she remained on Phicium (9. 26. 2). It is probable, however, that Milton uses 'Ismenian' in the general sense of 'Theban,' according to the practice of later writers (Stat. *Theb.* 1. 673; 7. 124). The Sphinx proposed the following riddle: What is that which has one voice, and goes on four legs, on two, and on three? While this remained unanswered the Sphinx continued to devour the Thebans, until Œdipus

6

finally guessed correctly that it is Man, who at first creeps, then walks upright, and at last goes with a staff. Thus he escaped destruction by the Sphinx, who threw herself down from the height. As his reward, he married the queen, who proved afterward to be his mother. This complication, with those which ensued, was a theme for tragic poets (*Pens.* 99). Of the extant plays, Æschylus has dealt with the legends in *The Seven against Thebes*, Sophocles in the *Œdipus Tyrannus*, the *Œdipus at Colonus*, and the *Antigone*, Euripides in the *Bacchæ* and the *Phœnissæ*, and Seneca in the *Œdipus* and the *Phœnissæ*. Tiresias (*P. L.* 3. 36) is the old seer, who throughout is the spokesman of the gods. He was blind because, as some say, he had revealed in his prophecy the secrets of the gods (Apollod. 3. 6. 7).

After Œdipus died, his sons, Eteocles and Polynices, quarrelled over the succession. Polynices, having withdrawn to Argos, gathered about him six other heroes, who encamped against Thebes. To these warriors Milton refers in *P. L.* 1. 578. They are described at length by the messenger in Æsch. *Seven against Thebes* 375–652, and a list of those who fought is given by Statius (*Theb.* 4. 1–344). Apollodorus also tells the story of the fight (3. 6).

THEMIS.—P. L. 11. 14; Son. 21. 2.

Themis, really a personification of justice, in Homer is the goddess 'who looseth and gathereth the meetings of men' (*Od.* 2. 68; cf. *Il.* 20. 4). Pindar mentions her as 'sitting (in judgment) by Zeus'; cf. *Hom. Hy.* 23.

In early days Themis presided over the oracle at Delphi, which later fell to Apollo (see Ov. *Met.* 1. 321 and *Deucalion*).

THESTYLIS.—L'Al. 88. See **Corydon.**

THETIS.—C. 877. See **Sea-gods.**

THONE.—C. 675. See **Helena.**

THRACIAN BARD.—P. L. 7. 34. See **Orpheus.**

THRASCIAS.—P. L. 10. 700. See **Winds.**

THYESTES.—P. L. 10. 688. See **Pelops.**

THYRSIS.—L'Al. 83; C. 494, 512, 657. See **Corydon.**

TIRESIAS.—P. L. 3. 36. See **Thebes.**

TITANS.—P. L. 1. 198, 510; 7. 605; D. F. I. 47; C. 804.

According to Hes. *Theog.* 133, 207, the Titans were sons of Earth and Heaven, and were named by their father. Apollodorus in 1. 1. 3 mentions six of them—Oceanus, Coius, Hyperion, Crius, Iapetus, and Cronus. In *P. L.* 1. 510 Milton speaks of Oceanus as the first-born, and as afterward deprived of his birthright by the younger Saturn (Cronus). Saturn usurped his rights by responding to his mother's appeal for vengeance upon Heaven, who had banished her sons, the hundred-handed giants (*Theog.* 164 ff.; cf. Apollod. 1. 1. 4). The brood of Oceanus is in part enumerated by Hesiod (*Theog.* 337-368). More than three thousand daughters had he, and as many were his sons, the rivers.

The battle waged by Cronus and the Titans against Zeus, is described by Hesiod (*Theog.* 664-721; cf. Apollod. 1. 2. 1). Both sides fought with such strength that the shock was felt even in Tartarus. Zeus hurled his thunderbolt, and blinded the eyes of the Titans, mighty though they were. At length by a compromise between Earth and Zeus, who promised to release her hundred-handed sons, the Titans were vanquished and hurled into Tartarus. See also *Saturn*, *Sea-gods*, and *Earth*.

TRITON.—C. 873; Lyc. 89. See **Sea-gods.**

TROY.—P. L. 9. 16; Pens. 100. See **Ilium.**

TRUTH.—D. F. I. 54; C. N. 141. See **Justice.**

TURNUS.—P. L. 9. 17.

In the enumeration of great epic themes in *P. L.* 9. 15-19 occurs the rage of 'Turnus for Lavinia disespoused.' The story is told in *Æn.* 7-12. Latinus, whom Æneas found reigning in Latium, had promised his daughter Lavinia to Turnus, but, warned by a dream, he made a final choice of Æneas. A Fury, sent by Juno, aroused the rage of Turnus (7. 413, 466), which was renewed in 12. 1-2. The character of Turnus is fierce and intrepid throughout the struggle.

TWINS.—P. L. 10. 674.

In the passage cited Milton speaks of a sign in the zodiac as 'the Spartan Twins.' This is a reference to the Dioscuri, Castor and Polydeuces, sons of Tyndareus and Leda of Sparta (*Od.* 11. 299; cf. *Il.* 3. 236 ff.). According to Hyg. *Astr.* 2. 22 they were changed into the constellation Gemini by command of Jove, as a reward for their mutual affection and fidelity.

TYPHON.—P. L. 1. 199; 232; 2. 539; C. N. 226.

Typhon, or Typhoeus, was the last and mightiest son of Earth (Hes. *Theog.* 821; Apollod. 1. 6. 3). He is described by Hesiod as having arms and feet invincible. From his shoulders grew a hundred serpents' heads whose eyes flashed fire, and from each was heard a voice, which resembled now a bull, now a lion, now a whelp, or a hissing serpent. Apollodorus says that above his thighs he was human in form, towering above the mountains, and striking the stars. Below his thighs he wore the great folds of serpents which rose about his head (cf. *C. N.* 226). Fire flashed from his mouth and eyes, and the gods fled before him. But Zeus met him in a battle whose shock was felt even in Tartarus, and, after vanquishing him with the thunderbolt, overwhelmed him, as usually related, beneath Ætna (cf. Æsch. *Prom.* 360 ff.; schol. on Pind. *P.* 1. 31; *P. L.* 1. 232). Pindar in *P.* 1. 32 speaks of the retreat of Typhon in the Cilician cave, which Apollodorus calls the Corycian cave. It was near the coast, about fifty miles west of Tarsus (cf. *P. L.* 1. 199). Nonnus speaks of Tarsus and Corycium as the scene of Typhon's exploits (1. 258).

The list of Egyptian gods in *C. N.* 211–226 is based upon Plutarch's treatise on Isis and Osiris. Typhon is the name which Plutarch gave to the Egyptian god Set, and it is to Typhon of Egypt that Milton refers in *C. N.* 226. The identification of Typhon with Set appears also in Herodotus (2. 156; 3. 5). According to Plutarch Typhon represents the power of evil as opposed to the power of good in the person of Osiris, his brother. The latter he entrapped in a chest, but an avenger of the crime appeared in the person of Horus, or Orus, the foster-son of Isis, the wife of Osiris. Typhon was vanquished in a single-handed combat. Plutarch says that in Apollinopolis the crocodiles were hunted down, from a belief that Typhon escaped from Horus in the form of a crocodile. But when Milton characterizes Typhon as 'huge' and 'ending in snaky twine,' he seems to adapt the Greek description as cited above.

TYRIAN CYNOSURE.—C. 342. See Calisto.

ULYSSES.—P. L. 2. 1019; 9. 441; V. E. 50; C. 637.

The relation of Ulysses to Laertes is beautifully set forth in *Od.* 24. 315-360. What use Milton makes of his story is discussed under *Alcinous, Hermes,* and, in connection with *P. L.* 2. 1019, *Scylla.*

URANIA.—P. L. 7. 1, 31. See Muses.

VENUS.—P. L. 5. 382; 9. 19; P. R. 2. 214; L'Al. 14; C. 124, 1002.

From Homer down, Venus (Aphrodite) is generally regarded as the goddess of love. The reference to her charmed girdle (*P. R.* 2. 214) finds an explanation in *Il.* 14. 187–221. Hera, in her preparation to beguile Zeus, applied to Aphrodite, and obtained on a false pretense 'the broidered girdle, fair-wrought, wherein are all her enchantments; therein are love, and desire, and loving converse, that steals the wits even of the wise.' Then, with the girdle in her breast, she met and fascinated Zeus. See *Jove.*

Milton (*P. L.* 5. 382) describes Eve as fairer than

> the fairest goddess feigned
> Of three that in Mount Ida naked strove.

To determine the poet's exact source in this case seems impossible. We find a reference to the story in a doubtful passage of the *Iliad* (24. 28 ff.). Hyginus (*Fab.* 92) tells it as follows. Discordia, who was offended because she was not invited to the wedding of Peleus and

Thetis, sent an apple for the fairest goddess. Venus, Juno, and Minerva each claimed the prize. The judgment was referred to Paris, who met the goddesses in Mount Ida and gave the prize to Venus. Cf. also Eur. *Iph. Aul.* 1289 ff.; *Troad.* 925 ff.; Paus. 5. 19. 1.

In *P. L.* 9. 19 is a reference to the *Æneid*, the story of 'Cytherea's son' (see *Juno*). The relationship of Æneas to the goddess is prominent throughout Vergil's epic (cf. 1. 229 ff.; 8. 370 ff.). The name Cytherea, frequent among Latin poets (*Æn.* 1. 257; Ov. *Met.* 4. 190; 10. 640), was probably derived from the island Cythera, sacred to Aphrodite (Paus. 3. 23. 1; Ov. *Her.* 7. 59; Verg. *Æn.* 1. 680; 10. 51).

See also *Adonis* and *Graces*.

VERTUMNUS.—P. L. 9. 395. See **Pomona.**

VESTA.—Pens. 23. See **Saturn.**

VULCAN.—P. L. 1. 732-751; C. 655.

The passage first cited is an adaptation to Milton's theme of the god Hephæstus, the Latin Vulcan. Diodorus Siculus says that men considered him the inventor of the arts of working iron, bronze, gold, silver, and, in fact, all the materials worked by means of fire (5. 74). Thus he is the patron god of all artisans. Milton's principal source, however, is to be found in Homer, where Hephæstus appears again and again as the god of fire, and the craftsman renowned for his skill (*Il.* 21. 331 ff.). Thus in *Il.* 18 we find him fashioning curious tripods (373), and he speaks of the 'cunning work of bronze, brooches, and spiral arm-bands, and cups, and necklaces,' which he had made for the gods (400 f.). Above all is the splendid armor of Achilles (478-613; cf. *Od.* 7. 92). As an architect he built his own house, 'imperishable, starlike, far seen among the dwellings of Immortals, a house of bronze' (370). In 20. 11 are mentioned 'the polished colonnades which Hephæstus in the cunning of his heart had wrought for father Zeus,' and we are told in 1. 607 that for each of the gods Hephæstus had built a palace. The glorious gates of the Sun, described by Ovid (*Met.* 2. 4-30), were made by Hephæstus, or Mulciber, a name connected with *mulceo*, to smooth, says Macrobius (6. 5. 2). Cf. *P. L.* 1. 740.

The story of his fall from heaven (740-746) seems to be founded upon the god's own account in *Il.* 1. 590 ff.: 'Yea, once ere this, . . . he (Zeus) caught me by my foot, and hurled me from the heavenly threshold; all day I flew, and at the set of sun I fell in Lemnos'; cf. *Eleg.* 7. 81; *Nat. non Pati Sen.* 23.

C. 655 is commonly referred to Verg. *Æn.* 8. 191 ff., where the monster Cacus is described as a son of Vulcan, 'illius atros Ore vomens ignis.' He was vanquished in a fight with Hercules, after attempting to overcome his foe by emitting great volumes of smoke (251–255).

WINDS.—P. L. 4. 329; 5. 16; 10. 695-706; D. F. I. 8; L'Al. 19; Son. 20. 6.

In the main Milton follows classical tradition when he makes the north the home of fierce winds (*P. L.* 10. 695). Boreas was generally supposed to come from Thrace (*Orph. Hy.* 80. 2; *Il.* 23. 229). In 697 the 'brazen dungeon' is evidently a reference to the lordship of Æolus over the winds in the Æolian Islands. With this expression may be compared Vergil's 'vinclis et carcere' (*Æn.* 1. 54). Valerius Flaccus describes the prison as 'in monte chalybs iterataque muris saxa' (1. 593). In Aristotle (*Meteor.* 2. 6) we find mention and description of most of the winds, and in fact, of the several passages in classical literature whose influence may be seen in these lines of *Paradise Lost*, the influence of Aristotle is most apparent, though Milton of course adds a suggestion of personification. According to Aristotle, Boreas, the north wind, Cæcias, the northeast, Argestes, the northwest, and Thrascias from north-northwest, form one group. The north winds bring the snow and hail. In *P. L.* 10. 697 the north winds are 'armed with ice.' The expression has been referred (Richardson in Todd) to Claudian 23. 69 ff.:

> Ceu turbine rauco
> Quum gravis armatur Boreas, glacieque nivali
> Hispidus et Getica concretus grandine pennas,
> Bella cupit, pelagus, silvas, camposque sonoro
> Flamine rapturus.

This military characterization of the winds is to be found elsewhere (Ov. *Met.* 1. 65; Verg. *Æn.* 1. 82), and is used again in *D. F. I.* 8, where Aquilo is called winter's charioteer.

According to Aristotle, Notus, the south wind, and Lips (Apricus or Afer, Senec. *Nat. Quæst.* 5. 16. 6), from west-southwest, form another group. Lips is moist (cf. etymology), and brings rain. He is described by Vergil as 'creber procellis' (*Æn.* 1. 85), and by Seneca as 'furibundus et ruens.' Eurus is an east or east-southeast wind. Zephyrus is the west wind. In the passage under discussion Milton follows Homer in making Zephyrus a stormy wind (*Il.* 23. 200, 208, 214, 215). In the *Odyssey*, however, it is soft and cool (4. 567), and by western writers is regarded as the gentle bringer of spring (Verg. *Georg.* 1. 43; Hor. *C.* 4. 7. 10; cf. *P. L.* 4. 329; 5. 16; *L'Al.* 19; see *Flora, Aurora*). By Lucretius it is called 'Veris prænuntius (5. 736). Favonius, another name of Zephyrus, occurs in *Son.* 20. 6; *Eleg.* 3. 47. The context in the sonnet suggests Hor. *C.* 1. 4. 1:

> Solvitur acris hiems grata vice veris et Favoni.

In *D. F. I.* 8 we find a reference to the story of the rape of Orithyia, daughter of Erectheus, king of Athens, by Boreas, or, as

Milton calls him, Aquilo (Plin. *N. H.* 2. 46). The story is told in Ovid, *Met.* 6. 677. When the god's prayers availed nothing, he raised a great storm, and bore the maiden away on his wings in a cloud.

WOOD-GODS.—P. L. 4. 707, 708; P. R. 2. 191, 297, 374; Pens. 134; C. 268; Lyc. 34.

Milton refers indefinitely to the wood-gods in *P. R.* 2. 297 (cf. 374), and elsewhere calls them by name. In *Met.* 1. 192 Ovid mentions the 'rustica numina, nymphæ, Faunique, satyrique, et monticolæ silvani.' See also *Pan* and *Nymphs*.

Faunus was a Latin divinity of the woods, sometimes confounded with the Greek Pan (Ov. *Fast.* 3. 84, 299–316). In Verg. *Æn.* 10. 551 he is called 'sylvicola.' In *Fast.* 5. 99 he is 'bicornis,' and in 101 'semicaper.' We find frequent mention of an indefinite number of fauni. It was when Silenus began his song 'that you might see fauns and wild beasts bounding to the measure' (Verg. *Ecl.* 6. 27; cf. *Lyc.* 34).

The fauns seem to have been the Latin form of the Greek *Satyrs*. Ovid (*Met.* 6. 392 f.) speaks of them as 'ruricolæ, silvarum numina, fauni, Et satyri fratres.' Horace (*C.* 2. 19. 4) mentions the 'aures Capripedum satyrorum acutas.' The ancients frequently represented them in the dance (Ov. *Met.* 14. 637; Hor. *C.* 1. 1. 31; Verg. *Ecl.* 5. 73), as does Milton in *Lyc.* 34.

According to Vergil (*Æn.* 8. 601), *Sylvan* was the god of the fields and flocks. Servius in his comment says that this was the popular belief, but that more strictly he was a god of the woods. The description of his grove (*Æn.* 8. 597–599) is in harmony with the descriptions in *P. L.* 4. 707; *Pens.* 134; cf. *Eleg.* 5. 121. The plural *sylvani* may refer to a whole class of wood-divinities, like those already described (Ov. *Met.* 1. 192; cf. *P. R.* 2. 191). See also *Eleg.* 5. 119–125.

Milton refers in *P. R.* 2. 191 to the fear which the nymphs had of different wood-divinities. Thus Syrinx (Ov. *Met.* 1. 692) is said to have escaped the satyrs more than once, and in *Fast.* 1. 397 we find the words, 'in Venerem satyrorum prona juventus.' Hor. *C.* 3. 18 begins, 'Faune, nympharum fugientum amator.'

INDEXES

I

INDEX OF AUTHORS

Achilles Tatius, 69.

Æschylus, xlii, lxxxiv, 14, 20, 28, 32, 34, 36, 61, 63, 68, 74, 80, 82, 84.

Ammian, 9, 37.

Anacreontics, 39, 44.

Anthology, Latin, 35.

Anthology, Palatine, 11, 31, 72.

Apollodorus, xlii, xliv, and N., 5, 7, 8, 13, 16, 17, 18, 19, 28, 35, 36, 37, 38, 41, 44, 69, 81, 82, 83.

Apollonius the Grammarian, lvii N.

Apollonius of Rhodes, xviii, xlii, xliv, 8, 13, 20, 29, 34, 35, 38, 43, 58, 69, 76, 77.

Apuleius, 26, 39, 44, 52, 53.

Aratus, xliii, 18, 35, 51, 70.

Ariosto, xlv N.

Aristides, 9, 39, 42.

Aristophanes, 42.

Aristotle, xliv N., 86.

Athenæus, xliii, lxvi, lxvii, 12, 59, 70, 77.

Augustine, 52.

Ausonius, 57, 65.

Bacon, xii.

Bion, 15, 54.

Boccaccio, xlv N., 27.

Bochart, xii, 7.

Boiardo, xlv N., 58.

Botticelli, lxvi, lxvii.

Buchanan, 61.

Callimachus, 20, 44, 50.

Catullus, 42, 46, 54.

Chaucer, xlv N.

Cicero, xliii, 25, 62, 75, 80.

Claudian, xii, xlii, 9, 29, 36, 42, 46, 63, 79.

Clement of Alexandria, 10.

Cypria, lxvii, 59.

Daniel, 48.

Dante, xxvii, xlv N., liii N., 15.

Dictys, 55.

Dio Cassius, 21.

Diodorus Siculus, xii, xlii, lviii N., 10, 17, 37, 43, 51, 60, 61, 72, 74, 77, 85.

Dionysius of Halicarnassus, 74.

Eratosthenes, 35.

Euripides, xlii, 4, 6, 10, 13, 15, 16, 20, 21, 26, 27, 31, 36, 43–47, 63, 66, 68, 69, 75, 80–82, 85.

Eusebius, xii, xlv N., xlvii N.

Eustathius Macrembolites, 4.

Eustathius of Thessalonica, 78.

Ezekiel, 3.

Fletcher, John, 50.

Fulgentius, 29.

Gellius, 49.

Geoffrey of Monmouth, 8.

Georgius Cedrenus, 63.

Gregory Nazianzen, 9.

Guido, xxvi, xlv N.

Hermippus, lxvi, lxvii, 59.

Herodotus, xlii, 8, 14, 23, 55, 69, 84.

Hesiod, xviii, xxi, xxii, and N.,
xxvii, xxxv, xlii, xliv, xlv,
lxix, lxx, lxxxiv, 7, 11, 15,
17–19, 22, 27, 30, 33, 34, 37,
38, 42–44, 46–48, 51, 54, 57, 60,
61, 63–66, 68, 70, 72–76, 78,
80–83.

Hesychius, 4.

Holbein, lxxiii.

Homer, x, xi, xviii, xxii N., xxvii,
xxxiv, xxxv, xlii, xliv, xlv,
lxix, lxxxiv, 3–7, 10–12, 14–17,
22, 23, 27, 28, 30–34, 36, 38,
40–44, 46–51, 53, 55–59, 61–65,
73, 75–78, 80–86; *scholia*, 11,
16, 49, 75; see Eustathius of
Thessalonica.

Homeric Hymns, xxii N., xlii,
lx N., 10–12, 14, 16, 20, 28, 29,
39, 42, 52, 54, 55, 58, 67, 71,
77.

Horace, xii, xxii N., xlii, xliv, 29,
36, 38, 51, 52, 54, 61, 65, 66,
70, 77, 80, 86, 87.

Hyginus, xliii, xliv, 5, 7, 16, 18,
19, 27, 30, 53, 55, 69, 70, 71,
75, 83, 84.

Isaiah, 48, 54.

Isidorus, 68.

Jerome, 46.

Job, xxvi, 48.

Johannes Phocas, 9.

Jonson, 46, 60.

Justin, 7.

Juvenal, 12, 13, 24, 25, 51.

Juvencus, 63.

Lactantius, xlv N., 27, 70.

Lavater, xlvii.

Leonardo da Vinci, lxxiv.

Libanius, 9.

Livy, 33, 49, 54.

Lucan, 8, 29.

Lucian, 3, 7, 31, 72.

Lucretius, xliii, 15, 53, 61, 86.

Macrobius, xliii, 7, 28, 48, 71, 72,
85.

Martial, 43, 59.

Memling, lxxv.

Moschus, 5, 57.

Nonnus, 18, 57, 84.

Orphic Hymns, xviii, xlii, lxvii,
lxix, 3, 15, 22, 52, 56, 59, 60,
63, 65, 67, 68, 72, 86.

Ovid, xii, xviii, xxi, xxvii, xxviii,
xxxiv, xxxv, xlii, xliv, xlv,
lxvi, and N., lxvii, lxix, lxx,
3, 5–16, 18–20, 22–32, 35, 36,
38–41, 43, 44, 46, 47, 50–61,
63–67, 69–80, 82, 85, 87.

Pausanius, xlii, 4, 6, 8, 9, 14, 21,
29, 33, 34, 39, 44, 54, 57, 62,
66, 67, 77, 81, 85.

Philostratus, 9, 51.

Pindar, xlii, xliv, liv, 4, 5, 7, 8, 11,
13, 17, 21, 30, 32, 37–40, 57, 80,
84; *scholium*, 84.

Plato, x, xi, xli, xlii, xlv, lix N.,
lxvi, lxx, 16, 20, 25, 35, 51,
52, 59, 61–63, 68, 70, 72–74.

Pliny, xlii, 4, 14, 21, 43, 52, 53,
70, 71, 77, 87.

Plutarch, xi, xii, xlii, xlvi, and
N., xlvii N., 6, 7, 11, 21, 22,
32, 54, 57, 74, 84.

Pollux, 16.

Pomponius Mela, 69.

Proclus, 63, 64.

Propertius, 40.

Psalms, xxvi N.

Quintus Smyrnæus, 76.

Raleigh, 7, 17, 57, 64.

Rembrandt, lxxiii.

Rubens, lxxvi, lxxvii.

Seneca, xlii, xlix N., 25, 29, 31, 41, 42, 46, 47, 65, 66, 78, 82, 86.

Servius, liii, 19, 29, 37, 39, 43, 45, 46, 48, 52, 64, 67, 70, 71, 76.

Shakespeare, xxiii, lxii, and N., 62, 79.

Silius Italicus, xxxiv, 49, 76, 79.

Sophocles, xlii, 15, 41, 47, 49, 51, 61, 68, 82.

Sozomen, 9.

Spenser, xx N., xlv N., xlvii N., 4, 37, 41, 42, 43, 76, 77.

Statius, 5, 12, 17, 27, 47, 57, 78, 79, 80, 81, 82.

Stesichorus, 12.

Stobæus, 20, 72.

Strabo, xlii, 3, 5, 8, 9, 23-25, 55, 58, 71, 75, 78.

Suidas, 24.

Tasso, xlv N.

Theocritus, xlii, xliv, 3, 4, 6, 24, 26, 29, 40, 44, 45, 54, 57, 58, 60, 63-65, 68; *scholium*, 3.

Theognis, 6.

Tibullus, 29, 47, 63, 78, 79.

Tzetzes, 34, 80.

Valerius Flaccus, 18, 45, 79, 86.

Valerius Maximus, 32.

Van Eyck, lxxv.

Vergil, x, xxii N., xxxiv, xlii, xliv, xlv, liii N., 3, 5, 6, 9-11, 14, 16, 17, 19, 22-26, 29, 30, 33, 36-38, 40, 41, 43, 45, 47-49, 51, 53-59, 61, 63, 64, 66-68, 71-74, 76, 77, 78, 80, 81, 83, 85-87; see Servius.

Watson, lxi.

II

INDEX OF PASSAGES FROM MILTON'S WORKS

In the citations from Milton's prose works the numbers refer in most cases to the volume and page of the Bohn edition (*P. W.*). The *Prolusions* and the *Authoris Pro Se Defensio* are cited from the edition by Charles Symmons, 1806.

PARADISE LOST

Book 1

Line	Page
6	56, 57
6 ff.	57
10	21, 57
15	56
57	44
196–208	xvi
197	xlviii
198	30, 37, 38, 48, 82
199	17, 30, 83, 84
208	xlvi
232	83
239	72
307	17
376	56, 57
376 ff.	57
446	3
508	46
509	30
510	76, 82
512	1, 74, 48
513	71
514	48
515	65
516	65
517	8, 10
518	49
519	74
520	42

PARADISE LOST

Book 1

Line	Page
521	74
543	21, 22, 62, 63
575–587	xvi
576	70
577	37
578	46, 81, 82
687	30
687 ff.	30
732–751	xix, 81
740	85
741	48
745	54
778	30, 37
784	28
780	70
786	xxv N.

Book 2

Line	Page
69	80, 81
150	62, 63
233	20, 21
245	6
252–258	xxii N.
306	xvi, 14
434–441	63
439	62, 63
506	72
530	71

PARADISE LOST

Book 2

Line	Page
539	xiv
539–628	xxxv, xxxvi
540–546	xiv, 41
542	41
551	20
570–576	73
574–586	72
596	36
604	72
604 ff.	72
614	80
628	xvi, xlviii N., 23, 45
643 ff.	81
645	xxii
655	xiv, 19
660	75
671	36
672	27
673–698	27
689–703	27
698	27
784–848	26
789	26
858	81
875	72
877–883	xxii N., 63, 73
883	33
884–906	22
891	22
894	22, 62, 63
895	21, 60
898–906	73
907	21
910	20
911	60
922	17
930	xxv N.
945	14
950	21, 22
960 ff.	xix
961	22

PARADISE LOST

Book 2

Line	Page
962	62, 63
964	3, 27, 66
965	20, 27, 73
967	30
969	22
970	21, 62, 63
986	62, 63, 64
988	21
1002	62, 63, 64
1005	48
1017	13
1017–1020	xvii N.
1019	75, 84
1036	62, 64
1037	60
1038	21

Book 3

Line	Page
14	72, 73
17	66
18	21, 62, 63
19	57
26–32	57
27	56
35	54, 81
36	69, 81, 82
51–55	lxviii
71	62
135	6
358	32
359	xix, 31, 32
421	21, 33, 62, 63, 64
424	62
455	60
472	31
522	xxv N.
558	35
568	42
568 ff.	43
603	41
604	76
726	28
730	29

PARADISE LOST

Book 4

Line	Page
205–287	xv, xxxv
240	6
250	xiv, xlviii, 42
265	20
266	39, 67, 68
267	38, 44, 68
268 ff.	20
270	70
271	19
272	9
273	8, 9
275 ff.	72
277	7
278	5
279	16, 71
329	86
355	42
453–469	xxi, 60
499	48
500	50
598	63
605	42
606–609	29
609	29
614	78
705–708	64
705–719	xvi
705 ff.	67
706	xlviii N., 64
707	64, 68, 87
708	87
713–719	xvii N.
714	68
717	41, 46
719	48
763	25, 26
776	xlvi N., 62
976	50
981	19
987	14
989	43
996	48
998	51

PARADISE LOST

Book 5

Line	Page
1	xxiii, liv, 14
2	liv
6	14
15	lv N.
16	xiv, 35, 86
41	29
57	6
106	63
124	14
139	xxiii
140	xxv N., 11, 12
166	xxv, and N., 53
186	xxiv N.
266 ff.	69
272	69, 70
277–287	xxii N., 41
285	41
300	13, 30
338	30
341	4
377–382	xiv, xvi, xlviii N., 50, 51, 55, 64, 70, 84
395	44
423	11, 12
427, 428	6
499	xxiv
633	6
642	6
645	63
658, 659	54
685	62, 63
700	63
760	53, 54

Book 6

Line	Page
1–15	xxvii, xxxv
2	14, 15
2–4	xxviii, xxix, liv, 44
4–11	33
12	liv, 14
13	15
14	62, 64

PARADISE LOST

Book 6

Line	Page
15	15
54	80
55	81, 83
100	xxv N.
320 ff.	xxii N.
321	6
332	6
338	xxv N.
358	xxv N.
390	xxv N.
406	62
407	63
409	63
475	6
640 ff.	83
644–646	xxii
711	xxv N.
749 759	xxv N.
770	xxv N.
829	xxv N.
859	36
871	21
871–875	xxii
881	xxv N.

Book 7

Line	Page
1	57
1 ff.	16
1–20	57
4	58
6	56
7	65
12	57
17	58
18	16
29	14
30	liv
30 ff.	liv N.
30–38	lxxii, lxxxxiii
30–39	lxi N.
33	16, 66
35	66

PARADISE LOST

Book 7

Line	Page
37	56, 58, 66
39	xlviii
105	62, 78, 79
131	53, 54
133	42
172	20
221	21, 22
238	80, 81
272	21, 22
276	30
370	11
370–375	xxiv N., xxvi, 14, 70
381	29
453	30
605	30, 82

Book 8

Line	Page
59	xxii N., xxvi
60	39
161	11
162	xxv N.
510	xvii N.
519	42
631	43
632	42

Book 9

Line	Page
14–19	xvi, 3, 46, 50, 51, 61, 62, 83, 84, 85
20–41	57
21	56, 57
49	42
65	xxv N., 62, 63
386	64
386–396	xvi, 28
387	28, 64
393	67, 70
395	19
369	48, 49
413	xlviii N.

PARADISE LOST

Book 9

Line	Page
439	4
439–443	xvi, xlix
440	3
441	4, 84
452	28, 64
503–510	xiv
506	17
507	32
508	7, 48, 49
522	xiv, 23
838	6
852	6
1000	30
1001	60
1029–1033	xxii N.
1044	78
1060	41
1111	6

Book 10

Line	Page
230	26
293	8
296	8
308	55
416	21, 22
425	53, 54
444	xiv, xliv N., 70
453	72
476	22
477	21, 22, 62, 63
525 ff.	38
531	71
539	xiv
560	36
580	1
580–584	xlvii, 74
581	34
583	65, 74
584	48, 71, 72
620	36
674	xiv, 70, 83
688	68

PARADISE LOST

Book 10

Line	Page
695	86
695–706	xliv N.
705	lv N., 86
707–710	30
857–858	51

Book 11

Line	Page
11	xlviii N., 28
12	27
14	82
129	47
131	13
133	41
135	53
173	14
175	xliv, 14, 15
184–203	xxii N.
185	48, 49
244	47
279	6
410	37
588	42
588 ff.	46
589	25, 42
591	45

PARADISE REGAINED

Book 1

Line	Page
57	44
456	xlvi
457	11
458	10

Book 2

Line	Page
173	67
173–191	xlvi N.
184 ff.	64, 67
184–189	64
185–191	xliv
186	10, 18
187	8, 9, 77

PARADISE REGAINED

Book 2

Line	Page
188	7, 67
190	1, 8, 48, 49, 61, 62
191	87
214	1, 48, 49, 84
215	xlviii
289–297	64
297	64, 87
355	58
353	36, 45
353–367	xix
353–365	xvi
354	64
355	28, 64
356	5, 60
357	42
358	xlviii N., 43
365	35
374	64, 87
403	xix, 39
596	39

Book 3

84	7, 48, 49, 54
85	26, 27

Book 4

259	54
260	10, 11
286–364	1
334	xlvii N.
339–348	xlviii
397	33
398	62
399	63
428	xliv
565	1
422	36
426	xxv, 14, 15
427	xxiv N.
428	14

PARADISE REGAINED

Book 4

Line	Page
560–576	xvii
563	8, 36
565	41, 48, 49
566	30
568	xliv N., 8
572	81
572–575	81
589	6
590	6
619	54

SAMSON AGONISTES

	xvii
27	xxv N.
100	nviii N.
499–501	xviii N., 1
500	80
501	80
716	46
1666	xviii N., 61
1699	xviii N., 69
1703	69
1707	70

ON THE DEATH OF A FAIR INFANT

8	86
15	xxv N.
19	xxv N.
23	8
25	10
40	xlviii, 31
43–46	xxiv N., 1, 48, 50, 65
47	30, 82
49	6, 83
50	51
54	51
56	xxv N.

AT A VACATION EXERCISE

Line	Page
5	79, 80
30–52	xli, lxviii, lxix, lxx
37	10, 11
38	40
39	1, 6, 48, 50
42 ff.	62
43	61, 62
46	60
49	4
50	84
53	56
93	xiv, 17, 30

ON THE MORNING OF CHRIST'S NATIVITY.

	xlvi, lxi N.
15	57, 60.
19	11
32 ff.	13
32	60
36	11
74	53
79	11, 12
84	xxv N., 12
85 ff.	xlvii N.
89	67, 68
103	28
135	74
141	51
141–143	51
145	xxv N.
173	xlvi
176	10
186	37
187	65
188	64
191	52
203	7
204	4
211–226	84
226	xliv N., 83
229–233	xxxiii
236	63, 79

THE PASSION

Line	Page
4	56, 57
13	xvii N.
14	41
23	10, 11
29	62, 63
30	63

ON TIME

2	44

AT A SOLEMN MUSIC

	lxx, lxxi
1	78

SONG ON MAY MORNING

1	53

ON SHAKESPEARE

12	10

EPITAPH ON MARCHIONESS OF WINCHESTER

17	46
18	45
18 ff.	46
26	54
28	34, 54
43 ff.	15
56	56

L'ALLEGRO

	xx, xliv, li, lii, liii, liv, lv, lvi, lviii, lxiv
2	19, 33, 62
3	72, 73
4	73
6	33
8	23
10	10
12	38
14	39, 84

L'ALLEGRO

Line	Page
15	38
16	16
17	liv
19	14, 39, 86
20	lv N.
25	64, 65
29	40
36	53, 64
54	14
59–62	xxxii
71	xxiv N.
81–90	24
125	45, 46
126	46
136	39
143–150	l x x x i, l x x x i i, lxxxiii
145	66
145–147	32
145–150	66
147	31
149	70

IL PENSEROSO

	xx, li, lii, lvi, lvii, lviii, lix, lx, lxi, lxii, lxiii, lxiv, lxv
10	56
17	lvii N.
18	55
19	19
21	lvii N., 64
23	74, 75
24	74
30	48
31–44	lx N.
45–48	liv N.
47	56
48	l, 48, 50
53–59	xxv N.
56	69, 80

IL PENSEROSO

Line	Page
58	62
59	28
59–62	xxxii
85–102	lx N.
99	68, 81
100	46
103–108	lxxxi, l x x x i i, lxxxiii
104	56
105	66
107	60
120	xlix N.
121	xxv N., 62, 63
122	14
123	liv
124	xix
133–146	64
134	87
135	lx N.
137	64
139–146	lxvii N., 79
142–150	xxxiv
146–150	78
147–150	79
154	37
157–166	lxxx
157–174	lx N.

ARCADES

	xix, 37, 66
1	64
16	28
18–23	xvi
20	52
21	71
23	50
30	5
30–31	xliv N.
33	xxviii, 64
43	50
44	l, 48
45	50

ARCADES

Line	Page
56	15
61–73	lxx
62 ff.	35
63	78
65	34
69	61
96	64
97	67
97 ff.	65
98	67
102	67
106	67

COMUS

Line	Page
	xvii, xix, xx, xxxvi, liv
1	48, 50, 65
1–4	xxxviii
1 ff.	xxiv N.
16	2, 6
18	61
18–27	xxxvii
20	1
24–29	76
41	1, 48, 50
46	16
49	75
50	23
50 ff.	24
51	11
54	64, 65
66	11
78	1, 48, 50
83	47
93–101	xxxix
95	xxv N., 11
96	12
97	12
113	xxxix
115–118	xxxvii
119–121	64
120	64, 65
124	25, 26, 84

COMUS

Line	Page
129	24, 25
130–135	29
132	72, 73
134	xxv N.
135	28, 29
136	25
136–142	xxxiii
139	14
141	11
143	25
145	25
153	23
175	67
190	xxv N., 11, 13
195	62
197	63
230	64
230–233	31
230–243	31, 64
237	60
244–257	24
249	80
252–257	31
253	23, 24, 78
254	xliv N., lxvi, 58, 64
257	xxiv, 31, 75
259	75
268	67, 87
275, 276	31, 64
289, 290	40
300	xxxix
334	21
341	18
393	42
422, 423	64, 65
441	28
441–552	xvi
442	28
445	25
447 ff.	38
448	55
453–463	lxi N.

COMUS

Line	Page
478	10
513–519	xlix
515	56, 57
517	23
522	15, 23
535	28
552	79
554	78
557	79
588	20
603, 604	72, 73
605	39, 40, 45
637	41, 84
638	39
641	36
655	85
661	9
662	8
676	40, 48, 50
701	50, 51
702–705	lxi N.
732–735	xxxvii
753	14
784–787	lxi N.
803	48
804	33, 82
805	74, 75
822	54
824	64
824 ff.	60
833	58, 60, 64
835	60, 76
838, 840	6
862	65
867–889	76
868–884	xxxviii
869	61, 62
870	76
872, 873	77
875	53
877	77
878–881	78
882, 883	64

COMUS

Line	Page
892	xxv N.
893	xxxviii
921, 923	7
959	42
962	xxiiii
963	41, 64
964	64
976–1023	xx
976–1011	4
977–1011	xxxix, xl
982	42, 43
986	xliv N., 38, 44
986 ff.	44
992	47
992–998	31
996	31
999	3
1002	84
1003	4
1003 ff.	26
1004	25
1011	xx, 48, 50

LYCIDAS

Line	Page
	liv
15	56, 58
16	48, 50
19	56
26	14
30, 31	xxiv
34	87
36	26
50	64, 65
56–63	lxxxii, lxxxiii
58	56, 58, 66
66	56, 58
68	6
69	61
75	34, 36
77	10, 11
82	1, 48
82–84	50
85	5

LYCIDAS

Line	Page
89	76, 77
90	61, 62
96	43
99	64
106	8, 10
132	5
133	56, 57, 58
133–151	57
148	10
168	11, 12
168–171	xxvi
175	6
183	37
187	xxiv

SONNETS

1, 4	44
7	48, 50
13	25, 56, 57
8, 9	56, 57
12, 6	8, 9, 52
7	xlvi N., 11, 12, 28
13, 4	55
10	10, 11
15, 7	xiv, 45
20, 6	lv N., 86
21, 2	82
23, 2	4, 26
3	41, 48, 49

ELEGIES

1, 62	4
63–73	xvi
64	49
65	72
74	72
2, 7	39
8	39
3, 26	77
32	12
41	47
46	43
47	86

ELEGIES

Line	Page
5, 37	50
62	72
91	77
97	25
98	26
105 ff.	46
117	65
119–125	87
121	87
6, 49	lx N.
52	25
55–78	liv N.
88	lx N.
7, 3, 4	25
17–47	26
21–24	45
81	85

IN OBITUM PROCANCELLARII MEDICI

10	41

IN QUINTUM NOVEMBRIS

69	33
148	43

IN OBITUM PRÆSULIS ELIENSIS

56	28

NATURAM NON PATI SENIUM

23	85
61	31
62	10
63	4

AD PATREM

21	66

EPITAPHIUM DAMONIS

1	65
52	67
99	77

PROLUSIONS (ed. Symmons)

6. 145	41
146	22, 27
152	23, 71
173	67

OF EDUCATION

3. 466 f.	67

OF REFORMATION

2. 411	45

REASON OF CHURCH GOVERN-MENT

2. 479	lxi
505	71

APOLOGY FOR SMECTYMNUUS

3. 100, 117, 118, lxi	

DOCTRINE AND DISCIPLINE OF DIVORCE

3. 227	74

EIKONOKLASTES

1. 330	4
395	45
484	51

AUTHORIS PRO SE DEFENSIO (ed. Symmons)

5. 291	25

HISTORY OF BRITAIN

5. 168	8

III

INDEX OF MYTHOLOGICAL NAMES AND SUBJECTS

Achelous, 5, 76.

Acheron, xxxv, 40, 72; see Rivers of Hades.

Achilles, 3, 5, 15, 42, 47, 48, 77, 85.

Actæon, 28.

Ades, see Pluto.

Admetus, 4, 27.

Adonia, xx, 4.

Adonis, 3, 4, 44.

Ægæon, 17.

Æneas, xxii N., 8, 40, 51, 56, 83, 85.

Æolus, xlvii N., 43, 86.

Æsculapius, 32.

Æson, 39.

Afer, 86.

Agamemnon, 44, 68, 78.

Aidos, see Justice.

Alcestis, 4.

Alcides, see Hercules.

Alcinous, 4, 11.

Aletheia, 51.

Alexander, 7, 49.

Alpheus, xliv N., 5.

Amalthea, xvi, xxxv, 5, 15, 72.

Amaryllis, 6.

Amazons, 6.

Ambrosia, 6.

Ammon, xlvii N., 72.

Amphitrite, 7.

Amymone, 7, 10.

Anchises, 8.

Andromeda, lvii N., 19, 35, 46.

Antæus, xliv N., 8, 30.

Antiopa, 8, 10, 49.

Aphrodite, see Venus.

Apollo, xiii, xvi, xlvi N., l, lxxxiv, 7, 8–13, 27, 28, 47, 52, 55, 71, 81, 82.

Aquilo, see Boreas.

Ares, see Mars.

Arethusa, 5.

Argestes, 86.

Argo, 13.

Argonauts, 66, 69.

Argus, 13, 42, 67.

Aries, 35.

Arimaspians, 14.

Artemis, see Diana.

Assyrian Queen, see Venus.

Astræa, 51.

Athene, see Minerva.

Atlas, xiv, 14, 42, 70.

Atreus, 68, 69.

Atropos, 34, 35.

Aurora, Eos, Dawn, Morn, Morning, xx, xxiv, xxv, xxvi, and N., xxvii, xxviii, xxxi, xxxiii, liv and N., lv, 14–15, 19, 39, 44, 53, 54, 55.

Bacchus, xix, xlvi, liii, liv, and N., 10, 15–16, 39, 46, 72, 77.

Bellerophon, lxxxiv, 16–17.

Bellona, 17.

Blessed Isles, 32, 43.

Boreas, 15, 86, 87.

Briareos, 17, 30, 81.

Brutus (of Britain), 7.

Busiris, 17.

Cacus, 85.

Cadmus, 17–18, 77.

Cæcias, 86.
Calisto, 18, 28, 49.
Calliope, xlviii, 58, 66.
Calypso, 62.
Carpathos, 77.
Cassiopeia, lvii, and N., 19.
Castalia, xvi, 9.
Castor, 83.
Cephalus, 14, 19.
Cerberus, xxxv, lii, liii N., lxv, 19, 73.
Ceres, 12, 19, 20, 29, 49, 72.
Chalybeans, xviii N., 20.
Cham, 7.
Chance, 20, 21.
Chaos, xviii, xix, lxxxiv, 21–22, 27, 29, 30, 60, 63, 73.
Charybdis, xix, 75–76.
Chimæra, xxxv, 16, 23, 45.
Chloris, see Flora.
Chrysaor, 37.
Cimmerian, lii, 23, 73.
Circe, xiv, xix, xx, xxxvi, xxxvii, xlvi, 16, 23–24, 29, 42, 59, 75, 78.
Clotho, see Fates.
Clymene, 10.
Cocytus, xxxv, 72, 73.
Comus, xxxiii N., xxxix.
Corydon, 24.
Cotytto, Cotys, xix, 24, 25, 29.
Cronus, see Saturn.
Cupid, xx N., 25–26, 28, 46.
Cybele, 24, 50, 71.
Cyllene, xix, 67.
Cynosure, 18.
Cynthia, see Diana.
Cynthius, see Apollo.
Cytherea, see Venus.

Dæmon, 37.
Damœtas, 26.
Daphne, xvi, xxxv, 9, 10.
Daphnis, 65.
Darkness, lii, 33, 63; see Erebus.

Dawn, see Aurora.
Day, xxvii, 33, 55, 63.
Death, 4, 26–27, 33, 78.
Delos, 8, 9, 28.
Delphi, 9, 10, 11, 71, 82.
Demeter, see Ceres.
Demodocus, lxix, lxx, 5, 11.
Demogorgon, 20, 22, 27.
Deucalion, xlviii, 27, 28, 30.
Diana, xx, xxxvi, xxxvii, li, 8, 11, 18, 28–29, 52, 54, 64, 65, 67, 79.
Dionysus, see Bacchus.
Dioscuri, 83.
Dis, see Pluto.
Discord, 20, 30, 84.
Dodona, 49, 50.
Dreams, 56, 79.
Dryades, 42, 65.

Earth, xxii N., 8, 13, 17, 27, 30, 38, 60, 61, 71, 74, 76, 82, 83.
Echo, xx, xxxvi, 31.
Eileithyia, 34, 54.
Electra, 68.
Elysium, xx, xlviii, lv, lxxxiii, 31–32, 43, 56, 67.
Eos, see Aurora.
Epidaurus, 32.
Epimetheus, lxxxiv, 46, 68.
Erebus, 19, 27, 29, 30, 33, 63; see Darkness.
Erinnyes, see Furies.
Eris, 30, 66, 73.
Erymanthus, xix, 67.
Eumenides, see Furies.
Euphrosyne, liii, liv, lxiv, 16, 38, 39; see Mirth.
Eurotas, 10.
Eurus, 86.
Eurydice, lvii, lxxxiii, 46, 66, 67.
Eurynome, xlvii N., 34, 38, 74.

Fama, see Rumor.
Fate(s), 20, 21, 27, 34, 35.
Faunus, Fauns, 87.
Favonius, 86.

Flora, lv N., 32, 35–36, 44.
Folly, lxiv.
Fortuna, see Chance.
Furies, xxxvi, 33, 34, 36, 66, 83.

Gaia, Ge, see Earth.
Ganymed, 36, 37.
Gemini, see Dioscuri.
Genius, 37, 50.
Geryon, 37.
Giants, xlviii, 30, 37, 38.
Glaucus, 16, 75, 77.
Gods of Olympus, xxi. xlvi, lxviii,
    11, 17, 30, 38, 48, 62, 71, 76,
    77, 80, 85.
Gorgons, xxxv, 23, 36, 38, 45, 55;
    see Medusa.
Graces, xvi, xx, xxii N. xxxv, l,
    liii, liv, 6, 11, 38–39, 44, 59, 65.
Griffins, 14.

Hades, 3, 4, 20, 22, 23, 27, 30, 33,
    38, 48, 50, 61, 66, 70, 72, 73,
    80, 81.
Hæmony, 39.
Hamadryads, 70.
Ham, see Cham.
Hammon, see Ammon.
Harmonia, 17, 18.
Harpies, xix, 23, 36, 39, 40, 45.
Heaven, 17, 30, 74, 76, 82, 83.
Hebe, 11, 39, 40, 49; see Youth.
Hebrus, 66.
Hecate, xix, xxxiii, xlvi N., 29.
Hector, 3, 48.
Helen, xxii, N., 28, 40, 41, 50.
Helicon, 56, 57.
Helios, see Sun.
Helle, 35.
Hemera, see Day.
Hephæstus, see Vulcan.
Hera, see Juno.
Hercules, xvii N., li, lxxxiv, 4,
    5, 8, 17, 37, 41, 45, 49, 85.
Hermes, xxii N., 13, 19, 24, 41–42,
    67, 68.

Hermione, 17.
Hesperides, xv, xvi, xix, xx,
    xlviii, 4, 5, 6, 42, 43.
Hesperus, Evening Star, 13, 42–
    43, 44, 46, 53.
Hestia, see Vesta.
Hippotades, 43.
Homer, 11.
Horror, 43, 44.
Hours, xvi, xx, xxvii, xxviii, xix,
    xxxv, xliv N., lxvi, lxvii, 11,
    12, 15, 39, 58, 59.
Hyacinth, 10.
Hydra, xix, xxxv, 23, 40, 45.
Hylas, 45, 60.
Hymen, 45, 46.
Hyperion, see Sun.

Iapetus, 7, 46, 68, 82.
Ida, lviii, 74, 75.
Ilium, lxix, 5, 6, 8, 15, 46, 47.
Ino, 53.
Irassa, 8.
Iris, xx, xxxix, 47.
Ismenian, 81.

Janus, 47, 48.
Japhet, see Iapetus.
Jason, 13.
Jove, xi, xx, xx, and N., xxi, xxiv,
    xxxix, xlvi, l, lvii, lviii N.,
    lxix, lxxxiv, 4, 5, 6, 7, 8, 10,
    13, 17, 18, 26, 34, 37, 38, 39,
    40, 41, 44, 47, 48–50, 51, 52,
    55, 56, 61, 68, 72, 74, 77, 80,
    82, 83, 84, 85.
Joy, 26.
Juno, xxii N., xxiv, xxviii, 6, 13,
    18, 31, 34, 40, 47, 49, 50–51,
    54, 79, 81, 83, 85.
Justice, 44, 51.

Ladon, xix, 67.
Laertes, 84.
Lars, 52.
Latona, 8, 11, 28, 50, 52–53.

Lavinia, 83.
Lemures, 52.
Lethe, xxxv, 72, 73, 80.
Leto, see Latona.
Leucothea, 55, 76.
Liberty, 53.
Libra, 49.
Lichas, 41.
Ligeia, 78.
Locrine, 7.
Love, see Cupid.
Lucifer, xxv, 15, 42, 53–54.
Lucina, 34, 54.
Lycæus, xix, 67.
Lycidas, lxxxiii, 54.

Mænads, lxxxiii, 16, 66.
Mænalus, 67.
Mæonides, 54.
Manes, 52.
Mars, lxix, 5, 11, 47, 54, 61.
Matuta, see Leucothea.
Medea, 29, 39.
Medusa, xxxv, 14, 38.
Megæra, 36.
Melancholy, lii, liv, lvi, lviii, lix,
    lxii, lxiii, lxiv, 75.
Melesigenes, 54.
Melicertes, 53.
Memnon, lvi, lvii N., 15, 55.
Menelaus, 31, 40, 41, 68.
Mercury, see Hermes.
Midas, 55.
Minerva, xiii, xx, xxii N., li, 38,
    47, 51, 55, 57, 72, 85.
Mirth, liv, lvi; see Euphrosyne.
Mnemosyne, 56.
Moly, xxi, xxxvi.
Moon, 28, 63; see Diana.
Morning, Morn, see Aurora.
Morpheus, lix, 56.
Mulciber, see Vulcan.
Musæus, 56.
Muses, lvii, lxxxii, 11, 54, 56–58,
    65, 66, 81.

Naiads, xix, xxxvi, xliv N., lxvi,
    5, 45, 58–60, 64.
Narcissus, xxi, 31, 60.
Nature, 13, 60, 61.
Neæra, 61.
Necessity, xviii, 34, 35, 61.
Nectar, 6.
Nepenthes, 40.
Neptune, xx, xxv, lxix, 7, 8, 10,
    17, 19, 47, 48, 61, 62, 72, 76,
    77.
Nereids, 12, 19, 24, 60, 64, 65, 76,
    77.
Nereus, 7, 76.
Night, xix, xxv, xxvii, xxxvi,
    xlvi N., lxxxiv, 13, 15, 19,
    22, 27, 29, 30, 33, 60, 61–62,
    64, 66, 79, 80.
Notus, 15, 86.
Nox, see Night.
Nymphs, xix, xxxvi, xxxvii,
    lxxxi, lxxxiv, 9, 24, 32, 42,
    58, 64–65, 87.

Oceanus, xlvi, 12, 34, 38, 76, 82,
    83
Odysseus, see Ulysses.
Œdipus, 81, 82.
Olympias, 7.
Olympus, xxviii, lxix, 15, 34, 56,
    57, 65, 74, 80; see Gods of
    Olympus.
Ophion, xlvii, 34, 74.
Ops, see Rhea.
Orcus, 20, 66.
Oreads, 28, 31, 64, 67.
Orestes, 68.
Orithyia, 86.
Orpheus, xvi, lv, lxxxi, lxxxii,
    lxxxiii, 16, 34, 46, 56, 58, 66–
    67.
Osiris, 84.

Palæmon, 53.
Pales, 67.

Pallas, see Minerva.
Pan, xvi, xix, xxxv, xxxvi, xlvii
  N., 39, 50, 55, 65, 67–68.
Pandora, 68.
Panope, 64.
Paris, xxii N.
Parthenope, 78.
Pegasus, 16, 17, 58.
Peleus, 3, 84.
Pelopidæ, 68.
Pelops, 68, 69.
Penelope, 28.
Persephone, see Proserpina.
Perseus, 14, 38, 46.
Phæacians, 4, 5.
Phaethon, 10, 12.
Phanes, 63, 64.
Philammon, 11.
Phillis, 24. •
Philomel, lix, 69.
Phineus, 36, 39.
Phlegethon, xxxv, 72, 73, 81.
Phlegra, 3.
Phœnix, xviii N., 69, 70.
Phrixus, 35.
Pleiades, xxvi N., 70.
Plenty, 5.
Pluto, 3, 20, 66, 70.
Plutonian Hall, xliv N.
Polydamna, 40.
Polydeuces, 83.
Pomona, 70.
Pontus, 76.
Poseidon, see Neptune.
Procne, 69.
Prometheus, 14, 34, 46, 48, 68, 80.
Proserpina, xvi, xxxv, 12, 19–20,
  29, 38, 49, 58, 66.
Proteus, 31, 76, 77.
Psyche, xx, and N., 26.
Pudicitia, 51.
Pygmies, 70, 71.
Pyrrha, xlviii, 27, 28, 30.
Pythian, 71.
Python, 71.

Quies, 79, 80.
Quirinus, 54.

Rhea, 19, 24, 34, 48, 50, 61, 71–
  72, 84.
Rhodope, 66.
Rivers of Hades, 72, 73.
Romulus, 54.
Rumor, 30, 73, 74.

Sabrina, xxxvii, xxxviii, xl, 60.
Saturn, xx, xlvi, lviii, and N.,
  lxxxiv, 3, 19, 34, 48, 50, 56,
  61, 72, 74–75, 82, 83.
Satyr, 50, 65, 87.
Scipio, 49.
Scylla, xix, xxxv, 19, 33, 75, 76.
Sea-gods, li, 76, 77.
Selene, see Moon.
Semele, 10, 49, 77.
Set, 84.
Sibyl, 10
Silence, 70, 80.
Silenus, Sileni, 42, 87.
Sirens, 75, 76, 78.
Sleep, xxxiv, xxxv, lxvii N., 33,
  56, 78, 80.
Somnus, see Sleep.
Sphinx, 81, 82.
Strife, see Eris.
Styx, xxxv, liii, 72, 73, 78.
Sun, xxvi, xxxii, xxxiii, liv, 11–
  13, 15, 23, 29, 30, 69, 71, 82;
  see Apollo.
Sylvan, Sylvans, xxxvi, 87.
Symplegades, 13.
Syrinx, 13, 67, 87.

Tantalus, xxxv, lxxxiv, 68, 80.
Tartarus, xxi, 22, 33, 48, 63, 72,
  73, 80–81, 83.
Tethys, 76.
Thammuz, 3, 4.
Thamyris, 81.
Thanatos, see Death.

Thebes, 17, 81, 82.
Themis, 28, 44, 82.
Thestylis, 24.
Thetis, 17, 77, 85.
Thrascias, 86.
Thyestes, 68.
Thyrsis, 24.
Tiresias, 27, 82.
Titans, xxi, xlviii, lxxxiv, 17, 30, 33, 38, 46, 48, 76, 81, 82–83.
Tithonus, 14, 45, 55.
Triton, 77.
Troy, see Ilium.
Turnus, 83.
Tyche, see Chance.
Typhon, xiv, xxii, xxxv, 30, 48, 83, 84.

Ulysses, xxi, li, 5, 11, 23, 34, 43, 53, 55, 57, 58, 62, 75, 76, 77, 78, 84.
Urania, 57.
Uranus, see Heaven.

Venus, xxii N., liii, liv, lxix, 3, 4, 5, 6, 11, 25, 26, 28, 39, 46, 47, 49, 51, 59, 84–85, 87.
Veritas, 51.
Vertumnus, 70.
Vesta, xx, lviii, and N., lix, and N., lx, lxi, lxiii, 72, 75.
Voluptas, xx N., 26.
Vulcan, xi, xix, 11, 40, 48, 51, 65, 68, 85, 86.

Water-nymphs, lxvi, 31, 60.
Winds, xliv N., 86, 87.
Wood-gods, 65, 87.
Wood-nymphs, xxxvi, lxvi, 28, 31.

Youth, 26; see Hebe.

Zephyrus, xx, liv, lv, and N., 15, 35, 39, 86.
Zeus, see Jove.

ERRATA

P. xxxiii, l. 19.   *For* sun *read* Sun.

P. lxi, last line.   Add *Apology for Smectymnuus, P. W.* 3. 100, 117, 118; *Reason of Church Government, P. W.* 2. 479.

P. lxxvi, l. 11.   *For* artist *read* architect.

P. 11, l. 17.   For *Schol.* read *schol.*

P. 15, ll. 26, 27.   *For* Milton's *Epist.* 18. 111, *read* Ovid, *Heroides* 18. 111.

P. 22, l. 4 from bottom.   *After Prolusions insert* ed. Symmons 6. 146.

P. 23, l. 14.   For C. 57 read *C.* 517.

P. 26, l. 1.   For *Æn.* 664 ff. read *Æn.* 1. 664 ff.

P. 26, l. 12.   *For* 7-17; 47 *read* 7. 17, 47.

P. 27, l. 5 from bottom.   *For* demogorgona *read* Demogorgona.

P. 28, l. 3 from bottom.   For In *Obit.* read *In Obit.*

P. 32, l. 22.   *For* Nymph *read* nymph.

P. 35, l. 28.   *For* 3. 5 8 *read* 3. 558.

P. 38, l. 2 from bottom.   *After* Hesiod *insert* (*Theog.* 907).

P. 42, l. 5 from bottom.   *For* 746 ff. *read Theog.* 746 ff.

P. 44, ll. 21, 23.   *For* Spring *read* spring.

P. 48, l. 2 from bottom.   For *Job* read Job.

P. 55, l. 14.   *After* told *insert* (6. 10).

P. 60, l. 1.   For *C.* 24 ff. read *C.* 824 ff.

P. 61, ll. 3, 4.   *For* Ovid, *Met* 1. 416 ff.) *read* Ovid (*Met.* 1. 416 ff.).

P. 64, l. 2.   *After* Homer *insert* (*Il.* 14. 259).

P. 65, l. 28.   *For* Ov. *Ep. read* Ov. *Her.*

P. 65, l. 32.   *For* 7. 7 10 *read* 7. 7; 10.

P. 66, l. 4 from bottom.   Add (*Met.* 11. 44-49).

P. 66, last line.   *Add* l. 55.

P. 67, l. 3.   *Add* ll. 62, 63.

P. 68, l. 10.   For *P. L.* 4. 66 read *P. L.* 4. 266.

P. 68, l. 10 from bottom.   For *Choephoræ* read *Choephori.*

P. 68, l. 8 from bottom.   After *Tauris* insert the *Electra.*

P. 72, l. 1.   *After* Ovid *insert* (*Fast.* 4. 219, 220).

P. 78, l. 27.   For *P. L.* 706 read *P. L.* 7. 105.

P. 86, l. 29.   *For* Apricus *read* Africus.